ASHES OF HAMA

RAPHAËL LEFÈVRE

Ashes of Hama

The Muslim Brotherhood in Syria

OXFORD
UNIVERSITY PRESS

OXFORD
UNIVERSITY PRESS

Oxford University Press, Inc., publishes works that further
Oxford University's objective of excellence
in research, scholarship, and education.

Oxford New York
Auckland   Cape Town   Dar es Salaam   Hong Kong   Karachi
Kuala Lumpur   Madrid   Melbourne   Mexico City   Nairobi
New Delhi   Shanghai   Taipei   Toronto

With offices in
Argentina   Austria   Brazil   Chile   Czech Republic   France   Greece
Guatemala   Hungary   Italy   Japan   Poland   Portugal   Singapore
South Korea   Switzerland   Thailand   Turkey   Ukraine   Vietnam

Published by Oxford University Press, Inc
198 Madison Avenue, New York, New York 10016

Published in the United Kingdom in 2013 by C. Hurst & Co. (Publishers) Ltd.

www.oup.com

Library of Congress Cataloging-in-Publication Data
Lefèvre, Raphaël.
Ashes of Hama : the Muslim Brotherhood in Syria / Raphaël Lefèvre.
p. cm.
Includes bibliographical references and index.
ISBN 978-0-19-933062-1 (alk. paper)
1. Jam'iyat al-Ikhwan al-Muslimin (Syria)—History. 2. Syria—History—20th
century. 3. Syria—History—21st century. I. Title.
BP10.J386L44 2013
322.4'2095691—dc23
2013014739

1 3 5 7 9 8 6 4 2

Printed in India
on Acid-Free Paper

CONTENTS

CONTENTS

CONTENTS

ACKNOWLEDGMENTS

I would like to thank all the people without whom this research project would not have become a reality. I am primarily indebted to Professor George Joffé who not only provided me with excellent supervision throughout my studies at the University of Cambridge but has also acted as an insightful adviser and a constant source of support ever since. My warmest thanks are also directed to Patrick Seale who, from the very beginning, supported my willingness to dig into Syria's history and shed light on previously little-discussed aspects by providing much advice. I am also deeply indebted to Ignace Leverrier whose expert knowledge of Syrian political life helped to guide me through the maze of Ba'athist politics. Without his numerous contacts and the quality of the material he kindly provided me with, this study would not have been possible. The same is true of Ahmed al-Othman whose generosity is a key pillar upon which this book rests. His willingness to introduce me into the world of the Syrian Muslim Brotherhood proved invaluable. In this respect, I am also thankful for the access I was granted to numerous leaders and rank-and-file members of the Islamist organization as well as their opponents from various fields—some of whom spoke on condition of anonymity. This study owes much to their trust. I would also like to express my warmest gratitude and friendship to Mehdi Laghmari in Paris, Mohammed Laroussi and Hadia al-Attar in Aachen, Abdullah Ali, Walid Safour, Obeida Nahas and Malik al-Abdeh in London, Emira Bahri and Yassine in Tunis, and Ahmed al-Othman in Istanbul and Paris, who all contributed greatly to the publication of this book by expressing their readiness to help translate original material from Arabic.

ACKNOWLEDGMENTS

I am also deeply grateful for Rana Kabbani's friendship and her early encouragements both of which acted as important sources of inspiration. Additionally, many experts and critical readers gave insightful feedback on earlier drafts of this study. In this respect, I am particularly thankful to Dr Bente Scheller, Dr Nikolaos Van Dam, Professor George Joffé and Professor Philippe Droz Vincent for their time. Needless to say, any mistakes that remain are entirely my own.

As this book went through several rounds of drafts and re-drafts, I am deeply grateful for all the time Anne Wolf, Anna Carden and Banu Turnaoglu spent reviewing earlier versions, giving substantial feedback. The staff at Hurst were also very helpful in this respect and in particular I owe much to Michael Dwyer who, by immediately giving his trust and confidence, made the publication of this book possible. The process of writing took a long time, however, and at times proved challenging. All my thanks go to Anne Wolf who, in addition to reading and editing successive drafts, also proved to be a constant and unyielding source of support. Finally, I would like to stress how much support I received from my family, whose sustained encouragement was a great source of motivation.

PROLOGUE

When references to the advent of an "Arab Spring" started to emerge after popular uprisings toppled regimes in Tunisia and Egypt, many commentators suggested it was unlikely that this revolutionary Arab mood would reach Syria.[1] They argued that the country's collective consciousness was still profoundly marked by the so-called "Hama rules"[2]— that an authoritarian regime can crush an opposition movement with the application of force on a brutal scale as the Assad regime did in Hama to crush an Islamist rebellion.[3] Throughout the month of February 1982, the Ba'ath regime's most loyal forces shelled entire quarters of the city and bombed many of its residential areas—leaving between 25,000 and 40,000 dead.

Analysts were right to point out the significance of the memory of the massacre in the hearts and minds of the Syrian people. What they failed to foresee, however, was that this collective scar would not forever restrain Syrians from defying the regime that rules over them. Instead, it would fuel such a degree of resentment and anger that the uprisings which started in March 2011 at Dar'a soon spread throughout the country with ever increasing pace and intensity. In virtually every Syrian city, the message of local opposition leaders and protest organizers soon boiled down to a simple sentence: "We will not let the massacres of 1982 be repeated!"[4]

Uprisings in Syria: the burden of history

Soon, however, these Syrians must have felt as if they were reliving their own history. In February 2012 Bashar al-Assad's younger brother Maher ordered a three week artillery siege of the Baba Amr quarter in Homs which left thousands of inhabitants dead—much as Hafiz al-Assad's regime henchmen had done to Hama exactly thirty years before.

The memory of atrocities suffered in the early 1980s by Syria's Islamists at the hands of the regime seemed to be an increasingly important mobilizing factor in the uprisings. A journalist, reporting on the revolt from northern Syria, observed: "A village elder with a handgun strapped to his side […] said he was arrested [in the late 1970s] as part of the regime's crackdown on suspected Muslim Brothers and served 15 years in prison. In Aleppo's countryside, the rebellion is fuelled by memories of that crackdown. Men in every village, it seems, can recite the names of men who were killed or disappeared into regime prisons or were forced into exile."[5]

It is against this background that the rebels' uncompromising demand for the overthrow of the regime should be understood: their call for revenge resonates with the country's bloody history of opposition between the regime and its Islamist rivals. "For me, the revolution started a long time ago, when my brother was arrested," confirmed a rebel in Damascus. "He was part of the Muslim Brotherhood's revolution of 1980." Then, "one day the mukhabarat intelligence men came in three cars and arrested him. Nobody knows where they took him—not even until now, 32 years later," he explained. "Now my revolution is getting bigger."[6]

But such a sense of historical continuity between the current uprisings in Syria and the situation prevailing in the 1980s is not only characteristic of anti-regime militants. Much of the support the Ba'athist rulers still retain among certain segments of the Syrian population is also framed in terms only understandable when seen through the prism of history. For instance, the apprehension voiced by members of minority communities about the demise of the secular Ba'ath regime and its potential replacement by a government dominated by Islamist forces emerged out of the fear that they could again be the target of violence perpetrated by extremist Sunni groups. The Alawis in particular, a religious sect from which most of the country's decision-makers come, have since March 2011 expressed their fear of a return to a situation similar to that which prevailed between 1979 and 1982. Then, sectarian provocations ignited by a handful of radical Islamic militants brought the country to the verge of civil war, drawing the various religious communities into a seemingly endless cycle of retaliation against one another.

Today, just as in the past, the Ba'athist rulers depict the revolt as the final act of Syria's long struggle "between Islamism and secular pan-Arabism"[7]—a way for the regime to stress its inclusive nature and contrast it to the supposedly polarizing demands of the rebels. In this framework, it is of little surprise that Bashar al-Assad's first instinct after the uprisings erupted was to blame them on the Syrian Brotherhood. "We've been fighting the Muslim Brotherhood since the 1950s and we are still fighting with them,"[8] he insisted in an October 2011 interview. But who are these "Syrian Brothers" the regime claims to be at war with?

Exploring the Syrian Brotherhood's legacy

Over the past thirty years, the Syrian Ba'ath has enjoyed a free hand to caricature its most influential competitor in terms closely associated with radicalism and violence. The regime's approach was exemplified in December 2011 after the Ba'athist rulers set up a fake Syrian Brotherhood website which was to claim the organization's responsibility for terrorist attacks that struck Damascus a few weeks later.[9] But, despite the group's repeated denials, published on its real website, the damage was done: amid the media frenzy, most Western and Syrian newspapers had already printed the news.[10] Since then, the regime's attempt to tarnish its powerful rival has been steadily successful—insofar as it has blurred the lines both inside Syria and abroad on what the Brotherhood's real intentions are.

Suspicion of the group's agenda is also heightened by a lack of detailed knowledge on the organization and its leaders. "The Syrian Muslim Brotherhood is considered more conservative than its Egyptian counterpart; the Syrian Brotherhood also had more history of violent resistance to the Assads. But not much more is known about the current internal dynamics of the group,"[11] a journalist from the *New York Times* acknowledged a year into the Syrian revolt. This lack of knowledge, in turn, seems particularly problematic in relation to the current uprisings as the biased nature or outright lack of information about the organization may have a significant impact on Western policy towards Syria.

This book attempts to bridge this gap in the available literature by providing an account as comprehensive and objective as possible of the Syrian Brotherhood's political history, ideological evolution and internal politics—free from regime propaganda. While there has been a considerable amount of work published on the Syrian Ba'ath—its ideological origins,[12] socioeconomic roots,[13] foreign policy[14] and the religious background[15] of its leaders—much less has been published on its Islamist adversary. There have been a few publications devoted to it but most were written in the early 1980s and, while the background information they provide is excellent, they lack the perspective needed to analyse the organization's modern evolution.[16] More recently, the short-lived alliance between the Syrian Muslim Brothers and the former Vice President Abdel Halim Khaddam has generated a renewed interest in the movement, but most of the journal articles published at the time tended to be more concerned with exile politics than with the group's internal dynamics.[17] All in all, the Syrian Brotherhood has received much less attention from journalists and academics alike than its Egyptian sister and this despite its considerably rich and eventful history.[18]

Since existing literature on the subject is scarce and given the extent to which current narratives on the organization are largely shaped by the regime's discourse, a significant effort was made in this book to reach out to members of the Syrian Muslim Brotherhood themselves. A series of long interviews were carried out with prominent leaders of the organization whose insights into previously little-discussed issues will provide experts and academics of Syria with useful material to reflect on. Aware of the risk of obtaining biased answers—because some events discussed are long past and some of the topics touched on arouse highly polarized views—the author was careful to select corroborated interview material. Leaders and members of each "group" within the organization were therefore interviewed—from the "Damascus wing" to the "Aleppo faction" and the "Hama clan". The information obtained was verified and confirmed by other more independent experts—analysts of the movement, former members of the organization or Islamists who never belonged to it. In addition, the Syrian Islamists' account, the first of its kind in the literature, was further checked by an equally comprehensive series of interviews held with senior or former prominent members of the Ba'ath regime who agreed to speak, sometimes on condition of anonymity, on the long struggle between political Islam and secular forces which has come to shape modern Syria.

The author's access to the memoirs of two former Syrian jihadists, Mustafa Setmarian Nasar—widely known as Abu Mus'ab al-Suri—and Ayman al-Shorbaji, as well as the autobiography of the former Brotherhood leader Adnan Saadeddine, was crucial insofar as it provided a surely biased yet insightful account of the Syrian jihad. Documents produced by members of al-Qaeda relating to Syria and found during the American raid on Usama Bin Laden's home in Abbottabad, Pakistan were also used by the author after they were made publicly available on the website of West Point's Center for Counter Terrorism (www.ctc. usma.edu). In addition, archival research was carried out in the original files of the British Foreign Office available at the National Archives at Kew and the Confidential Print at the library of the University of Cambridge. Reading the cables sent by successive British diplomats posted in Damascus was helpful in putting events back into their sociopolitical context, even though the restricted public availability of these documents (only released as late as winter 1964) limited the scope of such research. For their part, the cables sent over the last thirty years to Washington by the US Embassy in Damascus, now publicly available online (www.cablegatesearch.net), were useful as they provided a glimpse into more contemporary Syrian politics.

Structure and content of the book

This book will be chronological in form, privileging a historical rather than thematic treatment of political Islam's peculiar evolution throughout the twentieth century. In order to understand the moderate and, sometimes, more radical strands of thought informing Syrian representatives of political Islam to this day, it will first undertake an overview of the intellectual and political basis upon which their ideology is structured. Such an overview must, by its very nature, be only partial as its goal is to provide readers with a general understanding of the origins of Syria's Islamic movement; more detailed studies exist on the subject for those who are so inclined. The first section of this book, dealing with the inroads of political Islam up to 1963, the date of the Ba'athist takeover, will also examine the way in which Syria's Muslim Brotherhood initially managed to reconcile political Islam and democracy—the first experiment of this kind in the Arab world.

The second section of this book will look in more detail at the socioeconomic, political and ideological dynamics which have unleashed historic opposition, continuing to the present day, between political Islam and the Syrian Ba'ath. Particular attention will also be paid to the deadly wave of sectarianism which gripped the country's various religious communities in the late 1970s and early 1980s, with consequences so significant that they continue to be felt today. Even though a separate chapter deals with this complex issue, the 1970s uprisings must still be viewed in the wider political environment which encompassed them, as virtually all factors in that wider context overlap.

In the third section, particular attention will be devoted to the complex ideological and political circumstances in which Syria witnessed the rise of a violent and radical jihadist trend. First, the scene in which the radicalization of the Islamic movement took place will be set. This will involve a detailed discussion of the leadership crisis shaking Syria's Muslim Brotherhood at the time which laid the foundation for the departure of its more moderate members and the ascendance of a radical wing. Special attention will also be paid to the rise of a well-organized jihadist organization, born on the fringes of the Brotherhood, the Fighting Vanguard (al-Talia al-Muqatila), illustrating the extent to which the advent of a powerful jihadist stream in today's Syria is a likely development if a political settlement is not reached any time soon. The role of the Syrian Brotherhood in these developments will also be examined while bearing in mind the unprecedented human and political cost of the organization's opposition to Ba'athism.

The consequences of the Muslim Brotherhood's exile following the Hama massacre of February 1982 will be the topic of the final section of this book. Deprived of its most moderate voice inside Syria, the country's Islamic movement developed along divergent paths. One trend, a minority, continued its struggle against secularism on the global stage while preparing itself to return to Syria when time came. In the meantime, the Ba'athist authorities understood the power of political Islam and sought to tame the remaining expression of this political current to their advantage. The other strand, comprising the remnants of the Muslim Brotherhood itself, was forced into exile. While the organization was at first caught in a cycle of internal crisis, it was eventually able to recover its coherence and to restructure itself, to the extent that, by the time of the Arab uprisings, it would once again become the regime's most powerful political opponent.

PART I

POLITICIZING ISLAM
(1860–1963)

1

THE EMERGENCE OF A POLITICIZED ISLAM IN SYRIA (1860–1944)

While 1945 marks the official and organizational birth of the Syrian Muslim Brotherhood, its intellectual and political roots can be traced back to decades earlier. Some date the Syrian Ikhwan's foundation to the emergence of politically active *jamiat*, or clubs and societies, in the 1920s and 1930s. The proliferation of such societies certainly helped to foster an environment in which political Islam became more influential, as will be seen in the second part of this chapter. The success of these Islamic societies in 1920s and 1930s Syria also explains much of the populist discourse put forward by the Syrian Ikhwan in the 1940s and 1950s. The Syrian Brotherhood's intellectual foundations, however, are found in late Ottoman Syria when, between 1860 and 1914, the Salafiyya movement reached Damascus and became so influential in local Islamic circles that it would later shape the Ikhwan's reformist and moderate agenda between 1946 and 1969. Studying this movement is also important insofar as it greatly contributed to giving a militant taste to the rise of a politico-religious movement throughout the region, including the Syrian Ikhwan.

The Salafiyya movement sought to reform Islam from within in order to give the Arab world the resources deemed necessary to confront the challenges of European domination. The "Salafism" which would emerge out of this trend was therefore primarily intellectual and political

3

in its aims and peaceful in its means. Thus it had little to do with the "Salafist" descriptor attached to radical Islamists who today seek to literally emulate the way of life of the Prophet Muhammad and are sometimes willing to resort to violence. These are actually the product of a contemporary mixture of radical Salafism with the Saudi literalist movement, Wahhabism. The use of the term "Salafist" in the following pages and chapters therefore does not refer to current debates on Islam and political violence but rather to a revivalist and reformist movement which profoundly shaped the way in which religion came to take on a political hue at the turn of the twentieth century—laying down the ideological foundations for the rise of politico-religious movements such as the Muslim Brotherhood.

While the Salafiyya movement was regional in scope, it took different forms in each Arab country it reached. In Syria, the specific socioeconomic landscape and the country's sectarian makeup contributed to the rise of a particularly moderate politico-religious trend instinctively favouring political pluralism and religious tolerance. Understanding the ideological and historical context into which this trend emerged is crucial for it helps understanding the early moderation of the Syrian Brothers who were to embrace parliamentary democracy and sectarian tolerance at the dawn of Syria's independence in 1946.

The "Damascus school": the Salafiyya movement in Syria

Before investigating what intellectual substance is hidden behind references to the Salafiyya movement, a brief glance at the historical circumstances surrounding its emergence in the Middle East will help to illustrate the context in which it first appeared. By the middle of the nineteenth century the Ottoman Empire, long the dominant political and religious force in the region, had become a shadow of its former self. A thriving Islamic empire ruling over the Middle East and parts of Asia and Europe for centuries, it was now seriously challenged by the advance of Western powers keen on benefiting from the technological development they had enjoyed since the Enlightenment to gain a foothold in the rich and strategically important Middle East. In the 1820s and 1830s, the great European powers had started to challenge Ottoman authority on cultural and economic grounds and, by the 1870s and 1880s, relations between the two sides became more directly confrontational. The Russo-Turkish war of 1877 threatened the very seat of the caliphate and the borders of the Ottoman Empire were challenged by the French and the British who, by the early 1880s, had begun their military occupation of Tunisia and Egypt.

Challenged by European powers on every front—from technology to culture and political values—the elites of the Middle East reacted in two very distinct ways. Many pushed the Ottoman rulers to emulate and adopt the administrative, political and economic reforms which had seemingly enabled Western countries to reach their unprecedented might—a movement culminating in the Tanzimat reforms. Others, however, were convinced that imitating the West would not provide answers to the region's specific problems and that an indigenous response was instead preferable.

The most articulate proponent of the latter option was the Muslim activist Jamal al-Din al-Afghani (1838–97), who, through his active struggle against British imperialism in late 1870s India and Egypt, put forward a vision for renewing the strength of Islamic civilization across the Middle East and South East Asia. Travelling from Istanbul to Cairo, he gave public speeches drawing the masses in which he called for the unification of the entire *Umma*, the worldwide Muslim community. His attempts went beyond formulating a renewed vision of pan-Islamism. Strongly influenced by the power of nationalism, which he had witnessed during anti-British riots in India, he was convinced that a blend of patriotism and religious zeal would instil the enthusiasm necessary for revitalizing Islamic civilization. By referring to the Islamic community as a "nation", Afghani advocated a form of pan-Islamic nationalism resting on the faith and purity typical of the Age of the Prophet when Muslims enjoyed prosperity. What he meant was that Muslims could find in their own history and religion the tools necessary to effectively tackle the challenges emanating from the West.[1]

Afghani's call did not go unnoticed. At the time, Islam was becoming the target of many intellectuals within the Ottoman Empire for representing the seeming backwardness that was supposed to explain the Muslim world's comparative weakness vis-à-vis West—where the influence of religion in the political sphere had been at least partially sidelined. In response to such arguments, Afghani suggested that the problem lay not in Islam itself but rather in the traditionalism and conservatism into which it had fallen, and which gave a different taste to it according to where it was practiced in the world. This state of affairs, he contended, was at the root of the increasing fragmentation and divisions which plagued the unity of the Islamic world and weakened it in the face of the European challenge. In his view, only by stripping Islam of the numerous innovations and traditions in which it had been embedded since the emergence of various theological schools from the ninth century onwards could superficial differences between Muslims disappear. Purifying Islam of the unnecessary dogma that Sunni theologians had "corrupted" it with over several centuries was thus key to making the concept of *Umma*, or Islamic unity, more relevant. More united and therefore stronger, Muslims throughout the world would see their energies liberated and would find resources within their own civilization to help them face the threat of Western domination. What Afghani eventually sought was to reform Islam by advocating a return to the practice of the *salaf* (the "Great Ancestors" or "Rightly Guided Caliphs" who succeeded the Prophet Muhammad) at a time when the Islamic community was strongly united—hence the name given to the movement of Islamic reformism which he launched, Salafiyya or Salafism.[2]

Jamal al-Din al-Afghani's activism managed to instil enthusiasm for his pan-Islamic project and his reformist ambitions among the Muslim masses, particularly in India and Egypt, where he was active in struggling against British occupation. His advocacy also provided people in the Middle East and parts of Asia with a militant form of Islam which came to assume a strong political dimension—hence the use of the term "political Islam" to describe the subsequent rise of a myriad of politico-religious Islamic movements across the region. If Afghani brought the flag of Islamic liberation to the Muslim masses, it was nonetheless his prominent student and disciple, the Egyptian Muhammed Abduh (1849–1905), who took on the task of laying down the ideological foundations of the Salafiyya movement. More concerned with intellectual matters and education than with politics, Abduh was very active in trying to demonstrate the compatibility of Islam and much of the knowledge and technology that had allowed the West to reach its unprecedented might. In his view, the key to Europe's success lay in the way in which the Renaissance and Enlightenment had managed to bring forward "reason" as a main driver behind the philosophy guiding Western policies. If rationalism had allowed Europe to make considerable technological progress, most notably through the development of education in the field of science, then the Islamic world should also strive to make religion compatible with reason.

In this respect, Abduh sought to revive the legacy of the late Mutazilite theologians Ibn Rushd and Ibn Sina who had, in the medieval era, attempted to introduce reason as a way to interpret Islam and its scriptures in an effort to reconcile religion with Greek philosophy. Developing and updating their arguments, Abduh contended that revelation could not be opposed to reason since the latter would remain in harmony with God's word as long as knowledge was reached beyond doubt. The ideological and practical consequences of the Islamic reformer's "neo-Mutazilism"[3] were profoundly significant as they meant that any technological or intellectual progress made on the basis of harmony between revelation and reason would conform to Islamic principles and thus could not be charged with heresy. Concretely, this signified, for instance, a revival of interest in the Muslim world in the study of science and philosophy, subjects long considered "un-Islamic". Crucially, this new kind of "Islamic rationalism" was deliberately used by Abduh as an argument with which to oppose Western concepts such as secularism—in essence, a critique of religion's rationality. In many ways, reforming Islam from within was thus a means by which the entire Islamic community could tackle with indigenous tools the challenges of modernity.

Theologically, the consequences of Abduh's thought were also no less significant, for they came to represent the most significant challenge to the religious status quo that had dominated Islam since the ninth century. Since that time Islam had become engrained in a web of innovations introduced by various Sunni theologians who asked their Muslim followers to follow *taqlid* (emulation), not *ijtihad* (rational interpretation). Their fundamental opposition to the use of reason to interpret the Quran's "hidden meaning" was considered by both Jamal al-Din al-Afghani and Muhammed Abduh as one of the sources behind the Muslim world's backwardness at the time. What the "Islamic reformers" advocated, therefore, was a reopening of the doors of *ijtihad*, which would allow individuals across the Islamic community to rationally interpret the Quran's "hidden meaning" on matters related to the modern world.[4] This meant, however, that followers of Abduh and Afghani would be violently opposed by the local *ulama* (the religious establishment) who viewed the project of stripping Islam of its innovations as a direct challenge to their authority in the Muslim community. Despite

7

the *ulama*'s fierce opposition, however, the "Islamic reformism" of
Abduh and Afghani unleashed a wave of intellectual dynamism across
the Middle East which naturally reached late Ottoman Syria during the
1880s and 1890s.

Syria was perhaps one of the best places in the Middle East to offer a
listening ear to the teachings of the Salafiyya movement. Throughout
the thirteenth century Damascus had indeed been the home of Ibn
Taymiyya, one of the most prolific scholars (or *ulama*) in Islamic history,
whose insistence on the need for a greater role for *ijtihad* in applying the
early teachings of Islam would profoundly influence Muhammed Abduh
and his Salafi followers. Often seen as "the intellectual ancestor of
salafism,"[5] Ibn Taymiyya argued with passion that the innovations
ascribed to Islam by various theological schools betrayed *tawhid*—the
uniqueness of God. For instance, he considered it a polytheistic practice
for Sufis—a mystical branch of Sunni Islam—to seek a saint's intercession when, in his view, God alone should be worshipped. What this
medieval Syrian scholar unambiguously sought was to return Islam to
its "pure" foundations and to the original sources of Islamic religion: the
Quran and the *Sunnah* ("Prophetic traditions"). On this basis, he
strongly denied the validity of *taqlid* as a principle of jurisprudence,
since in his view it only encouraged the multiplication of innovations in
religion. Instead, he called on religious scholars to embrace *ijtihad* by
pronouncing legal rulings based on the interpretation of scripture. This
did not mean, however, that Ibn Taymiyya sought a greater role for
reason in Islamic theology. Instead, he vowed to subordinate its use to a
literalist interpretation of revelation—a strand of his thought which was
partially unsuccessful in his lifetime but profoundly inspired the rise of
the Wahhabiya movement in late eighteenth century Saudi Arabia.[6] At
any rate, the medieval Syrian scholar's advocacy of a return to the practice of the *salaf* as a means to purify Islam was embraced by Muhammed
Abduh and his Salafi followers who took on the task of reviving at least
parts of Ibn Taymiyya's legacy.

Rediscovered first by the Wahhabis at the end of the eithteenth century and then by Islamic reformers in Egypt and Iraq during the 1870s,
the writings of the medieval Syrian scholar quickly spread through
Damascus where the memory of his stay had died down over the centuries. In the Syrian capital, Ibn Taymiyya's teachings and writings were
revived by Abd al-Qadir al-Jazairi (1807–83). A hero of the resistance

against French occupation of Algeria, Jazairi later went to Syria from where, in the footsteps of Afghani and Abduh, he encouraged the local Muslims to seek the reform of Islam and achieve progress in order to fight Western imperialism. While he insisted on the harmony between rational knowledge and revelation, Jazairi also embraced a literalist interpretation of *Sharia* (Islamic law). According to the researcher David Commins, who studied in great detail the emergence of the Salafiyya movement in late Ottoman Syria, it was precisely Jazairi's own union of scripturalism with reason which would later become the hallmark of Syrian Salafi reformism.[7] In Jazairi's footsteps, other Damascene reformers such as Abd al-Razzaq al-Bittar, Tahir al-Jazairi, Jamal al-Din al-Qasimi and Salim Bukhari all proceeded to a selective revival of Ibn Taymiyya's thought.

While the medieval Syrian jurist certainly took them as a source of inspiration, they nonetheless fiercely rejected some of his views. In the framework of the peculiar socio-religious environment in which the Damascene reformers operated throughout the end of the nineteenth century—marked by the predominance of Sufi orders in religious life and the importance of religious minorities in Syria—Ibn Taymiyya's controversial rulings on these matters were bound to be unpopular. Often hailed as the "spirit of resistance" against the Mongol siege of Damascus in 1300, he sanctioned *takfir* (excommunication from Islam) and, as a consequence, jihad (holy struggle) against the "unbeliever" Muslim regimes set up by the Mongol invaders of Syria—who, because they were declared *kafir* (infidel), were now considered to be outside Islam, which meant that they could be killed. The Alawi, Druze and Christian minorities living in Syria were also targeted by this orthodox Sunni theologian. But it was for Sufism that Ibn Taymiyya reserved his harshest critiques. He considered, in particular, the almost mystic character of Sufi practices, such as seeking the intercession of saints and visiting tombs, as utterly "un-Islamic".[8] Several centuries onwards, however, the size of religious minorities had grown and Sufism had become a popular practice in Syria. This greatly encouraged nineteenth century representatives of the Syrian Salafi camp to support, in their overwhelming majority, peaceful coexistence with religious minorities. Also, even though Syrian Salafists regularly denounced the mystic dimension of Sufism, its very legitimacy within Syrian society was rarely questioned or criticized—with the exception of Abd al-Hamid al-Zahrawi.[9] Perhaps most importantly the Damascene reformists never condoned Ibn Taymiyya's tendency to practice *takfir* and jihad against governments judged "infidel" and therefore "outside Islam".[10]

This selective revival of Ibn Taymiyya's teachings by the Syrian Salafi camp of the nineteenth century greatly contributed to the emergence of a particularly moderate early brand of political Islam in Syria. While local Salafists advocated a return to the practices of Islam's forefathers, they also preached openness and an understanding of the changes in the modern world. David Commins thus holds that, in Syria, "salafism represented an adaptation to, not a rejection of, social change."[11] This strand of Islamic reformism, influential mainly in Damascus, came to be known as the "Damascus school" in contrast to the "Aleppo school", which was made up of religious scholars closer to Sufi than Salafi teachings.

But, as time went by, changing political circumstances also played an important role in fuelling debates on previously under-discussed topics. The late nineteenth century bore witness to a process of increased centralization of power in the Ottoman Empire which denied Arab provinces the degree of autonomy they had previously enjoyed. This was severely criticized by Salafist reformers who started to question the Islamic roots of Ottoman rule in Istanbul, advocating instead that "true" Islam could only be found in the Arab world, the birthplace of Islam. In Syria, two of the most prominent local reformers, Tahir al-Jazairi and Salim Bukhari, took on the task of reviving the Arab heritage of the Ottoman Syrian province. In 1906, another prominent Damascene Salafist, Muhibb al-Din al-Khatib, founded the Arab Renaissance Society in the Syrian capital, thereby also displaying his movement's commitment to an early form of Arab nationalism.

In addition, the Syrian Salafis came to embrace political ideas in tune with the mood of the time, such as constitutionalism and political liberalism. Since the 1890s the Salafis had argued in favour of the restoration of a constitutional government in Istanbul. When the Constitution was reintroduced after the Young Turks' 1908 coup against the Ottoman autocrat Abdulhamid II, the Damascene reformists provided theological backing for it. Jamal al-Din al-Qasimi passionately defended the principles of constitutional government in speeches and writings, contending that it could be interpreted through *ijtihad* as ensuring the application of precepts such as *shura* (consultation) and the preservation of public welfare—key Islamic tenets.[12] Open to external ideas and debate, the Damascene reformists came to embrace political views embedded in support for political liberalism and for an early form of Arab nationalism. The Syrian Salafists' activism, however, did not please everybody. Their plea in favour of *ijtihad* on the basis of the argument that local religious leaders brought too many innovations to Islam cast doubt on the *ulama*'s very competence, legitimacy and authority over Syrian society. The religious establishment was therefore particularly vocal in its criticism of the Islamic reformers—perhaps also because most *ulama* were then Sufis co-opted by the autocratic Ottoman rulers criticized by the Damascus Salafists.[13]

The Salafists' insistence on developing the use of *ijtihad*, however, did not mean they thought individual Muslims alone would be able to interpret the scriptures in a way consistent with reason and in reference to the early traditions of Islam. In their view, only qualified scholars should be granted the right to practice *ijtihad*—a somewhat elitist posture described as "patronizing"[14] by the Syrian Salafism expert David Commins. As will be seen in Chapter 5, where the background of the "Damascene Brothers"—those members of the Syrian Ikhwan most active in the capital—is studied, the elitist and chiefly intellectual component of Damascene Salafism was one characteristic of the leadership of Issam al-Attar over the Syrian Brotherhood throughout the late 1950s and 1960s, and one of the reasons behind a crisis of leadership within the Islamic movement. At any rate, the social elitism of the Damascene Salafists was already evident at the turn of the nineteenth century. Their disdain for practices popular at the time, such as Sufism, meant that their intellectual movement was bound to remain marginal. On the fringes, however, there emerged a handful of more populist figures organized in various increasingly influential Islamic societies. While the Salafiyya movement brought a political taste to Islam, these Islamic societies were to become the structures within which a popular version of political Islam would emerge—ultimately laying down the organizational foundation for the rise of Syria's Muslim Brotherhood.

Politicizing Islam: the rise of the "Islamic populists"

Jamiat, or societies and clubs dedicated to the promotion of intellectual or political goals, emerged all across the Ottoman Empire throughout the nineteenth century. Most were initially set up to advocate a series of reforms primarily relating to education. For instance, they argued for teaching of courses in the Arabic language and Arab history at a time when the Ottomans wished to pursue "Turkification" policies in their Arab provinces. Naturally, their plea became openly political with time, as their ultimate goal often clashed with Ottoman policies and participated in the rise of a popular Arab nationalist sentiment.

At first, Islamic reformers played a major role in favouring such a trend as the intellectual dynamism unleashed by the Salafiyya movement across the Arab world contributed to the early development of these societies. Prominent Salafists such as Muhammed Abduh and his associate Rashid Rida created influential newspapers and journals, like *al-Manar*, helping to spread their reformist ideas across the region. In Syria, Tahir al-Jazairi was one of the first to follow their path when, at the turn of the twentieth century, he created the "Benevolent Society", a *jamia* whose goal was to establish a library in Damascus tasked with gathering and making public all the major writings of earlier Islamic scholars of Arab descent, such as the Syrian Ibn Taymiyya.[15] In 1935, the Damascene Salafists were the main actors behind the birth of al-Tamaddun al-Islami ("the Islamic civilization"). The emergence of this society would mark the spread in Syria of Salafi-oriented Islamic *jamiat* primarily concerned with spreading Muslim education for boys and girls. By that time, however, the Damascene Salafists were already facing fierce rivalry from the right where a strand of less elitist Islamic activists, downplaying the Salafiyya's intellectual dimension, was gaining support from ever wider segments of Syrian society.

While the creed of al-Tamaddun was committed to the grand intellectual aim of seeking the reform of Islam from within, in order to face the challenges of the modern world, a new generation of Muslim activists had indeed emerged whose clear sociopolitical goals gave them a more populist outlook—hence the term "Islamic populists"[16] used by the researcher Elizabeth Thomson. Led not by major intellectual figures but instead by schoolteachers, lawyers and local sheikhs, these politically active societies strove to directly lobby the governments of the day to embrace educational reform and to uphold Muslim values. Also, while sharing the Damascene Salafis' ambition to save Islamic civilization through the spread of Muslim education, these societies appealed to the masses by emphasizing the traditions of Islam instead of focusing on its reform. It is therefore not surprising that many of them had major ties to influential Sufi orders popular in many Syrian cities like Aleppo and Hama. This broad-based appeal enjoyed by Syria's "Islamic populists" ultimately meant that their influence was not limited to the capital, unlike that of the elitist Damascene Salafists. While Damascus remained the birthplace of influential Islamic societies, such as Jamiat al-Gharra (1924), Jamiat al-Hidaya al-Islamiyya (1936) or Jamiat al-Ulama (1938), many more flourished throughout the country's other cities. In Aleppo, for instance, the emergence of Dar al-Arqam in 1935 was to represent a crucial development in the Syrian Islamic landscape. In the eyes of many members of the Ikhwan, this society was ultimately to inspire the creation of Syria's Muslim Brotherhood through the rise of several like-minded groups based in Hama and Homs, among other cities, called the Shabbab Muhammad.[17]

To understand the political activism and broad popular support which characterized such societies, a brief look at the sociopolitical circumstances surrounding their creation is needed. The 1920s and 1930s were indeed a time of profound change in the way Syrians led their daily lives. A foreign power, France, dominated much of Syrian political life throughout the Mandate period (1920–46). In addition to the challenge of foreign rule, which aroused strong anti-colonial sentiments, many of the traditions then still regulating Syrian society seemed to be on the verge of being challenged. Many Syrian Sunni Muslims were appalled by the introduction of French-imported secular norms which, in their eyes, threatened the Islamic traditions of the Syrian province. In addition, just as Western social and cultural norms were spreading throughout Syria, feminist circles started to publicly display their growing activism in the capital. Centuries of local traditions were upset in barely a decade. In economic affairs, the small urban traders and local artisans were the primary victims of the growth in foreign trade which seemed only to benefit a few major merchants. In addition, there were shortages of the most basic commodities. A British diplomat in post in Damascus in 1942 reported on bread shortages by pointing out that "bread queues start forming at 3am" while the overall price of wheat rose, in the same year, from £340 to £450 a ton.[18] The economic difficulties of the time were sometimes compounded by soaring inflation as urban migration exploded, disrupting the traditional social fabric of many cities by the same token.

In this context, only a spark was needed to fuel popular discontent. It was the French control of local education that acted as the catalyst, eventually enabling politico-religious *jamiat* to greatly reinforce their social base among Syrian Sunni Muslims. The most influential of these, al-Gharra (the Noble Society), was explicitly founded in 1924 with the goal of fostering an education for Muslim boys and girls thoroughly in tune with religious ethics. Al-Gharra was, at first, key in building several schools where such education could be received. Over time, the Islamic society's political agenda became clearer. When the local authorities allowed the building of many missionary Christian schools in Syria throughout the 1920s and 1930s, al-Gharra organized a series of street protests drawing the masses in the capital but also across Syria in cities such as Homs and Hama against what was widely perceived as part of a French plot to undermine Islamic values.[19]

One such prominent anti-French demonstration organized by al-Gharra took place in March 1939 when protests broke out throughout the country and slogans such as "France is the enemy of God"[20] were heard. Quite crucially, these mass demonstrations followed the introduction of a decree coming from Paris which introduced a "Personal Status Code" putting forward a series of secular reforms meant to replace the existing local traditions and customs in regulating citizens' lives in their private sphere. The measures included the right for Syrian individuals to disavow their religious affiliation, the obligation to register marriages with the state and the duty to follow civil law on matters related to issues not explicitly stated in the laws of their respective religious communities.[21] For many Muslims across Syria, such measures were unacceptable as they reversed centuries-long domination of Islamic law over civil common law. On the whole, according to Philip Khoury, a specialist on Syria during the French Mandate, it seemed as if "the French tried to reduce Islam in Syria to the status of one religion among many."[22]

During World War II, "Islamic populists" stepped up their activism in the political sphere. This time they focused their energies on polarizing Syrians for or against a highly symbolic change their society had been undergoing: the emergence of women's rights. Throughout the French mandate, women in Syria had received education and had become more visible in the public sphere. Some of them were very active figures in the philanthropic and political scene of the day—to the outrage of many religious sheikhs who saw this as the result of Western corruption of Islamic values. But what made women's rights a deeply controversial and salient issue was the fact that most of those who reached visible positions also happened to belong to Syria's elite, most often the wives or daughters of politicians or rich merchants. In this context, the struggle launched by the "Islamic populists" against women's rights gradually came to assume class overtones which made for a particularly explosive cocktail at a time of widening social inequalities among all Syrians.

The spark came on 11 May 1942 when al-Gharra gathered several hundred people in Damascus to protest against the "laxity of public morals"[23] after the wives of leading Damascene families had attended a theatrical show performed in the capital. What the Islamic *jamia* demanded from the prime minister, who then received a delegation from the group, was nothing short of "prohibiting women from going to cinemas and theatres" as well as the enforcement of "a return to their traditional Islamic code of behaviour and dress." Clearly, mobilizing in support of "Islamic morals" served the ambitions of al-Gharra, which positioned itself at the vanguard of the defence of traditions and Islamic values against the "corrupting" influence of Western culture. According to a British diplomat at the UK mission in Damascus, al-Gharra's attitude was nothing less than "the exploitation of religion to serve political ends."[24]

The newfound influence of the "Islamic populists" in the political sphere was made even clearer a few years later when al-Gharra took up the issue of the veil and politicized it to the extent that it would bring the Syrian government to the brink of collapse. As a chief symbol of Islamic tradition, the headscarf had been at the centre of controversy dating back to the late 1920s. It had opposed Nazira Zayn al-Din, a young Syrian feminist critical of the norms of veiling and seclusion, against Mustafa Ghalayini, a prominent Islamic scholar who argued in favour of upholding such traditions. The debate, at first led in elitist circles, spread throughout the Syrian public during the 1930s and 1940s and polarized it along ideological and political lines. While secular nationalist circles viewed unveiling as part of the project for emancipation from a seemingly backward Islamic culture, religious populists saw the headscarf as a symbol of resistance against Western oppression. In the nationalist fever that seized the country during the early 1940s, at a time when the French seemed to be constantly delaying their granting of independence to Syria, the arguments put forward by the "Islamic populists" were bound to be eventually victorious. This was acknowledged by Shukri al-Quwwatli, the leader of the secular National Bloc, who understood the influence of the "Islamic populists" and sought to benefit from it by allying with them. By the time the parliamentary elections of July 1943 came up, he had managed to recruit an al-Gharra leader to his electoral list, Sheikh Abd al-Hamid Tabba, and spoke in terms that appealed to the religious masses.

This Islamic-nationalist alliance represented a true breakthrough for the emergence of a clearly formulated brand of political Islam striving to push policy-making in a direction consistent with demands not limited to the field of education and morals but also covering politics and identity. In rupture with past practices, the nascent Islamic movement in Syria had come to exert a more direct kind of influence on the state. The alliance was short-lived, however, as its inherent contradictions came to the fore after barely a year, concentrating once again on the issue of the headscarf. Having lent its full support to Quwwatli, al-Gharra expected him to implement at least parts of the educational and social agenda the Islamic society had long since advocated. "The women's issue was seen as a test: if the government backed al-Gharra's demands, Tabba and others believed that the rest of al-Gharra's programs would see the light of the day",[25] as Philip Khoury has explained.

The occasion for such a test came on 20th May 1944 when Rafiqa al-Bukhari, the wife of the Minister of Education, scheduled the organization of a charity ball at the French Officers' Club in Damascus. When the leaders of al-Gharra learned that Muslim women might attend the event unveiled and in the company of men, they demanded that the government cancel the ball as an offence against public morality. Violent protests against unveiling erupted throughout Damascus, where estimates suggest they were supported by over 40 per cent of the population, before quickly spreading beyond the capital to reach Aleppo.[26] The issue of the veil, ever since the time of Nazira Zayn al-Din, had polarized Syrian public opinion. By the early 1940s, gender issues and class tensions had partially overlapped—as was visible through the concentration of protests in the disadvantaged Midan and Shagour quarters of Damascus in May 1944. Nationalism was also at play as, for the Islamic populists, upholding traditions such as the veil was the beginning of a process that would ultimately purge Syrian society of foreign influence and oust the French. Despite violent clashes with the police, the protests soon died down when, under intense Islamic pressure, the charity ball in Damascus and the formation of a women's club in Aleppo were cancelled.[27]

The "Islamic populists" had shown all the influence they could exert. In a clear break with the past practices of earlier *jamiat*, they had managed to politicize social and gender issues with the ultimate aim of influencing political outcomes. While they did not directly enter the realm of politics, claiming instead to be preoccupied solely by the defence of religious values, they started to enjoy a substantial political role. Their influence would greatly affect the emergence of a Syrian branch of the Muslim Brotherhood which, despite what its name may suggest, was not a direct import from Egypt but represented instead the merger of several of the aforementioned Islamic societies thriving in Mandatory Syria.

2

ISLAM AND DEMOCRACY

THE MUSLIM BROTHERHOOD IN POST-INDEPENDENCE
SYRIA (1946–1963)

While the Salafiyya movement's spill-over into Syria played a great role in building up the Syrian Muslim Brotherhood's intellectual foundations, the rise of Islamic societies throughout the 1930s and 1940s provided the political and organizational basis upon which the Islamic movement was to structure its actions. Thus the birth of Syria's Ikhwan in 1946 was very much the product of the country's particular socioreligious and political landscape. Such adaptability to local contexts would be a crucial feature of the Syrian branch of the Muslim Brotherhood as the organization came to be profoundly shaped by the moderate legacy of the Salafiyya movement's inroads into the country. The moderation and pragmatism of its historical leaders, Mustapha al-Sibai and Issam al-Attar, combined with the emergence of parliamentary democracy in post-independence Syria, are also factors explaining the Muslim Brotherhood's early commitment to peaceful participation in the Syrian political sphere.

Studying the political behavour and ideological rhetoric of Syria's Muslim Brotherhood between 1946 and 1963 will make clear that, for all the radicalization of the Islamic movement throughout the 1970s, the organization was in its origins a peaceful group committed to the principles of constitutionalism and political liberalism. It is also through the lens of the Brotherhood's moderate legacy, as illustrated in this section, that one can understand current Ikhwani claims that, despite radical episodes, the organization is now back to its "basics". Primarily political in its aims, the Brotherhood was to become violent only at the very height of the Ikhwan-Ba'ath confrontation, between late 1979 and 1982.

Learning the game of politics at the dawn of Syria's independence from France, the Syrian Brotherhood quickly professionalized its tactics and displayed a surprising degree of ideological flexibility—supporting political liberalism and an "Islamicized" version of socialism. Ultimately, however, the Syrian branch of the Muslim Brotherhood was bound to remain part of the wider Ikhwani framework which tied it to its Egyptian founders. The contradictions which would emerge out of such a situation, particularly when the Syrian Ikhwan were faced with the dilemma of whether or not to support the policies of Nasser—an Egyptian leader widely popular in the "Arab street" yet a major persecutor of the Egyptian Brotherhood—came to the fore in the late 1950s and early 1960s. Such weakness would, in turn, pave the way for the growing influence exercised over Syrian politics by the Ikhwan's main political competitor: the Ba'ath Party.

Egyptian roots

While the local branch of the Muslim Brotherhood was founded on socioeconomic and religious grounds specific to mid-1940s Syria, the group looked in its early years towards the original Egyptian movement for both intellectual and organizational inspiration. Here, a glance back at the historical and ideological circumstances surrounding the creation of the original Muslim Brotherhood will help to properly understand the underpinnings upon which its Syrian branch would build its activism.

The Muslim Brotherhood, or *Jamiat al-Ikhwan al-Muslimin* (also referred to simply as Ikhwan), was founded in Egypt in 1928 with the aim of becoming both the explicit political extension of the local religious clubs, or *jamiat*, and the intellectual heir of the Salafiyya movement. Thus the movement was openly dedicated to reviving the influence of Islam in Muslim societies. Hassan al-Banna, its founder, looked upon the earlier Salafi reformists as influential sources of inspiration. While he admired Jamal al-Din al-Afghani's political activism and call for a revival of Islam, he was also seduced by Muhammed Abduh's advocacy of a return to the tradition of the *salaf* as part of an effort to strengthen Islam from within. For Hassan al-Banna, if Muslims could regain the purity of faith which characterized the Prophet's generation and gave it strength, the *Umma* could once again successfully face the challenge of foreign domination.

All non-political efforts had to be concentrated on Muslim education as a first step towards the "moral re-armament"[1] of society. At a time when foreign cultural influence was gaining ground in Egypt, particularly through the British occupation, the Muslim Brotherhood's insistence on reviving Islamic values gave the movement a puritanical and conservative outlook which had not been characteristic of earlier Salafists but had gradually come to be embraced by later Islamic reformers such as Rashid Rida and Muhib al-Din al-Khatib. These two scholars were to exert much influence on the intellectual framework adopted by the Muslim Brotherhood as both sought to revive Ibn Taymiyya's literalism and call for jihad. So the doctrine put forward by the Ikhwan merged many strands of thought found in the dynamic legacy left by the Salafiyya movement, summed up by the slogan: "God is our purpose, the Quran is our constitution, the Prophet is our leader, jihad is our path and martyrdom for the sake of God is our noblest wish."[2]

Intellectually, what set Hassan al-Banna apart from his Salafist predecessors was his insistence on the comprehensiveness of Islam. The Islamic message, for him, was one that embraced all aspects of life. Not only did it obviously have a religious meaning, it also contained teachings which needed to be implemented in the social, economic, educational, cultural and political fields. In each area, from the individual to the public sphere, Islam had something to say which, if properly listened to, would eventually strengthen the Muslim community by giving rise to *nizam Islami*—a "true" Islamic order. In addition, Hassan al-Banna's comprehensive view of Islam—and his own personal background as a Sufi converted to the Salafism preached by Abduh and Afghani—meant that he naturally came to embrace both the spirituality of Sufism and the reformist impulse found in Salafism. According to Kamal al-Helbawy, a prominent Egyptian Brother, it was precisely Hassan al-Banna's inclusive vision of Islam that made his organization so appealing to millions of young Muslims first in Egypt and then across the region. The Ikhwan's historical founder himself is reported to have described his movement as combining at once "a salafiyya message, a Sunni way, a Sufi truth, a sports club, a cultural-educational union, an economic company and a social idea."[3]

This all-encompassing approach to Islam also made the Muslim Brotherhood a deeply political organization as, in order to implement the socioeconomic and cultural programme it had set out, power had to be achieved. The Muslim Brotherhood's early political activism set it apart from a Salafiyya movement which, if political in its aims, was essentially intellectual in its means.[4] Directly entering the political sphere was no longer considered a mere political right; it had become a religious duty. In Hassan al-Banna's words, indeed, "a Muslim will never become a real Muslim if he is not a politician and has a view for the affairs of his people."[5] The Brotherhood's early political activism led the researcher Paul Salem to characterize the organization as a "movement dedicated to defending and reasserting the place of Islam in society through educational and political means."[6] It took on the task, for instance, of exerting pressure on successive Egyptian monarchs, King Fuad and later King Farouk, in directions thought to be in accordance with the message of Islam.

By 1939, over two decades after its creation, the Egyptian Ikhwan had grown so rapidly in strength and influence that one of the movement's best analysts, Richard Mitchell, would describe the Brotherhood as "one of the most important political contestants on the Egyptian scene".[7] While at the time not formally a political party—its founder rejected the idea of party politics—the Ikhwan were still an organization capable of exerting such a degree of influence on Egyptian politics that the government decided to outlaw them in December 1948. The confrontational dynamic then unleashed would eventually encourage a member of the Ikhwan to carry out the assassination of the Egyptian prime minister, which would in turn lead to a fierce governmental response culminating with the assassination of Hassan al-Banna, followed by a long period of deep tension between Egyptian authorities and the Ikhwan.

One reason for the increasing perception of the Muslim Brotherhood as a threat to the Egyptian establishment was its organizational capability to mobilize thousands of people in mass protests across the streets of Cairo. More than just an intellectual trend or a *jamia* with socio-educational aims, the Ikhwan had, throughout the 1930s, become a true social movement backed by genuine popular support and with clear political goals. At a time when established political parties were often composed of Westernized elites, the message the Ikhwan strove to convey appealed to the Egyptian people through the perceived authenticity of their message: "Islam is the solution". The organization argued that, in order to face the cultural and socioeconomic challenges posed by the West, Egyptian Muslims had to restore vital values, taking as a starting point the original traditions found in Islam. The straightforwardness of the Islamic message was appealing to many as the Ikhwan's constituency was largely made up of the educated middle class comprising professionals, civil servants, artisans and petty traders. By linking traditional concerns—such as the enforcement of Islamic law and public morality—with contemporary national issues—such as independence and development—the Ikhwan managed to put forward a seemingly indigenous platform advocating, among other things, the rejection of Western values—then linked in the minds of many with foreign domination and the extravagant lifestyle of Egyptian elites.[8]

The Syrian branch of the Muslim Brotherhood

Owing its name to its Egyptian sister, the Syrian Muslim Brotherhood was born out of the personal ties and shared intellectual sensibilities developed by Syrian Islamic scholars with Hassan al-Banna during their religious studies at Al-Azhar University in Cairo. In 1933, Mustapha al-Sibai, a young Islamic militant from Homs, and Mohammed al-Hamid,[9] one of his classmates originally from Hama, went to the Egyptian capital in order to continue their study of Islamic law. There, they befriended the founder of the Muslim Brotherhood, gained extensive experience of the organization and even came to occupy influential positions within the Egyptian Brotherhood.[10] Upon their return to Syria, they strove to unify the several *jamiat* which had sprung up throughout the country during the 1920s and 1930s. The first congress gathering these religious societies together was held in 1937, but Mustapha al-Sibai waited until 1945 before giving the platform the official title of "Muslim Brotherhood". Reflecting upon this with a British diplomat during the summer of 1946, the founder of the Syrian branch of the Ikhwan explained: "various Muslim youth organizations had been inaugurated in Syria since 1936 but, in order that the French might not become alarmed, different names were given to the organizations in different part of the country; now that the reason for camouflaging the movement has disappeared with the cessation of French control, it has been decided to combine all of them in one organization, with the title of *al-Ikhwan al-Muslimin*."[11]

The first congress inaugurating the formal gathering of these Islamic societies into Syria's Muslim Brotherhood was held in Aleppo in 1945. The northern metropolis had been a major centre of Islamic activism throughout the 1930s, most notably through the work of Dar al-Arqam, a local *jamia* dedicated to the promotion of Islam's all-encompassing role in Syrian society by carrying out cultural, sporting and social activities. According to an account given by one of its former members who would later rise to assume leadership of the Syrian Brotherhood, Ali Sadreddine al-Bayanouni, Dar al-Arqam ("The Home of Arqam") could be distinguished from the Damascus-based al-Gharra by its open-mindedness and progressive spirit. "Dar al-Arqam was an Aleppine Islamic society which welcomed moderates and was open to various practices: it represented an ideology of the 'middle way', if you will, one consistent with the spirit of the 'Aleppo branch' of the Ikhwan, and which helps to distinguish from similar but less progressive organizations in Hama and Deir ez-Zoor, for instance,"[12] Ali Sadreddine al-Bayanouni explained.

Organizations similar to Dar al-Arqam—though, they might have slightly differed in their ideological and religious orientations, as Bayanouni suggested—flourished during the late 1930s throughout the country under the name of Shabbab Muhammad ("Muhammed's Youth"). When all of these *jamiat* merged under the umbrella of the "Syrian Muslim Brotherhood", they immediately provided the Ikhwani organization with an already constituted social base. Another advantage was that the Syrian Brotherhood was able to thoroughly structure its work and co-ordinate its actions in the country's various regions by relying relatively quickly on a clear hierarchy inspired by the Egyptian Ikhwan. From the outset, the Syrian organization worked on the following model: a Comptroller General would head an Executive Committee voted in by a wider Consultative Body (*Majlis al-Shura*) representative of the organization's regional and ideological diversity. The headquarters were located in Damascus and regional offices and sub-branches would ensure the collective yet hierarchical nature of the Ikhwan's work.[13] However, while the Syrian Brotherhood directly benefited from the organizational lessons drawn from the original Egyptian Ikhwan, the necessarily heterogeneous nature of the Syrian organization—both regionally and ideologically—would ultimately mean that any attempt on the part of one sub-group to seize the leadership over the others would lead to internal crisis (see Chapter 5).

The Syrian branch of the Ikhwan also looked to its Egyptian sister for ideological inspiration. Like Hassan al-Banna before him, Mustapha al-Sibai claimed that his programme was based on "trying to revive Islam from its current petrifaction" through "social reform" and the "liberation of Arab and Islamic people from foreign domination".[14] The Syrian leader also embraced his Egyptian mentor's conception of Islam as a comprehensive concept, seen as embodying "all aspects of life, political and social".[15] Islam—its teachings, law and culture—was here again perceived as the inspiration from which all socioeconomic and political reforms should be derived.

The common ideological background and striking organizational similarities between the two organizations did not mean, however, that the Syrian Ikhwan would merely be a representative in Damascus of the Egyptian Muslim Brotherhood, for the two groups retained their autonomy in two very distinct sociopolitical environments. Of course, as Mustapha al-Sibai confessed to a British diplomat, "the aims of the Ikhwan are similar in all countries and they co-operate on all political and social questions, keep in close contact and exchange information." But he also insisted that, even so, "the Ikhwan of Syria is administratively and financially independent and receives no instruction or orders from other organizations with the same name in Egypt or elsewhere."[16]

In addition, the discourse and practice of the Syrian Muslim Brotherhood at times also differed from Hassan al-Banna's original tone. For instance, since Syria's sizeable religious minorities—the country's Christians, Jews, Alawis and Druzes—had always been wary of the political influence Sunni Islamic organizations were capable of wielding, the Syrian Muslim Brotherhood tried from the outset to incorporate elements of moderation into its discourse. It stressed that "the People of the Book [the Christians and Jews] are entitled to protection and can expect to live in security under the laws of Islam"[17] and that "religion is brotherhood" while "sectarianism is enmity".[18] Similarly, owing to the Sufi background of many Syrian *ulama*, the Salafi-oriented intellectual founders of the Syrian Ikhwan strove to put forward a Sufi-Salafi synthesis which would set theological differences among members aside in order to focus on social and political work. Thus, while Mustapha al-Sibai was at times nicknamed the "small Ibn Taymiyya",[19] mainly for his critiques of Sufism, he is also remembered today for having been a relatively compromising figure working for Sufi-Salafi unity inside the movement. For the founder of the Syrian Ikhwan, Islam was "*'amal* [work and action] not *jadal* [controversial argumentation]".[20] This was also a feature shared by another prominent figure inside the movement, Muhammed al-Hamid based in Hama, of whom Said Hawwa, the future ideologue of resistance to the Ba'ath regime, said that he "believed that in order to stop the *ridda* ([apostasy]), Muslims must join hands despite their many controversies; and although he was a Hanafi Sufi, he had always declared his readiness to put his hand in the hand of the fiercest Salafi to stop this apostasy."[21] The prestige gained by Muhammed al-Hamid within the Brotherhood's ranks was to embody the Syrian Ikhwan's unique synthesis of the Sufi revivalist tradition, followed by many Brothers from Hama and Aleppo, and of traditional Salafism, present mainly but not exclusively in Damascus.[22]

It seems clear that the early pragmatism displayed by the Syrian branch of the Muslim Brotherhood with regards to Sufism and religious minorities was the result of the particular intellectual history which shaped the emergence of the Salafiyya movement in late Ottoman Syria. Damascus Salafists, such as Abdel Qadir al-Jazairi, always stressed the importance of building up healthy relations with religious minorities in Syria as well as with the popular Sufi sheikhs.[23] The ideas he put forward and the ideological flexibility he displayed gave rise, in the early 1900s, to a generation of Damascene Salafists who, like Muhammed al-Mubarak and Issam al-Attar, were to lead the Syrian Muslim Brotherhood into moderation throughout the late 1940s, 1950s and early 1960s (see Chapter 5).

Such pragmatism, combined with the relatively open political environment which emerged after Independence, meant that the Syrian Muslim Brotherhood would enter the political game and strive to challenge its competitors openly by forming a party and running for elections. This was a step that the Egyptian organization was not ready to take for while it tried to exert political influence on the rulers of the day, it did not yet wish to form a political party and continued to occasionally resort to violent activities.[24] In contrast, the Syrian Ikhwan proclaimed from the outset their commitment to a democratic form of government. In line with the Salafist tradition of Islamic reformism, Ma'ruf al-Dawalibi and Muhammed al-Mubarak, two politicians close to the Syrian Muslim Brotherhood, justified the inclusion of democratic practices in an Islamic state through the modernist postulate that Islam does not ordain a specific form of government but only lays down general principles which people are entitled to implement through *ijtihad* in accordance with the changing circumstances of their place and time. They insisted that the emergence of an Islamic state would not mean the advent of a theocracy as, while the elected ruler should indeed be bound by the rules of Islam, the real source of political authority lay in the *bay'a* (oath of allegiance) to the community. The political authorities should, in turn, consult this community through the mechanism of *shura* (consultation).[25]

In this context, the establishment in Syria of an Islamist party which would compete in the democratic sphere was a natural development which also grew from the pro-active views of the Ikhwan's Syrian leader, Mustapha al-Sibai, for whom "Islam teaches *tawakkul*—reliance upon God as the first principle of hope and action—not *tawakul*—fatalistic indifference and passive resignation."[26] By insisting on the indigenous Islamic roots of democracy, the Syrian Brothers were making it ideologically acceptable for the Ikhwan to directly enter the political game and participate in parliamentary democracy. As the researcher Stephen Humphreys put it, what at the time singled out the Syrian Ikhwan from their Islamic counterparts in the rest of the Arab world was that they were "militantly fundamentalist in tone but distinctly modernist in content."[27]

Competing for power in Syria's parliamentary democracy

A brief glance at the historical circumstances surrounding the Syrian Muslim Brotherhood's emergence as a political party will contribute to our understanding of the political platform put forward by the Ikhwan in the mid-1940s and their electoral successes. At the time of the organization's creation, Syria had just achieved independence from Mandatory France. Parliamentary sovereignty had been restored and the country was presided over by Shukri al-Quwwatli of the National Bloc, which had led the nationalist struggle against the French.

The National Bloc was heavily dominated by urban notables and rich landowners wishing to carry out a liberal reformist agenda; this, according to author Philip Khoury, had the consequence of hindering the growth of an organized urban proletariat and impeding the emancipation of an increasingly restless peasantry.[28] At first acclaimed for its leadership of the struggle against the French, the National Bloc quickly became seen as "widely corrupt and inefficient",[29] according to a foreign observer at the time, giving rise to a new generation of political parties wishing to tap into the disaffected urban and rural masses. This, combined with the seeming inability of the political establishment to deal effectively with the creation of the state of Israel in May 1948—reflected in Syria's defeat in the subsequent war—provided fertile ground for the rise of more radical political parties.

Leftist, nationalist and religious trends quickly developed. Akram al-Hawrani mobilized the peasantry in his home town of Hama where his Arab Socialist Party rapidly became an influential actor at the local and then the national level. Michel Aflaq and Salah Eddine al-Bittar, for their part, founded the Ba'ath ("renaissance") Party which originally centered its platform around the idea of Arab unity before giving it a populist and socialist spin by allying with Akram al-Hawrani's forces in February 1953. While the Ba'ath's socialist rhetoric was challenged by Khalid Bakdash's Syrian Communist Party and Antun Sa'adah's Syrian Social Nationalist Party, the pro-Palestinian rhetoric it displayed, which stemmed naturally from its Arabist ideology, found itself in competition with the Syrian Muslim Brotherhood's harsh attacks on Israel and plea for Islamic unity.

In that context, it is not surprising that the National Party—a newly established political platform stemming from the National Bloc—was challenged by a wide array of radical parties such as the Ikhwan and the Ba'ath in July 1947, when the first parliamentary elections since Syria gained full independence were held. Still in a state of genesis, the Muslim Brotherhood decided to join forces with the Rabitat al-Ulama (Union of Ulama), a group of religious scholars committed to implementing a conservative social agenda and opposed to Shukri al-Quwwatli's leadership of the country.[30] Although the success of the alliance remained modest, with only three candidates elected, it nonetheless seemed to represent a sufficiently threatening political challenge to the existing establishment given that the government subsequently dissolved the Union and transferred its property to the *Waqfs* (religious endowments) administration.

In addition, the authorities decided to temporarily suspend the publication of *al-Manar*, the newspaper edited by the Syrian Muslim Brotherhood.[31] This particularly repressive measure against the Ikhwan was representative of the government's concerns over the growth of the Muslim Brotherhood's popularity in Syria. While *al-Manar* had been a fairly successful newspaper from the outset, it had, by mid-1946, become popular to the extent that, according to a British diplomat at the time, the demand for it was even "greater than the supply" and its circulation was "larger than that of any other daily newspaper published in Damascus".[32] Beyond the Ikhwan's growing popularity, as shown by its fairly good electoral showing for such a new party, the July 1947 election to Parliament of three members of the Muslim Brotherhood also sent an important message to the rest of the world: the power of Islam's political message would ultimately make its way through elections to the ultimate benefit of the Ikhwan. As Mustapha al-Sibai proudly stated in a telegram he sent to Hassan al-Banna, the Syrian elections were "the first time official representatives of the Islamic idea are elected to parliament in any Islamic or Arab states".[33]

While the elections saw the consolidation of the National Party's power, an internal split within the political establishment emerged. This came to a denouement when politicians opposing Shukri al-Quwwatli's leadership decided to join the People's Party, an economically liberal Aleppo-based political grouping which would later exert a significant influence on Syrian politics. The internal wrangling inside the incumbent party, coupled with repeated student strikes and the defeat in the 1948 war against Israel, quickly led to a severe deterioration of the political atmosphere, leading the government to resign in November 1948. A few months later, in March 1949, Colonel Husni az-Zaim mounted a coup. Az-Zaim disbanded all political parties—including, in May 1949, the Ikhwan—and implemented a series of secularist reforms before he was ousted from power in August 1949 by Colonel Sami Hinnawi, who promised to restore civilian government and parliamentary democracy in Syria.

Elections to the Constituent Assembly were held in November 1949 in which the People's Party made a strong showing. Radical parties such as the Ba'ath and the Ikhwan also scored some success—gaining one and three seats respectively. This was also the first occasion on which the Muslim Brotherhood had run tickets on its own political platform, led by Mustapha al-Sibai, who was elected to Parliament alongside his colleagues Muhammed al-Mubarak and Arif al-Taraqji. Candidates affiliated with the Ikhwan but not officially part of the movement—such as Ma'aruf al-Dawalibi in Aleppo and Subhi al-'Umari in Damascus—were also successful. At that time, the Muslim Brotherhood's influence, while remaining weaker than that of established parties such as the People's Party, was nonetheless significant enough that two of its supporters, al-Dawalibi and al-Mubarak, were given ministerial posts in the December 1949 government led by Khalid al-Azm—becoming Minister of National Economy and Minister of Public Works respectively.[34] That prominent members of the Ikhwan became ministers also showed the extent to which the Syrian branch of the Muslim Brotherhood was a political force willing to display pragmatism, engage in coalitions and make compromises to exert influence on Syria's political life.

Defending Islam with pragmatism

Often portrayed by foreign observers as "religious fanatics",[35] members of the Syrian Muslim Brotherhood were in fact quite prepared to show pragmatism towards existing political authorities and embrace compromise as long as they felt that their interests and values were being advanced. Having agreed to join the December 1949 government, the Ikhwan made their pragmatism even clearer a few months later, in February 1950, when debates were initiated on the drafting of a new constitution at Syria's Constituent Assembly. A special committee had been set up to draft the constitution, made up of thirty-three members, chaired by People's Party leader Nazim al-Qudsi. One issue became particularly controversial: that of the relationship between religion and state. The Muslim Brotherhood, under the banner of the Islamic Socialist Front and in the person of Mustapha al-Sibai, who was on the committee, insisted that the constitution should enshrine Islam as the "state religion"—a demand that earned the support of many of Syria's *ulama*. Aware of the sensitive nature of such an initiative for Syria's sizeable religious minorities, Mustapha al-Sibai strove to emphasize the non-sectarian dimension of his plea. While insisting that Islam had the highest respect for Christianity and would not interfere in matters of personal status, he also argued that, should it be named the state religion, "our Parliament, deputies, laws and way of life will all remain but they will be reinforced by loftiness of spirit, purity of hand, moral probity and human nobility," concluding that "the only reason for establishing a state religion is to colour the state with a spiritual, moral hue so that regulations and laws will be carried out under the impetus of a deep, spiritual driving force."[36]

Mustapha al-Sibai must have proved quite convincing to the special committee, which eventually put forward a draft constitution stating, in its Article 3 that "Islam is the state religion; other divine religions and religious minorities will be respected." But when the draft reached the whole Constituent Assembly, debates on the subject became so violent that the government temporarily banned public discussion on the matter, fearing total chaos. When the matter was discussed again in Parliament on 5 September, continued opposition from most other political blocs eventually convinced Mustapha al-Sibai to negotiate a compromise. In exchange for accepting that Islam would not be considered the state religion, the Muslim Brotherhood managed to introduce a clause which made Islam the religion of the head of state and introduced *fiqh*—Islamic jurisprudence—as the main source of legislation. On the whole, the Muslim Brotherhood had fought with "noisy eloquence",[37] noted a British diplomat at the time, and had managed to give Islam a special role in the constitution which was subsequently approved by the Syrian Parliament. For the researcher Joshua Teitelbaum, this episode proved that "even religious fanatics can learn to be tactically patient and skilful."[38] It also showed the extent to which the Muslim Brotherhood had quickly become a significant actor in Syria's political life.

While Mustapha al-Sibai hailed the new Syrian constitution as an example of what the constitutions of Islamic states should be, and proudly defended the "Islamic element"[39] that he had managed to introduce into it, the pragmatism he had displayed did not please everybody. Syria's *ulama*, in particular, were outraged that the Muslim Brotherhood—which they had supported in the preceding elections—had so easily given up on the core demand of making Islam the state religion. According to Thomas Pierret, an expert on political Islam in Syria, the divergence between the *ulama* and the Ikhwan was not ideological, as both keenly defended the idea of making Islam the state religion, but tactical. While the former were profoundly attached to the Islamic values they professed every day in mosques, the latter had gradually become professional politicians, ready to engage in compromises if it advanced their interests and the values they claimed to defend.[40] In other words, the Muslim Brotherhood and in particular its leader, Mustapha al-Sibai, were "accused of being more interested in politics than in religion",[41] a British diplomat noted at the time.

The political activism displayed by the Ikhwan during the constitutional debates of 1950 was not, however, limited to granting Islam a formal role in the political system. Many members of the Muslim Brotherhood had taken part in the activities of the Islamic *jamiat* which, in the 1920s and 1930s, struck a populist tone by vehemently asking for a return to Islamic values against foreign cultural invasion. It was therefore only natural that the same populism would become a feature of the Syrian Ikhwan. Nawal al-Sibai, the niece of the first leader of the Syrian Ikhwan, remembered, for instance, her uncle's fierce public denunciations of the poems of Nizar Qabbani.[42] Throughout the late 1940s and early 1950s, the Syrian poet had published a series of romantic verses making explicit references to a woman's body, drawing the kind of outrage from conservative Damascene society on which the leader of the Muslim Brotherhood would be quick to capitalize. In the same vein, a political officer at the British Embassy in Damascus reported another instance of the kind of conservative populism practiced by the Muslim Brotherhood. "The Ikhwan al-Muslimeen have sent a written protest to the legation against the publication in *Britannia & Eve* of an illustrated article by Matania Muhammed, which shows the Prophet regarding Adam and Eve, the latter being assumed to represent Mohammed's wife and therefore being improperly dressed", read the cable. "Letters have also been written to the President of the Republic and the Prime Minister." "A Damascus notable has challenged Matania to a duel and applied for a visa to England for this purpose,"[43] the cable from the British Embassy in Damascus concluded with thinly veiled irony.

Unsurprisingly, the Muslim Brotherhood struck a similarly populist tone on the question of Palestine, vowing to fight "bloodily and cruelly until our country [Palestine] is restored to us."[44] Early on, the Syrian Ikhwan had displayed a particular kind of militancy when, upon its official creation, an article published in the organization's main newspaper, *al-Manar*, had "openly advocated that the Arabs should put into operation the secret decisions of the Bludan Conference of the Arab League and should resort to force."[45] It seems that the Syrian Brotherhood went as far as taking matters into its own hands. A political officer at the British Embassy in Damascus thus reported that, in the national debate on what should be done by the Arabs to recover Palestine, "foremost among the propagandists were the Ikhwan al-Muslimeen." As an example, he stated that following a ten-day trip by the organization's leader, Mustapha al-Sibai, in northern Syria, "to preach and inflame the youth of the country",[46] an "Arab Liberation Army" had been set up and tasked with recruiting volunteers to fight against Israel.

But beyond the Islamic rhetoric stemming from the Ikhwan's background, one could also interpret the activism displayed by the Ikhwan on the issue of Palestine as being directed at the political competition it faced on the subject from the Ba'ath Party. As a prominent defender of Arab nationalism, the Ba'ath also wished to show its pro-Palestinian credentials to a Syrian population increasingly disappointed with the way established political elites dealt with the issue.[47]

"'Islamic socialism': a Muslim drink in a Marxist cup"?

Besides playing up the issues of Palestine and the role of Islam in Syrian society, the Muslim Brotherhood also came to realize the importance of the so-called "social question" which had been raised in the early 1940s by the influential peasant leader Akram al-Hawrani. Throughout the 1940s and 1950s, the radical parties that emerged on Syria's political scene all strove to emphasize their commitment to a fairer social bargain which would benefit the lower middle classes frustrated by a growing divide between Syria's most privileged and the impoverished. This new generation of political parties incorporated ideological elements into their platform meant to appeal to the then-revolutionary mood which was gradually seizing Syria's urban populations, each on its own terms. While the Syrian Communist Party naturally emphasized its communist ideology, the Ba'ath Party insisted on its own brand of Arab socialism and the Syrian National Socialist Party put forward a national-socialist ideology. Meanwhile, the Muslim Brotherhood had also tainted its discourse with a degree of left-wing rhetoric, putting up candidates for election under the platform of the "Islamic Socialist Front" and pleading by the same token for the advent of an "Islamic socialism".

The doctrine of "Islamic socialism"—put forward by Mustapha al-Sibai in his *Ishtirakiyyat al-Islam* ("The socialism of Islam") published in 1959—represented the Syrian Muslim Brotherhood's first attempt at articulating a comprehensive ideology constitutive of a specifically "Islamic way" distinct from the values of the West and the East. For the Syrian Ikhwani leader, who subsequently became known as the "Red Sheikh",[48] true social reform could only be implemented through a framework based on Islamic teachings which would justify policies such as land reform. "The principles of Islam, our social situation and the obligation placed upon us by our religion to wipe out oppression and give human dignity to the peasants—all this renders the limitation of landed property legal in the eyes of the law and makes it one of the duties of the state."[49] In other words, what Mustapha al-Sibai sought was to emphasize the "socialist" aspects of Islam by portraying Muslim religion as a system of values that shared with socialism the goals of establishing social equality, eliminating hunger and poverty, and fostering education and opportunities for all. For al-Sibai, there was nothing more socialist than "the socialism of the fast during the month of Ramadan".[50]

In the early context of the Cold War, the Muslim Brotherhood's "Islamic socialism" and its attempt to strike a middle ground between the material systems of capitalism and communism meant that it had to walk a fine line between rejecting Western imperialism while not completely embracing the USSR—which, to the outrage of the Ikhwan, had voted in favour of the United Nations Partition Plan for Palestine in November 1947.[51] Gradually, however, the Ikhwan came to tacitly support the USSR in its struggle against the West. The rationale for this was quite clear and straightforward. The Syrian Brotherhood, according to a British diplomat, considered that "any enemy of the Western 'imperialists' was a friend of the Arabs and that therefore the Soviet Union and its policies should be supported."[52] This was a view particularly represented by Ma'ruf al-Dawalibi, a close associate of Mustapha al-Sibai, who advocated a rapprochement with the USSR and went as far as stating, during a visit to Cairo in April 1950, that "the Arabs would prefer to become a Soviet Republic rather than be judaized as a result of American pressure."[53] Other prominent members of the Islamic Socialist Front, such as Muhammad al-Mubarak, argued in favour of a Treaty of Friendship with the USSR.[54]

The growing sympathy displayed at that time by the Syrian Ikhwan towards the Soviets did not, however, translate into affection for Syria's communists. In fact, quite the opposite was true. If the Muslim Brotherhood was prepared to support Soviet policies in the Arab world in the name of the struggle against Western imperialism, it was not ready to condone the ideology professed by the followers of Khalid Bakdash, the leader of the Syrian Communist Party. Clashes between the Ikhwan and the Syrian communists were reported as early as May 1944, when the former accused the latter of spreading an ideology "contrary to the Muslim way of life".[55] "Combating communism in Syria" was even listed by Mustapha al-Sibai as one of the most pressing priorities of the Muslim Brotherhood, which had historically despised Marxism, seeing it as "anti-religious" and a "foreign doctrine not needed by Muslims because they already have a better one derived from Islam".[56] It is perhaps in this framework that Mustapha al-Sibai's "Islamic socialism" should be seen: wary of the threat represented by "Godless communism", the Ikhwani leader strove to provide the Syrians with an appealing ideological alternative. For him, "[Islamic] socialism should be embraced by every zealous defender of our nation who is anxious to avert the danger of extreme left-wing socialism."[57]

While the Ikhwan's struggle with domestic communism was certainly ideological, it was first and foremost political. During the 1940s and 1950s, the Muslim Brotherhood and the Syrian Communist Party fought to a large extent for the same constituencies made up of the educated, lower and middle classes found in urban areas. This was true to the extent that Mustapha al-Sibai's own family in Homs was itself divided between communists and members of the Ikhwan. In the social sphere, this meant that the Ikhwan devoted much energy to supporting workers' rights. The Syrian Brotherhood set up its own Workmen's Committees tasked with creating co-operative companies in which all workers participate and share profits. In addition, the Ikhwan was involved in offering loans to help small craftsmen open shops. It also assisted poor working men by providing them with medical care and offering illiterate people a free education.[58] In the Damascus trade unions, the Muslim Brotherhood's influence was growing.[59] By challenging communism on its own ground, the Syrian Ikhwan were "urging workers to abandon foreign doctrines, to rally to the Muslim Brotherhood and to follow the teachings of Mohammed rather than those of Stalin, Lenin and Molotov."[60] By the early 1950s, the social and economic activities of the Syrian Muslim Brotherhood covered so much of Syrian life that, according to one analyst, the organization had become "a state within a state".[61] But to what extent was it sincerely committed to a "new revolution",[62] as its historic leader once put it?

How far Mustapha al-Sibai's "Islamic socialism" was either a genuine attempt at social reform or a mere opportunistic bargain to attract the lower classes is still the subject of debate in Ikhwani circles today. While some hail al-Sibai's approach as a unique attempt to strike an "Islamist middle ground" between socialism and capitalism, others insist that the Ikhwani leader was a gifted and charismatic politician ready to use populist rhetoric in order to make his way through Syrian politics. The reality probably lies somewhere in the middle as a closer look at the substance found in the doctrine of "Islamic socialism" signals a moderate rather than revolutionary approach. While private property is seen as an "inalienable right", it should not be used as a "means of oppression and exploitation". Similarly, while the state should ensure the limitation of land ownership, this should be done with fairness and "not merely to satisfy rancour and vengeance". Striving to strike a fine line between capitalism and socialism, Mustapha al-Sibai concluded: "to the workers, [Islamic socialism] grants a decent standard of living and an assured future; to the holder of capital, it opens up wide horizons."[63]

At the time, however, the Ikwhani leader's mixed message seems to have stirred ambiguity, if not controversy, within his organization's ranks. It was well-known that Muhammed al-Hamid, for instance, despised the leftist rhetoric assumed by the Syrian Brotherhood upon the formation of the Islamic Socialist Front in 1950. Muhammed al-Mubarak, for his part, dismissed the Front as being a mere "Muslim drink in a Marxist cup",[64] which also led him to resign from the Ikhwan in 1954—although a British diplomat noted that "this seemed to make little difference to his continuous political activity" since "al-Mubarak was persistently referred to as a Brotherhood candidate".[65] Nevertheless, it seems that the rift which then emerged within the Ikhwan was quickly healed through the mediation of Hassan al-Hudaybi, leader of the Egyptian Muslim Brotherhood, who paid a visit to Syria in the summer of 1954. Mustapha al-Sibai's re-election at the helm of the Ikhwan a few weeks later sealed the controversy.[66]

One result of the internal debates amongst Ikhwani circles was that a clearer line gradually emerged in the mid-1950s. While the "Islamic socialist" rhetoric of the Syrian Brotherhood remained broadly similar, the organization nonetheless reinforced its links with the pro-business People's Party through the mediation of Mar'uf al-Dawalibi, who was affiliated with both organizations.[67] Current members of the Syrian

Ikhwan are also keen to remind their audience that, for all its left-wing populist rhetoric, the Muslim Brotherhood often came to be supported by economically liberal political forces. That was made clear, for instance, when those forces backed up Mustapha al-Sibai's candidacy against the Ba'athist candidate Riyadh al-Maliki in the 1957 by-elections in Damascus.[68] But these by-elections, lost by al-Sibai, also came to represent a turning point: they reflected the growing influence of the Ba'ath Party on Syria's political life and marked the first open political confrontation between the two forces.

Losing ground to the Ba'ath Party

Created in 1940 as a reaction to the continued French presence in Syria, the Ba'ath Party was, at first, a purely intellectual movement emphasizing Syria's nationalist struggle in pan-Arab terms. Led by the Christian Michel Aflaq and the Sunni Salah Eddine al-Bitar, it assumed a political nature only after the granting of independence when in 1946 it started to publish its newspaper, al-Ba'ath, and in 1947 held its first national congress. Initially, the main ideological drive behind the Ba'ath Party's emergence in Syrian political life was its insistence on the existence of an "Arab nation" whose particular historical legacy would give the Arab world sufficient strength, if united, to face the challenges of Western imperialism. Progressively, however, elements of socialism were also integrated into its revolutionary pan-Arab rhetoric. This culminated in the emergence of a doctrine of "Arab socialism" exemplified by the Ba'ath Party's merger with Akram al-Hawrani's Arab Socialist Party, forming an "Arab Ba'ath Socialist Party" in 1953.

Ideologically, the Ba'athists wished to draw a line between the communism inspired by Soviet Russia and the Arab socialism which had many of its roots in Tito's nationalist and social agenda. Politically and tactically, the alliance with Akram al-Hawrani's peasant movement considerably reinforced the Ba'ath Party's appeal across Syrian society and especially in rural areas. While a political analyst at the British Embassy in Damascus noted, in 1952, the "weakness" and "insignificance"[69] of the Ba'ath in Syrian political life, the same diplomat observed, in 1954, that "the growth and increased activity of this group [Arab Ba'ath Socialist Party] has been one of the main internal trends in Syria this year."[70] In terms of elected parliamentarians, the Ba'ath had gone from one seat in Parliament to twenty-two in 1954.[71] This can, of course, also be explained in terms of a regional trend, with the growth of secular, left-wing parties across the Arab world at the time. In Egypt, Gamal Abdel Nasser had led the Free Officers coup in 1952, which paved the way for his complete takeover of Egypt two years later. The Egyptian leader's Arab nationalist and socialist credentials certainly contributed to the spread of such ideology across the region. In Syria, the year 1953 saw "the increase in the strength of the left-wing"[72]—in particular in the army. But the Ba'ath Party's improving electoral fortunes should also be viewed against the backdrop of the Syrian Ikhwan's own announcement that they would not run for the 1954 electoral contest—a decision which surely greatly enhanced the Ba'ath Party's appeal as both movements were then competing for similar constituencies—the educated and nationalist lower and middle classes.

By 1954, the Muslim Brotherhood had decided to give up most of its political activities in a historical decision which would profoundly affect the movement's organizational capacity to effectively stand for elections. Here, two factors seem to have been at play: the impact of state repression and the influence of major political events in Egypt. The Syrian Ikhwan had suffered repression early on, when Husni az-Zaim declared after his December 1949 coup that he would first destroy the Communist Party before turning to the Muslim Brotherhood. Under az-Zaim's short rule, the movement was outlawed and steps were taken to limit its influence by, for instance, reorganizing the *Waqf*s administration.[73] While members of the Ikhwan returned to Parliament following az-Zaim's overthrow, their participation in Syria's political life only lasted a few years as, by November 1951, Colonel Adib Shishakli had taken over most of the country's institutions and installed a military dictatorship which lasted until February 1954. Shishakli's particular "toughness"[74] with regard to suppressing the Syrian Ikhwan was noted by a foreign diplomat at the time, who described the "numerous measures taken to suppress the Muslim Brotherhood and to weaken the hold of Islam" as "Colonel Shishakli feels that the Brotherhood had affiliations with foreign countries [Egypt] and that Islam is an aspect of Syrian life that he cannot entirely control."[75] In 1952, the leader of the Syrian Ikhwan, Mustapha al-Sibai, was imprisoned.[76] The heavy repression suffered by the Muslim Brotherhood during the three years of Adib Shishakli's authoritarian rule surely accounts for the movement's decision to shrink from politics and turn to politically neutral areas such as education and social work after the military ruler was ousted in 1954 and parliamentary democracy restored in Syria.

At the time, however, the Syrian Ikhwan's decision to temporarily retreat from politics was also, perhaps most prominently, affected by the political situation in Egypt, which presented it with a dilemma. The growing popularity of Gamal Abdel Nasser in Egypt and across the Arab world coincided with a dramatic increase in government repression of the Egyptian Muslim Brotherhood, culminating in January 1954 with the dissolution of the organization and the imprisonment of its leader, Hassan al-Hudaybi, who had succeeded Hassan al-Banna upon the latter's death. The repression faced by the Egyptian organization at the hands of the Arab world's most popular leader put the Syrian Ikhwan in a delicate situation: while it could only condemn Nasser's harsh measures taken again the Egyptian Brothers, it had to tone down its critiques of the Nasserist regime because of the risk that it would seem out of touch with an Arab street hailing the Egyptian leader as the hero of resistance to Western imperialism. In that context, staying out of politics was a way for the Syrian organization to avoid taking a firm stance on Nasserism. Its leadership thought that in this way it would neither have to condone Nasser—while betraying its Egyptian sister— nor to condemn him, with the associated risk of losing popularity in Syria. For Mustapha al-Sibai, often seen as a gifted politician, this did not however mean that members of the Syrian organization were prevented from running for election—as long as this was done on an individual basis not involving the broader movement. Thus, while the Syrian Muslim Brotherhood did not directly participate in the 1954 elections, Muhammed al-Mubarak and Ma'ruf al-Dawalibi, known Ikhwani sympathizers, still ran as independents and were elected to Parliament. Similarly, Mustapha al-Sibai ran independently as a candidate in the 1957 by-elections in Damascus, which he lost to the Ba'athist Riyadh al-Maliki.

Yet such an ambiguous policy could not last too long, and its contradictions came to a head a year later. By early 1958, the instability into which Syria's political system had been thrown following exacerbated tensions between civilians and the military and between the communists, Ba'athists and Nasserists led to the Syrian government's decision to ask Gamal Abdel Nasser to accept a merger between Syria and Egypt in a United Arab Republic (UAR). Forced to take a stand, the Syrian Ikhwan accepted a union which, ideologically, was hard to refuse given its declared commitment to pan-Islamism and pan-Arabism. Ideologically and politically trapped by the Syro-Egyptian union, the Syrian Brotherhood was one of the few important groups that did not participate in its breakup when, in September 1961, a heterogeneous civilian-military coalition orchestrated Syria's secession from the UAR. While the Muslim Brotherhood took part in the subsequent elections, held in December 1961, and won ten seats, its influence had already been greatly superseded by that of the Ba'ath Party which, beyond showing electoral success, had also been able to penetrate the army from the mid-1950s onwards.[77] A British diplomat had then warned that "it cannot be expected that [this group of Ba'athist officers], who have strong political feelings, are relatively numerous and hold many key positions, will stay quiet indefinitely."[78] That forecast was eventually proved right on 8 March 1963, when a group of Ba'athist and Nasserist officers carried out a coup d'état bringing them to power—a historical turn which would profoundly affect Syria's political and social institutions for the next forty years.

PART II

THE ISLAMIC OPPOSITION
TO BA'ATHISM (1963–1982)

3

THE ISLAMIC REACTION TO
THE BA'ATHIST REVOLUTION

The opposition between the Ba'ath Party and the Syrian Ikhwan which came to dominate much of Syria's political life between 1963 and 1982 was often portrayed by the regime as a struggle between modernity and religious fanaticism. Yet, although the Islamic opposition to Ba'athist rule over Syria naturally carried an ideological dimension related to the debate between political Islam and secularism, the roots of the clash were much more complex than the regime may have wanted to suggest. By the 1970s, large sections of Syrian society had become alienated by the regime's policies in virtually every aspect of life. The Syrian Ba'ath's pro-rural bias, its socialist policies, a growing sense that some regions were privileged over others, its sectarian makeup and, last but not least, a feeling that the ideology put forward by regime officials had not only been unsuccessful in mobilizing the masses but had in fact utterly failed—all these were elements fuelling strong popular resentment.

In this chapter, little reference will be made to the debate on whether the regime's sectarian features played a role in fomenting strong Islamic opposition to Ba'athist rule between 1963 and the crushing of the opposition in Hama in February 1982. As the issue of sectarianism in Syria is a very complex and highly sensitive one, it will be discussed on its own in the following chapter. It should be noted, however, that the roots of the increasingly polarized political atmosphere in late 1970s Syria can only be explained in reference to the overlapping of many factors. Devoting a distinct chapter to sectarianism does not mean, therefore, that the author believes the issue should be dealt with separately. Rather, it constitutes an attempt to simplify the reader's understanding of such a complex issue. In addition, while the sectarian question emerged with the advent of Hafiz al-Assad's rule over Syria in November 1970, or arguably with Salah Jadid's ascent to power in 1966, the roots of the Islamic opposition to Ba'athism can be traced back to the 1950s and 1960s. These were first and foremost the result of an ideological clash which was bound to happen given the two parties' inherently incompatible visions for Syrian society.

A clash of ideologies

There were political clashes between members of the Muslim Brotherhood and the Ba'ath Party from the early 1950s, following constitutional debates on the role of religion in Syrian society. However, the confrontation between the two political forces rapidly assumed a violent nature upon the Ba'ath Party's accession to power in March 1963. Ideologically, the Ikhwan and the Ba'ath Party were at odds. While the former had always argued that "Islam is both religion and state",[1] the latter insisted that "religion is for God, country is for all".[2]

Often portrayed as the "enemy of religion", the Ba'ath Party was, however, far from rejecting Islam in its totality. Michel Aflaq, its main ideologue, had been one of the first intellectuals to articulate a systematic explanation of Arab nationalism's unique relationship with Islam. Despite being a Christian, he argued that the whole Arab nation was inseparably connected with Islam and that Muhammad's life was the embodiment of "the nature of the Arab soul and its rich possibilities".[3] In an unorthodox twist, the Ba'athist ideologue considered that if the revelation had been given to the Arabs and to no other nation, then surely the Arab world could have faith in its destiny. Islam was also granted an important role in Ba'athist ideology as in Michel Aflaq's view, the emergence of the Muslim religion marked the birth of a "revolutionary movement that rebelled against a whole system of beliefs, customs and interests". In a thinly veiled attack on the Muslim Brotherhood, his harshest critique was directed at "those who seem to be the staunchest defenders of Islam" yet are themselves "the most unrevolutionary elements".[4] There is little doubt that, by identifying Islam with Arab nationalism, the Ba'athist ideologue hoped to convince the Arab street that embracing secularism did not mean rejecting religion. But, if Islam had an important place in Ba'athist thought, it was nonetheless a very unorthodox one—considering Islam as crucial not for the truth of its social and religious message but instead as a constitutive element of Arab nationalist consciousness.[5] To the religious Sunni community, the Ba'ath Party's ideology was nothing short of a betrayal of the essence of Islamic doctrine.

The troubles started as early as April 1964 with a campaign of agitation by prayer leaders who delivered inflammatory speeches against the advent of the secular Ba'athist regime. While street riots spread through most Syrian cities, they came to focus heavily on Hama, a stronghold of religious conservatism, where they took on a violent dimension and shaped the city's hatred for the Ba'athist regime for decades to come. According to Abdel Halim Khaddam, the Governor of Hama at the time who would rise to the Vice Presidency of the country years later, the troubles in the city began when three local schoolteachers were transferred in the middle of the school year to the far-off city of Deir ez-Zoor by local regime officials who accused them of spreading an anti-secular and, therefore, anti-Ba'athist message to their students.[6] Approved by Sheikh Muhammed al-Hamid from his pulpit at the Sultan Mosque, protests intensified in front of the school and quickly transformed into massive street demonstrations uttering slogans asking for the repeal of the decision and the ousting of the Ba'ath Party, the "enemy of Islam". The demonstrations gradually assumed a brutal dimension when a young Ba'athist militiaman, Munzir al-Shimali, was killed by the crowd, triggering fierce government retaliation.[7]

After two days of street fighting, the insurgents, led by a young Islamic activist, Marwan Hadid, took refuge in the Sultan Mosque where they had gathered weapons and ammunitions to resist the security forces. According to Muhammed Riyad al-Shuqfeh, a local leader of the Muslim Brotherhood in Hama who would later become head of the organization, Marwan Hadid's role in the April 1964 crisis was key as, despite repeated calls from the Ikhwan not to take up arms against the regime, the radical Islamic militant was nonetheless able to attract a sufficient number of followers to foment the armed insurrection.[8] In an atmosphere remembered as "electric"[9] by the former Governor of Hama, Prime Minister Amin al-Hafiz and General Salah Jadid decided to force a breakthrough by ordering the armed forces to bombard the Sultan Mosque, something which would be remembered by many Hamawites and religious Syrians as an act not only of Ba'athist secularism but also unyielding atheism. Strikes and anti-regime protests exploded throughout the country, only calmed by the resignation of General Amin al-Hafiz, associated in the minds of many Syrians with the harsh repression of the Hama riots. After the mediation of Sheikh Muhammed al-Hamid, who strove to find a negotiated solution to the twenty-nine-day crisis, the radical insurgents led by Marwan Hadid finally surrendered.[10]

At the time, the Ba'ath Party's line was still influenced by its historical founders, men such as Michel Aflaq and Salah Eddine al-Bitar, who would temporarily assume the premiership after Amin al-Hafiz's resignation. Although they were secularists, most of them were nonetheless of Sunni confession and, therefore, had respect for other religious traditions. However, as the balance of power among religious communities inside the army progressively changed in favour of the minorities (see Chapter 4), so did the orientation of the Syrian government. Originally led by the historic civilian founders of the Ba'ath, the regime soon became dominated by men originating from the military, whose minority and often rural background gave them a more radical outlook. Their ascent culminated in General Salah Jadid's coup in February 1966, after which the regime started to be referred to as the "neo-Ba'ath"[11]—a term designating the radically left-wing social and economic policies adopted by the Syrian government from 1966 until 1970. The already existing rift between the Islamic opposition and the Syrian Ba'ath only widened with time as religious Sunni Muslims seemed to become the target of a regime intensifying its involvement in the appointment of clerics, bringing the *Waqf* institutions under increasing government control and prohibiting religious teaching outside the mosques.[12]

Only a spark was needed to ignite the situation again. This came when a highly symbolic article written by a Ba'athist officer, Ibrahim Khlas, was published in April 1967 in *Jaysh al-Sha'b*, the journal of the Syrian army, which inflamed the community of religious Sunni Muslims because of its anti-religious content. In the article, the Ba'athist officer claimed that "until now, the Arab nation has turned towards Allah […] but without success as all [religious] values made the Arab man a miserable one, resigned, fatalistic and dependent. We don't need a man who prays and kneels, who curbs his head and begs God for his pity and forgiveness. The new man is a socialist, a revolutionary."[13] Ibrahim Khlas went on: "the only way to establish the culture of the Arabs and to build Arab society is to create the new Socialist Arab man who believes that God, the religions, feudalism, imperialism, the fat cats and all the values that dominated the former society are nothing but mummies embalmed in the museums of history."[14] Upon the publication of the article, mass anti-regime protests broke out in most Syrian cities. In Damascus, Sheikh Hassan Habannaka, who had turned against the regime after losing a contest for the post of Grand Mufti to Sheikh Ahmad Kuftaro, led fierce anti-regime sermons which inflamed the population of the Midan quarter, where the *souk* closed for days.[15] Calm was only restored when, having realized the extent of the alienation the article had engendered, the Ba'athist authorities sacked Ibrahim Khlas, brought him to trial and publicly dismissed the article as being part of a "reactionary Israeli-American plot […] to drive a wedge between the masses and their leadership".[16] The protests, however, represented a growing cultural gap putting an increasingly secular and left-wing leadership at odds with the conservative bastions of Syrian society.

In November 1970 Hafiz al-Assad, Defence Minister under the "neo-Ba'ath", launched the "correction movement"—a successful *coup* attempt against Salah Jadid, with the declared objective of moderating the Ba'athist stance on socioeconomic issues. At first, his arrival in power provided the Islamist opposition with breathing space as the new leader seemed keen to cultivate close links with a constituency that had been humiliated by Salah Jadid. Upon assumption of power, Hafiz al-Assad multiplied the gestures of appeasement towards the *ulama* and the Sunni Muslim community. He raised 2,000 religious functionaries in rank, increasing their salaries as well, appointed a religious scholar as Minister of *Waqfs*, encouraged the construction of mosques and revived the Islamic formulation of the presidential oath in the Syrian constitution.[17] In addition, the new Ba'athist leader sought to cultivate a public image associated with a personal commitment to Islam. While participating on a regular basis in public prayers and religious ceremonies, he published a special edition of the Quran with himself photographed in uniform on the first page, organized local elections in which the Muslim Brotherhood supported conservative candidates, and personally undertook the 'Umra to Mecca—the "minor" pilgrimage at an irregular time.[18] The official support he obtained from a few co-opted *ulama*, such as the late Grand Mufti Sheikh Ahmad Kuftaro and the Kurdish scholar Said Ramadan al-Buti, was meant to provide an Islamic stamp of approval for the policies of his regime.[19] The early years of his leadership were therefore marked by a general improvement of relations between the Islamic opposition and a Ba'athist regime now publicly committed to rectifying its early left-wing secular tone in favour of "preserving the Islamic identity of the country".[20]

In this context, the community of religious Sunni Muslims could only have been bitterly disappointed when, in January 1973, Hafiz al-Assad published a draft Constitution which provoked a storm of protests and riots all condemning the "irreligiousness" of the document. In fact, while the draft implicitly mentioned Islam by naming the *Shari'a* ("Islamic law") as a main source of legislation, it did not include the special status that had been given to it by the 1950 Constitution—which stated that the religion of the head of state should be Islam.[21] The protests condemning the "Godless" Ba'athist regime originated again from Hama but quickly spread to other cities before reaching the popular Midan quarter of Damascus, where the influential Sheikh Hassan Habanakah rallied thousands of angry pious Muslims. The Islamic opposition to the draft constitution was coordinated by a young ideologue of the Syrian Muslim Brotherhood, Said Hawwa, who set up a nationwide network of *ulama* dedicated to enhancing coordination amongst all Islamic actors.[22] According to the researcher Thomas Pierret, Said Hawwa and the Ikhwan envisioned using the Syrian *ulama*'s anger against the draft Constitution in order to rally them into a more active opposition to the Ba'athist regime.[23] Realizing that the Islamic credentials he had been so keen to put forward were on the verge of disappearing, Hafiz al-Assad ordered the Syrian Parliament to add an article stipulating that "the religion of the President of the Republic is Islam". However, he rejected demands that Islam should be declared as the "state religion" and, in a thinly veiled attack on the Islamist opposition, instead stated that "true Islam should be far removed from narrow-mindedness and awful extremism as Islam is a religion of love, progress, social justice and equality."[24] By that time, the Islamic opposition to Hafiz al-Assad's rule had come to represent not only a rejection of Ba'athist secularism but also a denunciation of the regime's increasingly visible Alawi face, which made the debate on the 1973 Constitution all the more prescient.

A clash of constituencies

Although the struggle between the Ba'ath and the opposition in the late 1970s and early 1980s was often framed in terms referring either to the "Godless Ba'ath" or to the "fanatical Ikhwan", it would be a mistake to view the confrontation as one fought on purely religious grounds. Behind the bitterness felt by Sunnis towards the Ba'athist regime lay a more profound socioeconomic resentment which widened the social base of the Islamic opposition. The Ba'ath Party's ascent to power in 1963 had led not only to a transformation in the status of the Alawis and to the emergence of a secular ideology but also to the complete overturning of the traditional structures of political and socioeconomic power which had dominated Syria for centuries. The new regime had thus upset traditions in every area of life, sidelining an increasingly vocal group of people disaffected by Ba'athist policies and the new rulers.

One of the most visible aspects of the advent of the new regime for the Syrian population, according to a Ba'athist source who remembered this period, was the "youth" and "inexperience"[25] of the new Ba'athist rulers. Politics in Syria, along with the control of the country's economy, had in fact long been dominated by urban Sunnis from the upper classes. In the post-independence era, the picture had remained broadly similar. As the heroes of the independence struggle against the French had mostly been wealthy Sunni merchants and intellectuals from the urban centres, they inherited the country's political and economic institutions in 1946 and dominated Syria until the early 1960s.[26] However, the political parties they controlled, such as the National Bloc and the Aleppo-based People's Party, rapidly became discredited by their seeming inability to cope effectively with the many problems facing Syria's lower and middle classes. In addition, these traditional parties showed little interest in exploiting the potential for mass mobilization which existed in the countryside, where over two thirds of the Syrian population lived. Other newly formed, more radical political groupings such as the Ba'ath, the Syrian Socialist National Party (SSNP) and the Arab Socialist Party were quick to realize the benefits of appealing to this promising yet still untapped potential support base.

By the early 1950s, the Ba'ath Party had become a vehicle through which many Syrians from modest socioeconomic backgrounds could achieve their political ambitions. The core of Ba'athist politicians in the early 1960s could thus be defined as "those Syrians of the lowest socioeconomic background to whom a high school education was available."[27] For the author Michael Van Dusen, the significant aspect of the 1963 coup was the unprecedented socioeconomic profile of the new rulers. "The real and the only revolution in Syria since independence," he argued, "has been the transformation of the salient political elites."[28] A study carried out by the researcher Alasdair Drysdale, who tried to come up with an identikit of the typical Ba'athist ruler, confirmed the radical transformation of Syria's ruling class. While upper-class members of the Aleppo, Hama and Damascus bourgeoisie used to make up the majority of the country's rulers, after 1963 and, more significantly, following the advent of the "neo-Ba'ath" in 1966, Syria was now ruled by young men of peasant origin, often belonging to a religious minority and geographically coming from the most deprived areas of the countryside, from Latakia but also, in lesser proportions, from Deir ez-Zor and Dar'a.[29] A new elite was in place, antagonistic to the traditional holders of power on every account. It was with their deprived origins in mind and a revolutionary Ba'athist ideology in hand that the new rulers were dedicated to overturning the existing traditional socioeconomic and political order.

To achieve the socioeconomic transformation of Syria to which the Ba'ath Party was committed, full use was made of tools such as land reform and nationalization. At the time, a popular slogan of the Ba'ath Party was: "The Land to Him Who Works It".[30] From 1963 to 1966, the goal of the Party was therefore twofold. While it strove to keep the promises it had made to its rural constituency, it aimed by the same token to perpetuate the dominance of its peasant leadership over Syria by sidelining once and for all the traditional Syrian economic elite. With the aim of breaking up the existing neo-feudal sociopolitical structures which had previously benefited rich landowners, the Ba'ath Party embarked on a campaign of radical reforms favouring the peasants. First, it drastically accelerated the pace of land expropriations which had been carried out between 1958 and 1961 in the framework of the UAR, thus definitely breaking up the quasi-monopoly of a few rich families over vast Syrian lands.[31] This also meant that redistributed land would benefit previously landless peasants, the proportion of whom dropped from 70 per cent to 30 per cent over a short period of time.[32]

Secondly, the advent of the more left-wing "neo-Ba'ath" in 1966 ushered in a policy of "state land ownership" through which confiscated land was transformed into state farms and cooperatives. This meant, among other things, that the state would be able to provide credit and production supplies to the peasants, thereby breaking their dependency on rich middlemen and landlords who used to loan them money at substantial interest rates.[33] A General Peasants Union was also created, first as an institutional rural grouping aimed at balancing the traditional leadership, before it became a tool for mass mobilization in the hands of the Ba'athist rulers.[34] The aggregate effect of the land reforms carried out by the new rulers quickly proved successful. While the landed upper class numbered 39,640 in 1960, this figure had decreased by a factor of four to 8,360 rural notables by 1970.[35]

Having politically sidelined the traditional elite by taking over the country's institutions in 1963, the Ba'athist rulers had also managed to overturn the economic order on which the old landed elites had been relying for their power. This would prove a crucial factor in encouraging the old elite to support the Islamic insurrection of the late 1970s and early 1980s in a place like Hama—where their political and economic influence was threatened by local Ba'athist authorities of rural extraction, committed to crushing these traditional holders of power. Throughout the 1970s, the Ikhwan strove to appeal to the upper land-owning class which had been severely hurt by Ba'athist policies such as land reform and the substitution of state rural credit for private money lending. The networks linking the Brotherhood and the rich landowners, which had been formed in the 1950s through a tacit electoral alliance between the Ikhwan and the Aleppo-based People's Party, were reactivated. By 1980, the Brotherhood's programme made it clear that only land already belonging to the state would be distributed to landless peasants in the event of an Islamist takeover. In exchange for such a guarantee, rich notables started to provide money to the Ikhwan and engaged in conspiracies with them in order to topple the Ba'athist regime.[36]

In addition to the traditional elite, an increasingly vocal constituency became disaffected by Ba'athist policies: the urban middle classes. The pro-rural bias of the post-1963 rulers had led them to focus on the peasants' living conditions in the countryside, with policies often coming at the expense of the urban masses which would form the most significant social component of the Islamic opposition to the Ba'athist regime. Traditionally, the Muslim Brotherhood had always been seen as a natural ally of the economically liberal middle class Syrians working in the *souk*. Religion and economics were deeply intertwined as many low-income sheikhs combined their religious activities with being a petty trader or an artisan. Usually located in the old quarter of the city, the *souk* was a stronghold of conservatism and a guardian of tradition—values embodied in the activism of the Muslim Brotherhood. For various reasons, this urban-based and religiously-oriented small-trading class rapidly became an important constituency for the Ikhwan. The organization, in turn, emphasized the sanctity of "free enterprise" and "private property".[37] Even though they emphasized their commitment to social justice through "Islamic socialism", the Brotherhood's commitment to liberal economic values certainly reflected the interests of its main constituency. A clash of constituency and of ideology was thus bound to happen with the Ba'ath Party which, by 1953, had strengthened the socialist aspect of its programme through an alliance with the left-wing leader Akram al-Hawrani, giving birth to the Arab Socialist Ba'ath Party.

Since the Ba'ath was from the very beginning committed to "categorically rejecting the capitalist outlook",[38] according to the words of its co-founder Michel Aflaq, the socialist policies enacted after 1963 soon came to have a devastating effect on the economically liberal small-trading class of the urban areas. While the activities of some merchants, such as the import and export of goods, became integrated in nationalized public bodies, other traders were affected by the changing patterns of industrial and agricultural policies and by the exponential growth of bureaucracy. Led by the Ikhwan, strikes broke out in 1964 and 1967 in the *souk*s of Aleppo, Homs and Damascus, where the powerful Chamber of Commerce demanded the repeal of restrictions on foreign trade and guarantees against further nationalization.[39] By the mid-1970s, Assad's promise of liberalizing the economic system had been only partially fulfilled. Persisting state restrictions on private capital and trade infuriated the small traders and *souk* merchants who took their anger to the streets. In a deliberate act of defiance, the cooperative stores, which had become a symbol of failed Ba'athist socialist policies, were among the first establishments to be destroyed by members of the Brotherhood during the protests that took place in Aleppo throughout March 1980.[40]

According to Raymond Hinnebusch, the Syrian Ikhwan had, by the late 1970s, become "the most implacable opponent" of the socialist Ba'athist policies as well as "the forward arm of the endangered urban traders".[41] This was reflected through the Brotherhood's political programme which, when it was published in 1980, made much room for the defence of values such as the "right of ownership of private property", "freedom of trade" and "encouragement of private investment in the national economy".[42] In addition, the nature of the language employed was unambiguously tailored to the attention of this social group, with a reference to the public sector suggesting that it should be "purified" of its "laziness and incompetence".[43] For Raymond Hinnebusch, it was thus quite clear that "the pro-capitalist, anti-statist bias of most of [the Muslim Brotherhood's 1980 political] programme is unmistakable."[44]

Interviewed Muslim Brothers, for their part, do not shy away from defending their liberal economic orientation and sometimes go as far as stating that the early "radicalism"[45] which foreign observers noticed in Mustapha al-Sibai's vision for an "Islamic Socialism" was in fact "purely rhetoric".[46]

The pro-rural bias of the post-1963 rulers led them to focus on the living conditions of the peasants in the countryside, with policies often applied at the expense of the urban masses. For instance, the decline in cotton production, which can be interpreted as a result of Ba'athist agricultural and industrial policies, combined with the subsequent rise in the price of this commodity, did significant harm to the economic life of small-scale, *souk*-based urban manufacturers.[47] Artisans and petty urban traders were also among the first victims of the socialist programme carried out by Hafiz al-Assad, despite his promise of pursuing more liberal, "redressed" economic policies. Indeed, while the Syrian President had overseen a fourfold increase in public spending between 1970 and 1974, inflation had by 1976 reached a rate of 30 per cent, leaving many urban workers unable to keep up with the rise in daily living costs.[48] For instance, while a small apartment in central Damascus might have cost 50,000 Syrian pounds in 1970, it had by 1977 increased eight times in value and would increase tenfold in the next decade.[49] The rise in prices in the cities was also a consequence of the regime's attempt at "ruralising"[50] the urban centres by encouraging rural-urban migration. If this provided the Ba'ath with a political stronghold in the cities, it also alienated the traditional urban inhabitants who viewed new arrivals with suspicion. This pattern of socioeconomic transformation led the author Patrick Seale to suggest that "men whose self-esteem was rooted in the old quarters of the cities where life had not changed for generations found themselves devalued and uprooted."[51]

The ideological failure of Ba'athism

The severe inflation which hit the Syrian economy during the mid- to late-1970s also symbolized, for many, the failure of the socialist economic policies that had been an important aspect of Ba'athist doctrine since the late 1940s. This was, however, only one of the many ideological contradictions which came to discredit Ba'athism. The rulers, whose ideological heart lay in the prestige of the Arab nation's historical and cultural heritage,[52] utterly failed to live up to their promises of developing a foreign policy genuinely guided by Arab nationalism. The first recognition by the Ba'ath that it would prove difficult to reconcile the national destiny of "Greater Syria"[53] with a broader, shared cultural and ideological Arab heritage came to the fore shortly before it took power when, in 1961, it joined the separatist movement leading Syria to quit its short-lived union with Egypt (1958–61). Subsequently, despite repeated attempts to frame Syria's foreign policy in terms which emphasized the country's belief in Arab nationalism, through alliances with Egypt and Jordan in the 1967 and 1973 wars against Israel, for example, the foreign policy developed by Ba'athist rulers was predominantly nationalist in its aims. Syria's historic rivalry with its Iraqi neighbour, despite the ideological (Ba'athist) and ethnic (Arab) similarity of the two regimes' composition, was a case in point. The relations between the two countries declined so much that, when the Iran-Iraq war broke out in September 1980, Hafiz al-Assad backed the Iranian regime—notwithstanding the many ideological and historical contradictions which Ba'athist support for a religious, Shi'ite-oriented Persian regime could entail.

The Arab nationalist credentials of the regime also became severely tarnished by Hafiz al-Assad's June 1976 decision to send a 30,000-strong Syrian military force to Lebanon in order to crush the Palestinian Liberation Organization (PLO), which had just allied with leftist Lebanese forces in an attempt to break the status quo at the Israeli border. The Syrian army forged a tacit alliance with the pro-Western Lebanese Christian Maronites and idly stood by when their militias, the *Kata'ib* (Battalions), entered the Tal al-Za'tar camp and slaughtered around 3,000 Palestinians. "Assad's relations with the Palestinian resistance had long been highly ambivalent: in theory, it was [the Ba'athist regime's] heart and soul, in practice it was a constant source of trouble,"[54] explains Patrick Seale. But many, even inside the Ba'ath Party, criticized the intervention as representing "a complete betrayal of what the Ba'ath stood for".[55] For these critics, "the lion of Arabism was slaughtering Arabism's sacred cow".[56] Even Salah Eddine al-Bitar, co-founder of the party, asked how it was that Syria, as a "beating heart of Arabism", could have sided with the Christian isolationists on a course so foreign to its traditions.[57]

This raises another question, that of the evolution of political elites within the party itself and the effect this had on the nature of the ideology put forward by the rulers of the time. "Ba'athism" itself became rapidly discredited as Salah Eddine al-Bitar and Michel Aflaq, the major intellectual founders of its doctrine, were quickly sidelined when the military members of the Ba'ath took over the direction of the Party after Salah Jadid's coup in 1966. The two founders fled to Baghdad, where the "old guard" of the Party joined the Iraqi Ba'ath—thereby leaving open and public the ideological and personal struggle which had been taking place within the Syrian Ba'ath. The confrontation became so bitter and embarrassing for the Syrian regime that Hafiz al-Assad was reported to have sent an assassination squad to eliminate Salah Eddine al-Bitar at his home in Paris.[58] By the mid-1970s, these internal bloody power struggles coupled with the Ba'athist rulers' inability to provide the Syrian people with a clear sense of direction had spread an atmosphere of disenchantment with the promises which the Party had made to the masses upon its accession to power.

In addition, under Hafiz al-Assad's rule the Ba'ath Party itself became a secondary institution, its members and leaders being sidelined from taking part in the regime's most important decisions. This was a result of the obvious lack of enthusiasm expressed by Ba'athist leaders when Hafiz al-Assad took over the regime through an internal coup in November 1970. The Ba'ath Party had, by a heavy majority, favoured General Salah Jadid in its power struggle against Assad, whose more economically liberal "corrective movement" was in a minority inside the Party. Upon his ascent to power, the President thus had to compromise and form a government dominated by the Ba'ath. But when, in 1971, the Party, by thirteen votes against five, refused Hafiz al-Assad's proposed puppet-candidate for the post of Party Leader, it became clear that the President had to act in order to tame Ba'athist dissidents.[59] This was done, but at the expense of the Party itself, now weakened and sidelined from effectively participating in decision-making. From a one-party system, the regime had transformed into a one-man show. For Abdel

Halim Khaddam, a former Vice-President of Syria and long-time member of the Ba'ath, the Party itself thus quickly became an additional victim of Hafiz al-Assad's personal rule.[60]

Widespread elite corruption also fuelled popular resentment and gave credit to the idea that the domestic situation in Syria was more than a mere consequence of the doctrinal and political failure of Ba'athism; it had its roots in the utter lack of ideological commitment manifested by its rulers. Indeed, according to Abdel Halim Khaddam, "Ba'athism" came to serve as a mere "ideological blanket",[61] used to legitimize the enrichment of specific individuals and communities. One of the regime's stalwarts, for instance, who served in various economic portfolios in the mid-1970s, was revealingly nicknamed "Mister Five Per Cent"[62] in reference to the margins he made through the significant commissions received during his tenure. Patronage, cronyism and corruption spread through the ranks of the army, the Ba'ath, the bureaucracy and the military, leaving Syria's rulers as well as the ideology they claimed to represent more isolated from society than ever.

By the late 1970s, popular unrest had spread through nearly all major cities in Syria. The reasons for discontent were various and often overlapped, hence the difficulty in singling out one factor. The Alawi background of many Syrian rulers was one reason for popular Sunni discontent—but one among many, and a sufficiently complex one to dedicate a whole chapter to it in this book (see Chapter 4). The anger expressed at the regime Hafiz al-Assad headed was also directed at the rural origins of the new ruling class and at the socialist policies it implemented. It was this explosive sociopolitical setting paved the way for the emergence of a social base for political Islam in Syria. Alienated by the overturning of traditions, many Syrians became increasingly attracted to the Islamic movement which was to pose the most significant challenge yet to the Ba'ath regime.

Urban uprisings

By the end of the 1970s, virtually all of Syria's urban centres had been touched by unrest to varying degrees. Nowhere was this more significant than in Aleppo and Hama, two major cities combining many of the religious, socioeconomic and political grievances which ultimately pushed their inhabitants towards the streets in mass anti-regime protests led by the Muslim Brotherhood. However, by at least partially meeting the demands of the local elites in most of the cities, the regime managed to retain its grip on the country. The crushing of the Hama revolt of February 1982, where the bloody death toll could have raised the anger of many protesters from Aleppo to Damascus, was instead met with calm and seeming indifference.

In Hama and Aleppo, the situation had been precarious for quite some time as their inhabitants had felt increasingly estranged from the centres of power since the Ba'ath Party's takeover in 1963. In many ways, the landed Sunni elite of both cities represented the traditional Syrian ruling class which the rural and minority-dominated Ba'athist rulers had aimed to destroy. Everything was thus done to reduce the influence of the Hamawite and Aleppine ruling classes which had long dominated the Syrian political scene through the People's Party. In practice this meant, for example, that the proportion of Aleppine politicians represented in Syrian cabinets had dropped from 20.3 per cent in 1942–63 to 5 per cent by 1976. Most significantly perhaps, while Aleppo comprised 20 per cent of the Syrian population, the Regional Command of the Ba'ath Party included only four representatives from the city, or 8 per cent of the seats, in 1963–66, and none in 1966–76.[63] Under the Ba'ath regime, Aleppo, which had in the post-independence period wielded a considerable political influence, was marginalized from all centres of power. In Hama, the resentment which many of the city's inhabitants felt towards the regime was more focused on the actual policies implemented. On an economic level, Hama had indeed been targeted by Ba'athist land reforms as the city comprised a high concentration of rural notables who owned much of the vast surrounding areas. This meant that, at the political level, the once influential rich Hamawite families such as the Keilanies and the Barazis had seen their power considerably decrease under the local Ba'athist rulers.[64]

Politically isolated, the urban inhabitants of Hama and Aleppo had thus also become the primary victims of the economic policy of the Ba'ath regime. As a result of the agricultural policies put forward in the late 1960s, the bulk of cotton production had shifted from being centered in the north-central part of the country to becoming concentrated in north-eastern Syria, leaving many unemployed in the surroundings of the two cities. In addition, the regime's industrialization policy concentrated on increasing the role of petroleum production in the Syrian economy. This was, however, done at the expense of cotton production, for which the total acreage fell from 220,000 hectares in 1971 to 185,100 in 1976, raising the price of textiles.[65] The aggregate effect of these agricultural and industrial policies of the early 1970s was to sharply increase the level of unemployment in Hama and Aleppo, where much of the economy depended upon small-scale manufacturing, to the extent that the author Fred Lawson interpreted the uprisings that swept through both cities in the early 1980s as a violent reaction of the *souk* traders against the regime's policies.[66] Politically and economically marginalized by the Ba'athist rulers, Hama and Aleppo also came to resent more vocally the secular orientation of the minority-dominated Syrian regime. Both cities had indeed long been bastions of religious conservatism. In Aleppo, religious *jamiat* such as Abi Dharr were influential and *ulama* such as Sheikhs Muhammad Abu al-Nasr al-Bayanuni and Zeinedin Khairallah had the popular following needed to mobilize the masses in anti-regime demonstrations. Hama, for its part, was famous for its uncompromising spirit as a result of the violent rebellions led by local sheikhs against the French in 1925–27 and against the secular Ba'athist rulers, most notably in 1964 and 1973. By the late 1970s, the city had become a hotbed of radical Islam where the sermons of local anti-regime Islamist activists such as Marwan Hadid, Said Hawwa and Muhammad al-Hamid were carefully listened to.[67] In both Aleppo and Hama, the situation, it seemed, was ripe for social unrest.

By 1980, many of Syria's urban centres were touched by mass protests, from Jisr al-Shugour to Homs and Deir ez-Zoor. In Hama and Aleppo, however, mass demonstrations were taking place on an unprecedented scale. Significantly, the spark which came to enflame the precarious situation encountered in both cities had religious roots. In Aleppo, a large-scale massacre of Alawi military cadets in June 1979 had triggered a repressive response on the part of the local Ba'athist authorities who had gone as far as imprisoning the Imam of Aleppo's Grand Mosque for his links to Husni Abu, the regional leader of the jihadist group the Fighting Vanguard (al-Tali'a al-Muqatila) and also happened to be his son-in law. The arrest, which symbolically took place only a few days before the religious celebrations of Eid al-Adha in November 1979, sparked an unprecedented wave of outrage among the Sunni community of Aleppo which quickly moved into the streets of the northern metropolis.[68] The protests, organized by the Muslim Brotherhood, lasted for several months before reaching a peak in March 1980 when they were joined by the professional unions asking for the release of political prisoners and by the *souk* traders, who carried out the longest strike in their history.[69] However, despite sporadic violence and occasional attacks on government buildings, the demonstrations at Aleppo remained relatively peaceful.

In Hama, sectarian strife had ensued after a truck driver from the city was murdered by an Alawi peasant from a nearby village, triggering the first wave of mass protests in November 1979. These were followed by a series of other urban demonstrations which culminated in February 1982 in demands from the local leaders of the Muslim Brotherhood and the Fighting Vanguard that the city's inhabitants stand up violently against the regime. According to Abdel Halim Khaddam, former Vice President of Syria, calls for jihad launched from minarets were then followed by the killing of over seventy Ba'athists by Islamist militants, ushering in a cycle of "irrational and disproportionate revenge"[70] which would lead Syria's elite troops, overwhelmingly Alawi in their composition, to slaughter between 25,000–40,000 of the city's inhabitants. However, when news of the Hama massacre reached Aleppo in late February 1982, the northern metropolis kept relatively quiet. Was this the result of a "Hama trauma",[71] as suggested by interviewed Syrian Brothers, or were the reasons for the post-1982 relative calm deeper than the fear of large-scale state repression?

Although the fear of a disproportionately harsh regime response to mass protests certainly played a role in discouraging large-scale demonstrations following the Hama massacre, the differentiated positions of the local elites seem to have played an even more important role. According to the former Vice President Khaddam, what made the scale of the Hama revolt possible was the strong local alliance struck between Akram al-Hawrani's powerful peasant movement, the urban merchants, the Ikhwan and the rural notables.[72] The rich landed Hamawite families which formed the core of the local elite until the mid-1960s had been so hurt by the Ba'athist land reforms that, by the late 1970s, they had joined the anti-regime protests, providing money and weapons to the protesters, thereby indirectly encouraging the radicalization of the opposition movement.[73] In Aleppo, the situation had been very different. Local demands voiced by the Aleppine elite were partially met by a Ba'athist regime striving to negotiate its way between repression and conciliation. While several hundred Aleppines were arrested or killed after the March 1980 protests, the regime also sent a message of conciliation by dismissing the Governor of Aleppo, a brutal Ba'athist officer whose rural roots in the region of Deir ez-Zoor had irritated many in the northern metropolis. Instead, an Aleppine lawyer was nominated in a move thought to appeal to the Lawyers' Union which had been very active in the anti-regime protests. By nominating as mayor of the city an Aleppine architect with much influence in Damascus, the regime also strove to appease Aleppo's cultural and political elite which had been resentful of the way the previous urban policies had been carried out locally.[74]

Despite sporadic attacks, Damascus remained relatively quiet throughout the late 1970s and early 1980s. A few spontaneous protests broke out, led by the religious Zayd movement and *souk* merchants, but these were swiftly repressed by the Defence Companies of Rif 'at al-Assad, Hafiz's brother, who had been entrusted with keeping the capital safe from protests. According to Abdel Halim Khaddam, it was clear for many inside the Ba'ath that Damascus constituted a "red line"[75] which the protesters could not be allowed to cross; if they did, they could very well drag down the entire regime. This is perhaps why Hafiz al-Assad, aware of the Ba'ath Party's lack of popularity inside the capital, endeavoured to co-opt the Damascene economic and political elite in the early 1970s. Prominent Sunni Damascenes were nominated to key posts in the bureaucracy and the security services. In addition, their proportion inside the Regional Command of the Ba'ath Party rose from 2 per cent in 1963 to 25 per cent in 1976.[76] Most visibly, the local merchants of the Damascus Chamber of Commerce brought their unconditional support to the Ba'athist regime in exchange for a lifting of restrictions on the import and export of goods, precisely at a time when the Aleppo *souk* traders were starting a long strike.[77]

By 1982, the regime had managed to reassert its authority over the whole country. The urban uprisings which had swept through Syria's major centres, Aleppo and Hama in particular, had been put down by conciliation, repression, or a combination of both. Local elites played a significant role in every city by stirring up or calming down the popular anger expressed by the urban population. By the early 1980s, however, the confrontation between the Islamist opposition and the Ba'ath regime had become so intense that it had alienated large corners of Syrian society.

ISLAMIC REACTION TO BA'ATHIST REVOLUTION

The Islamic movement, which had led the anti-regime protests, had become dominated by a new generation of radical activists who increasingly employed heated religious rhetoric and were even prepared, if deemed necessary, to resort to political violence to achieve their goals—thus putting the country on the brink of a sectarian civil war.

4

"A MINORITY CANNOT FOREVER RULE
A MAJORITY"

By the late 1970s, much of the Islamic opposition to the Syrian Ba'ath had become framed in sectarian terms. This reflected an effort on the part of some Islamic militants to portray the struggle against the regime as a "Sunni awakening" which, by making it clear to the country's primarily Alawi leaders that "a minority cannot forever rule a majority", was drawing mass support from Syria's largely Sunni Muslim population—whether pious or not. Deliberately exposing the "sectarian face" of the regime would broaden the scope of popular support for the Islamic movement. Even though this strategy was the work of only a handful of radical activists, a self-described "vanguard" whose overtly sectarian outlook and violent militancy would bring the country to the verge of civil war, it managed to exacerbate the struggle between a popular Islamic opposition and a regime keen to reinforce its power base by drawing increasing support from its key constituencies—the country's minority religious communities in general and the Alawis in particular.

Those militants who strove to put forward such a sectarian strategy will be the topic of Chapters 5 and 6. This chapter will primarily examine the socioeconomic, religious and political dynamics which led to the emergence of an environment propitious to the rise of a radical and sectarian Islamic trend—thereby providing a sought-after opportunity for the regime to use overwhelming force to crush not only these militants but also the wider Islamic and non-Islamic opposition to Ba'athist rule. It is also important to note that the sectarian tone assumed by the Islamic opposition was not a purely religious phenomenon arising from Ibn Taymiyya's earlier condemnations of the Alawis. Rather, it reflected the increasingly vocal bitterness felt by Syria's Sunni majority at the concentration of power in the hands of a selection of Alawi officers. Whether or not the ascent to power of the "Nusayris", as the minority community is often referred to negatively in Islamic literature, was part of an "Alawi plot" destined to take over Syria will be debated in this chapter.

It is also worth noting that understanding the historical background against which the sectarian struggle developed in late 1970s Syria—a country long hailed as exemplary for the peaceful coexistence of religious minorities—is also key to analysing the contemporary implications of a conflict revived by the regime's crushing of the Syrian opposition in 2011 and 2012.

Sunnis and Alawis: a history of mistrust

If the Ba'athist officials of Alawi faith have sometimes been described as the "Mamluks of modern times",[1] it is because the community to which they belong has historically been one of the most oppressed and marginalized of all social groups in Syria before some of its members took over the most significant political, economic and military Syrian institutions in the mid-1960s—much like the Mamluks did in thirteenth century Egypt.

The Alawis, comprising approximately 11.5 per cent of the Syrian population, form part of a religious community heavily concentrated in the small mountain villages spread throughout the Latakia region in the north-west of the country. Fitting the traditional pattern of socioeconomic and political dominance of Middle Eastern cities in the countryside during Ottoman times, the Alawi peasants cultivated the soil of the upper-class Sunni and Christian landowners from the towns of Latakia, Jablah and Banyas, in exchange for an often meagre income. Their living standards were never enviable. According to the author Hanna Batatu, a researcher who studied the social roots of Syria's ruling class in great detail, "the conditions even of the more independent and less downtrodden Alawi peasants in the inaccessible mountainous regions became so deplorable that they developed after World War I the practice of selling or hiring out their daughters to affluent townspeople."[2]

In addition to being economically dominated by the urban center, the Alawis traditionally suffered a measure of social and religious oppression from the ruling Sunnis, representing 69 per cent of the Syrian population, who at times accused the minority religious community of being "heretical". The doctrine of the Alawis, founded in the tenth and eleventh centuries as an offshoot of Shi'ism, evolved over time to include elements thought to be inspired by Greek philosophy, Phoenician Paganism, Judaism, Zoroastrianism and Christianity.[3] In practice, this has meant that the Alawis have subscribed to unorthodox views such as believing that Ali is the incarnation of God himself, adopting the idea of a divine triad and adhering to the concept of an esoteric religious knowledge which can only be revealed to a few.[4] Several works published in the 1930s and 1940s go as far as strongly suggesting that Alawism has encouraged wine-drinking, male sodomy and incestuous marriages among the members of this community.[5] Whether an accurate reflection of reality or not, such perceptions gained ground and encouraged the discrimination perpetuated by many orthodox Sunnis against those whom they saw as being "heretical Alawis" who did not belong to Islam. Crucially, the longstanding Sunni disdain for Alawi beliefs and practices was also theologically backed by a *fatwa* ("religious ruling") from the medieval Syrian scholar Ibn Taymiyya. In Taymiyya's view,

these people called Nusayriyya [...] are more heretical than the Jews and the Christians and even more than several heterodox groups. Their damage to the Muslim community [...] is greater than the damage of the infidels who fight against the Muslims such as the heretic Mongols, the Crusaders and others. They do not believe in God [...]. They are neither Muslims, nor Jews, nor Christians.[6]

Socially marginalized, economically exploited and religiously isolated, the Alawis saw the advent of the French Mandate in Syria (1920–1946) as an opportunity to obtain autonomy in the region of the Jabal al-Nusayriya, surrounding Latakia, where they formed 62 per cent of the local population. The French quickly realized the opportunity to use Alawi resentment against the rest of the Syrian population and pursued a policy of divide-and-rule aimed at curbing the rapidly expanding Arab nationalist movement, led in Syria by Sunni and Christian intellectuals.

However, by briefly providing the Alawis with a country of their own, "the State of the Alawis" (1920–1936),[7] the French ended up reinforcing the longstanding mutual distrust between Sunnis and Alawis—the former accusing the latter of being traitors to the Arab cause and pro-Western in their orientation. In fact, the British Embassy in Damascus reported the "constant visits", between 1941 and 1945, that the military and political officers of the French Consulate in Latakia paid to Suleyman al-Murshid, a popular Alawi leader seeking independence for his province—offering to clandestinely supply him with 3,000 rifles, it was reported.[8] In fact, it is believed that French help to Alawi separatists continued until after Syria's independence—and was then still significant to the extent that it pushed the central government in Damascus to issue a decree declaring the Alawi region as "a forbidden area in which foreign consuls should not exercise any of their functions".[9] On the whole, British diplomats concluded with a zest of irony that "the French have for some time been working for unity among the Alawis, but not for unity with the rest of Syria."[10]

The Sunnis, who had managed to perpetuate their economic dominance throughout the French Mandate era and had been at the forefront of the independence struggle, inherited the political institutions of Syria in 1946.[11] According to a foreign observer, Sunnis have since that time shown a "regrettable tendency to assert [the domination of their community] at the expense of other communities".[12] They quickly destroyed the remnants of the "State of the Alawis", crushed the separatist Alawi rebellion led by Suleyman al-Murshid and re-integrated the region of Latakia into the whole of the country. By then, Sunni resentment at Alawi separatism had become such that, in the vote on a law abolishing the autonomy of their region, the Alawi members of parliament in Damascus did not even dare to vote against it for fear of retaliation against them. Indeed, a British diplomat reported in March 1946, "When the resolution [...] was passed in the Syrian Chamber of Deputies on December 19th, only two Alawi Deputies happened to be present and they both declared subsequently that the nationalist feeling during the sitting was so strong that it would have been impossible for them to make any protest without endangering their lives."[13]

By 1947, Sunni political dominance over the Latakia region, and therefore, over the Alawis had become so significant that it led the Oriental Secretary and the Military Attaché of the British Embassy in

Damascus to note, after a tour of north-western Syria, that "it was noticeable that all the senior Government officials were Sunni Muslims and that Alawis were largely shut out from posts of responsibility."[14] This was a state of affairs a leader of the security services in Latakia did not try to deny, explaining to a British diplomat who, in turn, reported the content of the conversation to London:

He said that the Alawis were dissatisfied that the Syrian government had given most of the government posts in the region to Sunni Muslims of Latakia and Tartous. He explained that it was difficult, however, for the government to do otherwise since for the past twenty years the Alawis had generally co-operated with the French against the central government whereas the Sunni Muslims of Latakia and Tartous had not done so; it was therefore natural that the central government would appoint to government posts the people on whom they had learnt to rely.[15]

This was, of course, something the most influential Alawi figures of the region were not prepared to accept. They accused the central government of exercising "uncontrolled authority in the area", carrying out "malpractices" and "withholding the constitutional rights from the Alawi people".[16] On the whole, they remained "deeply distrustful of the intentions of Sunni Muslims",[17] a British diplomat concluded.

Discriminated against in political, religious and socioeconomic terms, many Alawis left their countryside during the immediate post-independence period in order to join two of the few institutions providing them with upward mobility and inside which their power would ultimately prevail after the coup of 8 March 1963: the army and the Ba'ath Party. It was through their prominent position in these two key institutions that members of the Alawi community would become the new masters of Syria. To paraphrase the author Martin Kramer, the situation thus seemed rich in irony: the Alawis, having been denied a state of their own by the Sunni nationalists, were about to take all of Syria instead.[18]

The "revenge of a minority"?

Scholars of Syrian politics have long debated the extent to which the Alawi-dominated Ba'ath regime was consciously driven by a purely sectarian motivation. Some, such as Annie Laurent and Matti Moosa, have argued that the Alawis' ascent in the Ba'ath regime was always part of a "plan for a future takeover of the government"[19] in order to get their "revenge".[20] Others, such as Daniel Pipes, agree and have gone as far as quoting alleged clandestine meetings of Alawi leaders in the 1960s to demonstrate that, from the very beginning, sectarian loyalties shaped the nature of a regime which, in his view, would ultimately become an "Alawi dominion".[21] But was the Alawis' ascent to power really the product of a conscious attempt at enhancing their communal power?

In many ways, it can be seen as only natural that the growing Alawi resentment at the Sunni domination over the country would find its expression through the armed forces and the Ba'ath Party. The latter had been established as a political platform by Salah Eddine al-Bitar and Michel Aflaq, of Sunni and Christian confessions respectively, in a move symbolizing the Party's attachment to the notion of a secular state in which "Arabness" rather than religion would bind citizens together. The secular aspect of Ba'athist ideology was to prove quite attractive to religious minorities such as the Christians, Druzes, Ismailis and Alawis. Indeed, according to an analysis provided by a British diplomat posted in Damascus in 1947, religious minorities were at the time increasingly worried by the emergence of a growingly vocal Islamic current in post-independence Syria.[22] Furthermore, the Ba'athist blend of revolutionary socialism and pro-rural bias which emerged out of the 1953 alliance with Akram al-Hawrani proved attractive to members of the lower and lower-middle classes of Syria's countryside, including many Sunnis but also Alawis, located mainly in the deprived and rural region of Latakia. More than a conscious attempt to deliberately infiltrate the Ba'ath on a communal basis, the ascent of the minority inside the party should thus be viewed as a phenomenon largely explained on the basis of the "qualitative break"[23] which, according to Hanna Batatu, was proposed by way of a political platform offering the Alawis equality with other citizens.

In parallel, another reason behind the Alawis' growing influence in the Ba'ath Party was their increased prominence in the army officer corps—a significant proportion of whom also belonged to the influential Military Section of the Ba'ath Party. The Alawis' over-representation in the Syrian armed forces was partly due to the legacy of the French Mandate during which the *politique minoritaire* of "divide and rule" inclined the French to recruit as many non-Sunni Arabs (Druzes, Ismailis and Alawis) as possible to fill in the ranks of Syria's Troupes Spéciales. Upon Syria's independence from France, the bulk of the Troupes Spéciales were integrated into the newly formed Syrian army[24]—hence the initial prominence of Alawi soldiers among national troops. Perhaps most significantly, though, the deprived socioeconomic situation in which many Alawis found themselves did not allow them to pay the *badal* (financial substitute), a tax of 500 Syrian pounds which would exempt young Syrians from undertaking the obligatory two and a half years of military service. While, as a general rule, that amount was affordable for an urban Sunni of humble outlook, for an Alawi of peasant extraction it represented several seasons of arduous labour, making it difficult for many inside the community to escape military service. Ultimately, however, the Alawis' ascent to prominence inside the officers' corps was the result of the internal divisions which plagued Sunni officers' ranks and pitted them against each other along political, regional and class lines—while Alawi officers, for various reasons, remained, at least temporarily, a relatively cohesive bloc.[25]

After Egypt's Gamal Abdel Nasser shut down the Syrian multi-party system in 1959 within the framework of the newly formed United Arab Republic (1958–61), a core group of Syrian Alawi officers based in Cairo became involved in the establishment of the Ba'ath's secret Military Committee—a confidential paramilitary platform which would later take a leading role in the Ba'athist coup of 8 March 1963. After the Ba'ath Party's accession to power in Syria on that date, an internal struggle inside both the army and the Ba'ath was played out along overlapping sectarian, regional and socioeconomic lines, culminating in the coup of 23 February 1966, which saw the advent of a more radical, disproportionately rural and minority-dominated regime.[26] As a result, during the period of this "neo-Ba'ath", Alawi officer representation inside the Syrian Army increased from 30 per cent in 1963–66 to 42 per cent in 1966–70. Similarly, the proportion of Alawis in the Syrian Regional Commands of the Ba'ath Party, the most influential decision-making organ of the Party, had risen significantly from 14 per cent in 1963–66 to 23.4 per cent in 1966–70.[27] Inside the army, bitter rivalry between regional factions did not end until the remaining non-Alawi blocs were neutralized in 1969, paving the way for an intra-Alawi confrontation between Salah Jadid and Hafiz al-Assad, of whom the latter ultimately prevailed through another coup on 12 November 1970. The symbol was powerful: Hafiz al-Assad became the first Syrian President of Alawi faith, thereby formally overturning the traditional pattern of oppression which his community had suffered for centuries.

As the rise of the Alawis inside the army and the Ba'ath Party became more pronounced, so too did the favouritism from which the minority religious community could benefit. Not only did Alawis receive preferential access to public sector jobs, but health care and education efforts were also concentrated on the Latakia region so as to reduce inequality between members of the community and the rest of the country.[28] Private and public investment also came to be concentrated in the north-western part of Syria, where in the early 1970s a university was established in Latakia, a cement works factory set up in Tartus and an oil refinery built in Banyas.[29] While the regime strove to find rational grounds for most of these investments, certain examples of obvious regional and sectarian preference have sometimes been harder to justify. The French sociologist Michel Seurat reported, for instance, that among a group of 100 students from Tartus selected to undergo professional training in the USSR, one was Christian, two were Sunnis and 97 were Alawis in an area where 55 per cent of members belonged to the latter religious community.[30] At the national level, especially in the army and the upper echelons of the bureaucracy, sectarian favouritism also seemed to spread. A Syrian Muslim Brother living in exile recounted that, when doing his military service at the Tartus Air Academy, he was surrounded by 1,200 fellow cadet officers amongst whom only 99 were Sunni, Christian or Druze; Alawis represented the remaining 98 per cent of the corps and controlled the most important positions.[31] While such examples have only anecdotal value, they still convey the atmosphere of the time which, in certain sectors of Syrian society, led to the perception that the Alawi-dominated Ba'athist regime had, in fact, become an "Alawi regime" seeking to assert the domination of one community over others.

By the end of the 1970s, the Alawis had managed to secure a grip on the political, economic and military levers of power in Syria. At first glance, this seems to confirm the old assertion of Jacques Weulersse, one of the earliest authors of scholarly work on the Alawis, that a minority can rule a majority so long as it wields an unquestionable political, military and economic superiority over it.[32] But was the sectarian nature of the Assad regime always as clear-cut as this?

The "Alawization" of the Syrian regime: myth or reality?

While Hafiz al-Assad's Sunni Islamic opponents have often portrayed his regime as being overtly sectarian from the outset, it is nonetheless worth noting that the Syrian President strove to moderate the sectarian antagonism he inherited from his radical "neo-Ba'ath" predecessors—at least in the early years of his rule. Until 1976, Hafiz al-Assad thus oversaw several substantial increases in Sunni representation in Syrian cabinets (+10.5 per cent between 1966–70 and 1970–76), the Syrian Regional Commands of the Ba'ath Party (+18 per cent between 1966–70 and 1970–76) and the military (+15 per cent between 1966–70 and 1970–76).[33] Some Sunnis officials, such as Mustafa Tlass or Abdel Halim Khaddam, rose to prominent positions, Minister of Defence and Foreign Minister, later to become Vice President, respectively. It should be added that these increases in Sunni representation inside the country's most significant decision-making bodies often came at the expense of non-Alawi minorities (Druze, Ismailis and Christians) and of other Sunnis originating from the cities of Aleppo and Hama.

In fact, one of the earliest acts of Hafiz al-Assad's presidency was to forge an informal alliance with the Sunni bourgeoisie of Damascus, offering this key constituency high-level positions in the bureaucracy and the Ba'ath Party in exchange for political support. A former senior Syrian diplomat whose family background is rooted in the traditional Sunni Damascene bourgeoisie thus recalled that when Assad took over as President, he immediately proposed key positions to his father, then a doctor, first as Dean of the Faculty of Medicine at the University of Damascus, before making him Minister of Health.[34] Yet, if Hafiz al-Assad first strove to downplay the sectarian dimension of his rule by co-opting Sunnis into visible positions, why did his Alawi background become an issue so salient that, by the late 1970s and early 1980s, it seemed to have brought Syria to the brink of civil war? Here, at least two factors seem to have been at play: the increasingly radical nature of the Islamic opposition and the growing perception that the Assad regime was behaving in a sectarian way both domestically and externally.

Indeed, even though Hafiz al-Assad relied during his presidency on a power base composed, in order of importance, of his family (with his brothers Rif'at and Jamil in key positions in the army), his tribe (the Numailatiyyah section of al-Matawirah), his religious community (the Alawis) and senior Ba'athist officials from the countryside (the northwest and north-east of Syria) as well as from the capital, it was nonetheless the Alawi dimension of his rule that attracted most attention. This was mainly because, throughout the 1970s, the thorny issue of the sup-

posedly non-Islamic nature of Alawism resurfaced. In January 1973, the
enactment of a "secular" Constitution was perceived by many inside the
Islamist opposition as symbolizing the fusion of the two worst sins: the
secularism of the Ba'ath and the supposed anti-Sunnism of Hafiz al-
Assad. As a result, the Syrian President had to introduce a clause making
it mandatory for the head of state to be a Muslim, but he felt insecure
enough to ask the Shi'ite Lebanese cleric Musa al-Sadr to produce, the
same year, a *fatwa* asserting that Alawis belong to Shi'ism and are therefore Muslims.[35] In parallel, he strove to obtain the official support of a
few co-opted Sunni religious scholars such as the then Grand Mufti
Ahmad Kuftaro and the Kurdish sheikh Said Ramadan al-Buti, who tied
their own destinies to the regime by blindly praising it in return for privileged access to decision-making circles.[36]

It was not long, however, before the sectarian powder-keg exploded
again, with lasting consequences this time. In June 1976, Hafiz al-Assad
dispatched 30,000 Syrian troops to Lebanon with the goal of restraining
the leftist-Palestinian alliance which Kamal Jumblatt, the Druze leader
of the left-wing Lebanese National Movement (LNM), had struck a
little earlier with Yasser Arafat, the head of the Palestine Liberation
Organization (PLO). While Hafiz al-Assad's decision to order the military intervention in Lebanon was driven by a perception that this would
enhance Syria's security interests, it was nevertheless interpreted by the
majority of Syrians as a deliberate act of anti-Sunnism. To them it
seemed as if it was their President's Alawi faith that had driven him to
take sides in the early stages of the Lebanese civil war, defending and
supporting the pro-Western Christian Maronite minority in their struggle against the Sunni Palestinians. If the Lebanese episode severely tarnished the Arab nationalist credentials of the Ba'ath regime, it also drew
a renewed attention to the Alawi background of its rulers.

That perception, in turn, was partly the result of a campaign started
by an increasingly radical section of the Islamic opposition against Hafiz
al-Assad's rule. Since the Hama riots of April 1964, the jihadist current,
at the time led by Marwan Hadid, had grown more and more vocal in
the Syrian Islamic movement (see Chapter 5). While the reasons behind
the increased radicalization of the Islamic opposition go beyond the
regime's policies in Lebanon, that, it can be suggested, helped fuel Sunni
resentment. At any rate, many inside the Islamist movement started to
emphasize the distinctly "Nusayri", or Alawi, nature of the Ba'ath

regime. In a radical move, the Syrian Ikhwan's chief ideologue at the time, Said Hawwa, started referring to Ibn Taymiyya's *fatwa* against the minority community. Increasingly, Syrian Islamic publications such as *Al-Nadhir* referred to the Ba'athist regime as embodying the "Alawi enemy", or these "infidel Nusayris who are outside Islam".[37] According to Nikolaos Van Dam, by framing its struggle in increasingly sectarian terms, the Islamic opposition hoped to polarize antagonisms in Syrian society around the confessional axis. This, in turn, was expected to gather the key support of Sunnis who were less religious, possibly even Ba'athist, to whom the regime appeared to be more and more tainted by a sectarian colouring, and who were increasingly attracted by the popular Islamic slogan of the time: "a minority cannot forever rule a majority".[38] The renewed anti-regime campaign launched from 1976 until 1982 by the Islamic movement was not, however, limited to harsh verbal attacks seeking to delegitimize the regime on sectarian grounds. It also had a violent component.

At first, a campaign of assassinations directed at prominent Alawi members of the Ba'ath regime was launched by the leaders of the Fighting Vanguard, a well-structured jihadist network with loose connections to the Muslim Brotherhood (see Chapter 5 and 6). A prominent member of the Syrian *mukhabarat*, or security services, was killed at Hama in 1976, the rector of Damascus University and a professor at Aleppo University were both shot in 1977, and close security aides to Hafiz al-Assad perished in 1978, among many others. However, what was at first targeted violence soon transformed into indiscriminate sectarian killing. A former senior Syrian diplomat, whose father was a minister of Sunni faith in Hafiz al-Assad's government, recalls: "all my Alawi friends, whether close to the regime or not, were afraid of seeing a plastic bag on their doorstep, possibly hiding a bomb."[39] The tipping point was reached on 16 June 1979, at the Aleppo Artillery School when a Sunni Ba'athist staff member, Captain Ibrahim Yusuf, assembled the cadet officers of Alawi faith in the dining-hall before letting in jihadist gunmen affiliated with the Fighting Vanguard who then slaughtered eighty-three of them, wounding many others.[40]

Between 1979 and 1982, faced with a violent Islamic insurrection that based its opposition on sectarian grounds, Hafiz al-Assad took steps to reinforce his grip on Syrian institutions. In 1979–80, he proceeded to purge hundreds of Sunnis from the army and the Ba'ath. He also came to rely more heavily on the one group he could expect loyal support from: the Alawis.

Atmosphere of sectarian civil war

In August 1980, at a high-level meeting of Alawi leaders in Hafiz al-Assad's home town of Qardaha, the Syrian President allegedly went as far as encouraging the members of his religious community to "enter the society and challenge the Sunni bourgeoisie in the economy".[41] Alawis were increasingly mobilized: they would either throw all their weight behind the regime or face an uncertain future. "Working for cohesion […] was the strong fear among Alawis of every rank that dire consequences for all Alawis could ensue from an overthrow or collapse of the existing regime,"[42] explained Hanna Batatu. This dynamic was also confirmed by the former Syrian Vice President, Abdel Halim Khaddam, who sees "the regime's fear of collapse"[43] as a reason behind the increased mutual dependence of the Alawi community and the Assad system. By 1980, Syria was on the brink of a sectarian civil war. The Aleppo Artillery School massacre carried out by Sunni extremists had indeed managed to polarize Syrian society to an unprecedented extent and, by the same token, destabilized the regime of Hafiz al-Assad as never before.

By the admission of one radical Islamic activist, the goal of the massacre of the eighty-three Alawi cadets at Aleppo had been to "sow sectarianism similar to that in Lebanon".[44] In that endeavour, the Sunni extremists were successful insofar as the attack triggered a wave of state repression mainly directed at the regime's Sunni opponents who fought back, bringing Syria to the verge of a violent cycle with no end in sight. Just a few days after the June 1979 massacre, the *mukhabarat* were, according to one report, already detaining an estimated six thousand people in and around Aleppo.[45] However, when the popular sheikh of the Rawda Mosque, Zeinedin Khairallah, was briefly detained by the Ba'athist authorities on the eve of Eid al-Adha, the streets of Aleppo quickly filled with several thousand angry protestors on violent demonstrations culminating in the killing of eighteen Alawis by the crowd.[46]

Sectarian strife was not limited to the northern metropolis. It soon reached Latakia in a symbolic move signifying the spread of sectarian violence in a city that was predominantly Sunni but which also counted a sizeable Alawi minority, located at the heart of a predominantly Alawi region. In late August 1979, the Alawi sheikh Youssef Sarem was assassinated in the coastal city, inaugurating several weeks of violent clashes between Sunnis and Alawis. Clashes of a similar nature in Hama and Homs were reported. Most significantly, perhaps, it was in the armed forces that sectarianism quickly spread following the massacre at the Aleppo Artillery School, threatening to cause a split in the Army and bring the Ba'athist regime to a state of implosion. The day after the Aleppo massacre, clashes between Alawi and Sunni cadet officers erupted at the Homs Military Academy, which only calmed after a visit by the Sunni Defence Minister, Mustafa Tlass. Similar clashes erupted in several units of the Syrian army stationed in Lebanon. In Berze, near Damascus, a Sunni soldier from the Special Units slaughtered thirteen Alawi officers before killing himself on 15 July 1979. According to Michel Seurat, the seeds of sectarianism planted by the Aleppo massacre had spread so quickly within the armed forces that, by the end of the summer of 1979, it seemed as though there were "two Syrian armies" separated along confessional lines. While it is difficult to assess how far this represented the reality at the time, the Alawi-dominated regime felt sufficiently threatened for Hafiz al-Assad to order the dismissal of over 400 Sunni officers.[47]

Very often, state repression itself assumed a sectarian nature as the units sent to crush the opposition and detain suspected terrorists were predominantly Alawi in their composition. While Hafiz's own brother, Rif'at, was in charge of the Defence Brigades, famous for being disproportionately Alawi in composition and ruthless in action, other prominent members of the minority community were in charge of the security apparatus, such as Ali Haydar, leader of the Special Forces, and Ali Duba, head of Military Intelligence, among others. According to Walid Safour, director of the London-based Syrian Human Rights Committee (SHRC), "it became sufficient to be a religious Sunni Muslim to be arrested and tortured".[48] Now living in Britain, Walid Safour was a secondary school teacher in Homs where he was arrested in 1979 by Military Intelligence for his alleged links to the Muslim Brotherhood before being tortured, according to his own account, by Muhammed Ibrahim al-Shaar, a local Alawi security officer who would later rise to the post of Minister of the Interior. In many instances, the regime's declared goal of "tracking down the Muslim Brotherhood", an organization supposed to be behind the sectarian provocations of the radical Islamic militants, merged with a determination on the part of Alawi-dominated security forces to humiliate and crush its primarily Sunni opponents.

Inside the regime, the President's own brother, Rif'at, called at the 7th Congress of the Ba'ath Party, in December 1979, for a "national purge" which could be carried out by setting up "labour and re-education camps in the desert" since no sacrifice would be too great to "defend the revolution". This Ba'ath Party Congress marked the rise of Rif'at to a position of unprecedented influence. At the same time, however, Patrick Seale suggests that, if "the iron-fist methods he put into practice probably saved the regime, it also changed its character".[49] A few months after the Congress, an editorial in *Tishrin*, the mouthpiece of the Assad regime, warned that "armed revolutionary violence" would be used in order to defeat the "reactionary violence".[50] On the ground, the shift came about shortly afterwards when, on 10 March 1980, the government struck a severe blow to anti-regime protesters who had just set fire to a Ba'ath Party local headquarters at Jisr al-Shughur, a small town in the mountains between Aleppo and Latakia. Helicopter-borne troops of the Special Forces were flown in, and after two days of a search-and-destroy operation, two hundred people had been killed.[51]

Aleppo, then a centre of gravity of the Islamist opposition, became the target of state repression again. By mid-March 1980, units of the Third Army Division entered the city, their commander, General Shafiq Fayadh, warning the townspeople that he was "prepared to kill a thousand men a day to rid the city of the vermin of the Muslim Brothers".[52] The city was occupied by additional troops from the Special Forces and the Defence Brigades. It is estimated that, during the year the city was occupied, the security forces killed between one and two thousand people, some at random, many in summary executions. At least eight thousand more were arrested.[53]

In the public mind, however, it is the city of Hama that has received the most attention. As the particular dynamics leading to the February 1982 Hama massacre are complex and can only be fully understood by also considering the internal wrangling within the Syrian Islamic movement between its most moderate and radical members, it will be examined in greater detail in Chapters 6 and 7. It is nonetheless worth noting that the Hama massacre remains, to this day, one of the most traumatic experiences lived by those Syrians who poured out into the streets of the country's cities in the late 1970s and early 1980s. Faced with an Islamic insurgency that was on the verge of taking Hama back for its pious Sunni Muslim inhabitants after a long occupation by government troops, Hafiz al-Assad decided to make an example of the city, showing how much it would cost for Syrians to rebel against his rule. As an illustration of the intensity of the fighting throughout February 1982 in Hama, it is difficult until today to assert precisely how many Syrians lost their lives. While initial reports suggested 10,000 civilians were killed,[54] other reports put the number as high as 40,000.[55]

It was then, in the early 1980s and in the context of a tense and emotion-filled political atmosphere, that Hafiz al-Assad proceeded to a late "Alawization" of the regime he was heading. As Syrian society was gradually splitting along sectarian lines, so the Syrian President's dependence on his Alawi kinsmen intensified. But it is also important to keep in mind that, in spite of the late "Alawization" of the Assad regime, the country was still firmly ruled by one man, Hafiz al-Assad. While his former Sunni friend and colleague, Abdel Halim Khaddam, recognized that "Hafiz did use the broader Alawi community to save the regime", he nonetheless asserted that "despite all the rumours there never was an 'Alawi plot' to take over Syria: the Assad regime should not be seen as the rule of one confession over others but rather of one man over others."[56]

PART III

THE RISE OF JIHADISM IN LATE 1970s SYRIA (1963–1982)

5

THE RADICALIZATION OF THE ISLAMIC
MOVEMENT (1963–1980)

By the late 1970s and early 1980s, the Islamic movement's overtly sectarian tone and the violent actions of some of its most radical militants had brought the country on the verge of a sectarian civil war, with an unprecedently high human cost. Jihadist elements committed to using violence against regime targets were multiplying their initiatives and ultimately came to dominate a radicalized Islamic landscape. For its part, the Muslim Brotherhood's leadership was increasingly under fire from certain segments of its membership who asked that the organization pledge to do whatever was necessary to protect the country's Sunni Muslim population—which could mean toppling the Assad regime. As certain leaders of the Ikhwan were themselves convinced of the need to resort to weapons, the organization plunged into armed struggle—a move culminating in the Brotherhood's endorsement of jihad against the Syrian Ba'ath in late 1979, and which will be studied in greater detail in Chapter 6. But why and how did the Muslim Brotherhood, an organization known as much for its moderate leaders and its message of compromise as for its political participation in Syrian political life and its past rejection of violence, become dominated by radical elements wishing to put it at the forefront of the violent anti-regime struggle?

The answer to this question is a complex one as it lies at the intersection of at least two mutually reinforcing trends which met in the mid-

1970s. By that time, a distinctively jihadist trend, which had emerged in mid-1960s Hama, had widened the scope of its support to the rest of Syria and would greatly contribute to the overall radicalization of the Islamic movement. Its organization, the Fighting Vanguard, was situated on the fringes of the Ikhwan and is still remembered today by many Syrians who most often associate the group with an uncompromising and radical opposition to the Ba'ath. Furthermore, by 1975, the leadership of the Muslim Brotherhood had switched to the "Hama clan" whose particular militancy would play a key role in the violent confrontation that the struggle against the Ba'ath assumed. This was the indirect result of a leadership crisis which plagued the Ikhwan's ranks throughout the 1960s and eventually pitted the organization's Damascene members, known for their moderation, against more radical members originating in other parts of the country, including Hama. In order to understand the extent to which this leadership crisis indirectly contributed to the Ikhwan's radicalization, particularly through the ideological and political void left after the split of their "Damascus wing", we will start by analysing the roots behind the moderation of the Damascene Brothers before going on to study the explanatory factors behind the crisis of leadership.

The moderation of the Damascus Ikhwan

Despite what its name might suggest, the Syrian branch of the Muslim Brotherhood was not formed out of one single coherent organization or *jamiat*. Rather, it regrouped various Islamic societies which had sprung up throughout Syria in the 1930s and 1940s. Thus the Syrian Ikhwan have been characterized since their foundation by their deeply heterogeneous geographical, cultural and ideological composition. Most notably, this has meant that Ikhwani members from different parts of Syria have often identified themselves with the group which they come from geographically—each "faction" being characterized by its own peculiar political history and shaped by its local culture and its immediate sociopolitical environment.

While today most analysts distinguish the "Hama clan" from the "Aleppo faction", such a distinction was throughout the 1960s superseded by the antagonism that developed between the "Damascus wing" of the Syrian Muslim Brotherhood and a "Northern axis" composed of Ikhwani members from Aleppo, Hama, Latakia and other cities. The schism that emerged between the two branches would have profound ideological and political consequences as, after it came to a head in the early 1970s, increasingly radical Ikhwani activists came to dominate an organization from which the moderate members of the "Damascus wing" had become marginalized. The split, which will be analysed more closely in the following paragraphs, would have far-reaching consequences on the overall evolution of the Islamist movement in the late 1970s and early 1980s. In order to understand the extent to which the departure of the moderate Damascene Brothers from the Ikhwan contributed to the organization's subsequent radicalization, special attention should be paid to the reasons behind the moderation shown early on by the "Damascus wing", a special breed of moderate Islamists who led the Muslim Brotherhood from the time of its creation until the leadership crisis of the late 1960s.

By the time of the emergence of the Muslim Brotherhood in Syria, most Damascene members of the organization knew each other and, as admitted by a prominent Damascene Brother, already formed a core group within the movement.[1] Stemming from the conservative bastions of Damascene society, members of the "Damascus wing" often belonged to the intellectual elite and exercised professions such as lawyer, university teacher or religious scholar. Family ties united many Damascene Brothers among themselves and organically linked them to members of the Islamic reformist movement of the nineteenth century. Indeed, they were often associated with the Salafiyya trend which had emerged in Damascus in the late 1860s, an intellectual and sometimes even familial affiliation which profoundly influenced their views on politics, religion and society. For several reasons, detailed below, their own proximity to the Salafiyya movement encouraged their adoption of particularly moderate and reformist views and therefore, indirectly, surely contributed to the advent of a Syrian branch of the Muslim Brotherhood willing to play the game of democracy and pragmatism as described in Chapter 2.

Generally speaking, the rise of the Salafiyya trend in Ottoman Syria was largely confined to Damascus where most intellectuals and religious scholars affiliated with the Islamic reformist movement were based, with the notable exception of Abdel Rahman al-Kawakibi in Aleppo. In the capital, the Syrian heirs of Muhammed Abduh and Jamal al-Din al-Afghani had given rise to an intellectual movement advocating the reform of Islam and its adaptation to the requirements of the modern world. Salafist scholars such as Abdel Razzaq al-Bitar and Jamal al-Din al-Qasimi had argued in favour of a "selective revival" of Ibn Taymiyya's legacy which would allow for a greater use of *ijtihad* in order to make such modern concepts as democracy and constitutionalism compliant with Islam while rejecting the medieval Syrian jurist's most extreme positions on topics such as excommunication and Sufism. By blending the modernist thinking of Muhammed Abduh with the reformist impulse found in Ibn Taymiyya's teachings, the Damascene Salafists were to distinguish themselves from the orthodox Damascene *ulama*, or religious establishment, who were often Sufi. Through the lens of the confrontation which took place between these two religious forces at the turn of the twentieth century, one can also interpret the Damascene Salafists' adoption of ideas embedded in Arabism and political liberalism as a reaction against the alliance which the local religious establishment had made with the autocratic Ottoman authorities of the late Tanzimat period.[2] Progressively, the Salafists' opposition to the orthodox *ulama* and their call for religious reform came to take on a political meaning influenced by growing calls on the part of Islamic reformers such as Abdel Qadir al-Jazairi and Salim al-Bukhari to replace autocratic Ottoman rule over Syria with a local—Arab—parliamentary government respecting liberties and the principle of constitutionalism. At the turn of the twentieth century, Damascene Salafists opposed the orthodox *ulama* allied with the autocracy of Abdulhamid II by elaborating arguments to justify constitutional government in Islamic terms; Jamal al-Din al-Qasimi, for instance, used *ijtihad* to make constitutionalism comply with the early Islamic principles of public welfare and avoiding harmful things (*i'tibar al-masalih wa dar al-mafasid*).[3]

The special creed of Islamic reformers which emerged in late Ottoman Syria and, for religious and sociopolitical reasons, embraced political liberalism, continued to flourish throughout the early years of the 20th century in Damascus. Many of them, professors, lawyers, doctors or religious scholars, became involved in religious societies which sprang up at that time. More particularly, al-Tamaddun al Islami can be seen as the society that apparently best represented their religious and political views and whose journal, *al-Tamaddun*, came to reflect the early moderation and rationalism of the Salafiyya tradition. In its columns, the Salafist scholar Bahjat al-Bitar argued in favour of equality between men and women and better relations between the Sunnis and Syria's religious minorities. Motivated by the concern to restore the authenticity and strength of Islamic civilization in the face of foreign occupation embodied by the French Mandate in Syria, the men of al-Tamaddun naturally rejected the import of Western cultural and social influence. At the same time, they always retained a degree of openness towards the political ideals promoted by the West which did not seem to infringe upon Islamic values, such as parliamentarianism and political pluralism.[4]

More intellectual than political, the Damascene *jamiat* nonetheless comprised members who, like Mehdi al-Istambuli, Muhammed al-Mubarak and Issam al-Attar, became involved in the establishment of the Muslim Brotherhood in Syria during the mid-1940s. Thus naturally characterized by an openness to democracy and political freedoms, these historical Damascene figures of the Syrian Ikhwan were a key driving force behind the organization's acceptance of Syria's nascent parliamentary political system. Using the principle of *ijithad*, Muhammed al-Mubarak for instance justified the inclusion of democratic practices in the Ikhwan's doctrine by suggesting that Islam does not ordain a specific form of government but only lays down general rules which are to be implemented through rational discretion in accordance with the changing circumstances of their place and time.[5] By stressing the modern relevance of early Islamic concepts such as public opinion (*al-rai al-'amm*), popular consciousness (*al-Amir al-sha'bi*) and consultation (*shura*), the Salafist Damascene members of the Muslim Brotherhood strove to incorporate values stemming from political liberalism into a seemingly authentic Islamic doctrine of democracy.

This did not mean, however, that they identified their vision of an Islamic democracy with the European and, perhaps most significantly, the French model. Early on, they strove to promote the vision of a democratic "Islamic state" in which, according to Muhammed al-Mubarak, Islam is both religion and state, making *shari'a* (Islamic law) the main source of inspiration for lawmakers.[6] This was again in line with the spirit of the Damascene Salafists who, in the columns of *al-Tamaddun*, always rejected the French notion of secularism under the guiding idea of opposing state involvement in the religious sphere, rather than claiming that religion should be separated from the state.[7] Striving to draw a fine line between adapting to the realities of the modern world and claiming to represent a return to the authenticity of the early Islamic message, the Damascene Salafists marked the Muslim Brotherhood early on with their moderate fingerprint.

However, they did not shy away from taking populist positions at times, many of them for instance joining the more conservative al-Gharra in its May 1944 protests against the Western dress code of certain Syrian women (see Chapter 2). Questioned on this opportunistic alliance of the Damascene Salafis with more reactionary political forces, Mohammed Hawari, one of the leaders of the Damascene Brothers, acknowledged that "in order to win over the public support, we had to ally from time to time with al-Gharra whose strong popular base, especially in the Midan quarter of Damascus, gave it much influence at the time."[8] It is also possible that the Damascene Brothers were at times influenced by the emergence of a more doctrinal wing within their camp, represented by rising figures such as Zuhair Shawish, Muhammed Surur and Muhammed el-Abdeh, all inspired by the more literalist and orthodox vision of Islam promoted by the "attenuated Wahhabism"[9] of a conservative religious scholar residing in Damascus, Nasir al-Din al-Albani. All in all, however, the Damascene Brothers and their Salafi followers always strove to promote the moderate vision of an Islamic state shaped by democratic forces and social reform, never calling for armed struggle against successive political regimes.

The peaceful and moderate political platform put forward by the Damascene Brothers would profoundly mark the years during which one of their most prominent leaders, Issam al-Attar, took over the reins of the Syrian Ikhwan, between 1957 and 1969. Under the leadership of Mustapha al-Sibai, who, despite being from Homs, shared many of the intellectual and political orientations of the Damascene Brothers, Ikhwani members from the capital such as Muhammed al-Mubarak had already risen to prominence.

When Mustapha al-Sibai became weaker after a debilitating stroke in 1957, he gradually relinquished his leadership to the young, well-read Damascene and former high school teacher Issam al-Attar, a move formalized after al-Sibai's death in October 1964. At first, al-Attar, then the leading figure of the Muslim Brotherhood's "Damascus wing", concentrated his efforts on spreading the Islamic message to the masses through education and preaching rather than through political activities. This was especially the case during the short-lived union with Egypt, lasting from 1958 to 1961, during which political parties were banned and the Muslim Brotherhood dissolved. The organization soon returned to politics, however, when a group of officers led the Syrian split from the United

Arab Republic, in 1961. Elections were held and the "Islamic Front", the political label of the Ikhwan, won ten seats, Issam al-Attar being elected member of Parliament for the district of Damascus. This was a brilliant electoral success for the Muslim Brotherhood, which was offered ministerial responsibilities in the government formed after the elections by Ma'ruf al-Dawalibi, himself a figure close to the Islamic movement.

The return to parliamentary democracy in Syria proved difficult, however, as most political parties had become weak after Nasser's suppression of parliamentary activities during the time of the UAR. But, as political instability was growing, with governments succeeding one another and the army taking a leading role in directing the country's institutions, the moderate, Damascene imprint on the Muslim Brotherhood also became clearer.

In a move symbolizing the Damascene leadership's attachment to parliamentary democracy and peaceful political change, Issam al-Attar crucially refused to take part in a coup d'état prepared in 1962 by Abdel Karim Nahlawi, an officer who had already taken a leading role in the Syrian split from the UAR. "Nahlawi proposed me to join him in overturning the government but I refused, I am a man of principles and I never thought that military involvement into politics could bring any good to democracy,"[10] the historic Damascene figure explained in an interview. A few months later, as the political crisis was deepening, Issam al-Attar was summoned to the presidential palace. In an act reflecting the Muslim Brotherhood's rapidly growing political influence, the President, Nazim al-Qudsi, proposed to the leader of the Islamic Front that he should form a government and become Prime Minister. According to Issam al-Attar, the President posed two conditions for taking up the premiership. First, the Ikhwani leader, who had been an early supporter of the UAR, would have to renounce for good the idea of a reunification with Egypt. Second, he would have to support the large-scale and violent repression of all the other political forces which the President and the army were in the midst of preparing. That night, the leader of the Muslim Brotherhood walked out of the presidential palace having refused to become Syria's Prime Minister, in a move on which he still prides himself, "having supported the principles of liberty and justice which I have always cherished in my heart".[11]

Issam al-Attar's important decision, however, was far from achieving a consensus of approval inside his organization. Until today, some within the Ikhwan's ranks still criticize Issam al-Attar for his handling of the situation at the time, pointing out the "historic mistake" which he made by refusing to take up power and leaving a political void quickly filled after the Ba'ath takeover in March 1963. This would be one of the many criticisms formulated against the Damascene leader which eventually led to his resignation from the leadership of the Muslim Brotherhood in the late 1960s, with profound consequences for the overall evolution of the Syrian Islamic movement.

The split of the "Damascus wing"

From the outbreak of the leadership crisis within the Syrian Muslim Brotherhood until its resolution in 1972, the organization went through a period of confusion during which Ikhwani members, mostly from Damascus, became progressively marginalized by a "northern axis" comprising Brothers originating from Latakia, Aleppo, Hama and other cities. Today, most analysts refer to the split which emerged at the time as resulting from the tensions which, in Syrian politics and society, have historically plagued relations between Aleppines and Damascenes. But, while geographical factionalism certainly played a role in the unfolding of the crisis, it would be a mistake to view the rising tensions within the organization at the time as being a purely regionalist phenomenon.

In many ways, the difficulty in analysing the deep roots of the emergence of the leadership crisis arises because many of its protagonists give different reasons for the tensions, depending on the camp to which they belonged. Having a discussion with members of the Ikhwan on the split of the Damascene Brothers from the mother organization remains delicate as this episode underlies the many political, personal and, to a certain extent, religious and ideological differences which have plagued the Muslim Brotherhood's ranks—with significant consequences on the movement's shape ever since.

In order to properly understand the root causes of the split of the late 1960s, a deconstruction of the reasons given by each camp is necessary. The "Damascus wing", on the one hand, has often suggested that its leadership became marginalized throughout the 1960s because its moderate ideology of endorsing parliamentary politics and rejecting the use of violence against the regime had itself become a minority position within the organization at a time when young Syrians increasingly embraced the jihadist struggle led by the Fighting Vanguard.

On the other hand, however, members who belonged to the "northern axis", which challenged Issam al-Attar's leadership in the late 1960s, often mention the Damascene leader's over-reliance on a small clan of followers originating from the capital. This, in their view, gave the Syrian Muslim Brotherhood a regional, almost clannish structure, which had not prevailed at the time of Mustapha al-Sibai's tenure as leader of the organization. Some also raise the issue of Issam al-Attar and his Damascene followers' Salafism, a religious tendency that has been criticized for its harsh line on Sufis, who form an overwhelming majority of Muslims in the cities of Aleppo and Hama. Finally, Issam al-Attar's continued leadership of the Islamic movement, despite his forced exile from Syria, is often cited as the main reason why groups not belonging to his "Damascus wing" rebelled against him, claiming that in a time of crisis for the Ikhwan, who started to suffer from fierce Ba'athist repression from the mid-1960s onwards, the organization could not afford to have a leader removed from the country and from its most pressing concerns.

While all these factors certainly played a role and, to a certain degree, sometimes overlapped, others seem to have merely served as a pretext for what was, in the end, a purely political split. The supposedly ideological divergences between the two groups belong to that last camp of pretexts used to explain the crisis. At the time, the leadership of the Muslim Brotherhood—whether its members came from Hama, Damascus, Aleppo or elsewhere—never questioned the movement's commitment to democracy and non-violence. A few young activists had decided to adopt a more radical stance against the Ba'ath regime but they remained, throughout the 1960s at least, a minority on the fringes of the Muslim Brotherhood. Although Issam al-Attar had been criticized by Hamawites such as Said Hawwa for calling for an end to the jihadist violence that had burst out at Hama during the April 1964 riots against the Ba'ath, the most senior Ikhwani figures from the city, such as Muhammed al-Hamid, nevertheless sided with the Damascene leader's non-violent position. This happened again when, in January 1965, Issam al-Attar asked the hundreds of Ikhwani members who had gathered at the Umayyad Mosque in Damascus for an anti-regime rally to remain peaceful and reject calls for a confrontation with the Ba'athist security forces.[12] All in all therefore, the attitude adopted with regards to the Ba'athist regime throughout the 1960s did not, at this stage, become an issue so significant that it created splits at the leadership level.

If claims that ideological differences led to a leadership split need to be strongly qualified, the same is true for the accusation that Issam al-Attar surrounded himself with solely Salafist followers who exclusively originated in the Syrian capital. Here, it is worth stressing that, for many Ikhwani members who belonged to the "northern axis", the issues of Salafism and geographic factionalism overlapped as Issam al-Attar's religious inclination had roots in the emergence of the Salafiyya movement in late Ottoman Damascus. Until today, the former Damascene leader is sometimes criticized by prominent Sufi figures inside the Muslim Brotherhood for having surrounded himself with Salafists, such as Mehdi al-Istambuli and Zuhair Shawish, who did not hold favourable views of the Ikhwan's Sufi members. Seemingly backing their claims, some academics have suggested that the Salafism of certain Damascene Brothers played a role in the deterioration of relations with Sufi *ulama* and Muslim Brothers coming from other cities. For example, Umar Faruk Abd Allah, author of the most detailed account of the Syrian Muslim Brotherhood written in the early 1980s, wrote, "Because the Salafis often condemned the traditional schools of Islamic law for alleged deviation from the Qur'an and *sunnah* and took even harsher positions against the Islamic tradition of Sufism, al-Attar never enjoyed a favourable relation with the Syrian *ulama* who, as a rule, follow one of the traditional schools and often are Sufis."[13] Such claims have been supported by key personalities belonging to the "northern axis", whose members are often associated with powerful Sufi orders such as the Naqshbandiya in Hama.

The argument, however, can be countered on the grounds that some inside the "Damascus wing", such as Muhammed Hawari or Hassan al-Houeidi, did not follow the Salafist doctrine preached by Issam al-Attar and instead remained faithful to a Sufi order and a Sunni school of jurisprudence. Thus, the fact that Issam al-Attar's Salafism became an issue for some inside the Ikhwan should be seen not as a religious quarrel between Sufis and Salafists but rather as the product of a growing resentment on the part of many belonging to the "northern axis" at the fact that Salafi-affiliated Damascene Brothers were, for a time at least, monopolizing the leadership of the Ikhwan. Their Salafism, as a product of the peculiar sociopolitical and religious environment specific to the Syrian capital, was therefore rejected more for symbolizing the leadership of the "Damascus wing" than for its religious meaning.

Indeed, it cannot be denied that during at least some of the time of Issam al-Attar's leadership of the Muslim Brotherhood the levers of power in the organization became increasingly centered on its Damascene members. From Zouheir Salem to Ali Sadreddine al-Bayanouni, key Ikhwani figures quote the Damascene leader's "geographic factionalism" as having been the driving force behind the rebellion led by the "northern axis" against the "Damascus wing".[14] It is true that, from the mid-1960s onwards, Issam al-Attar tightened his grip on the organization by surrounding himself with mostly Damascene colleagues. While in the early 1960s, the Executive Committee, the top decision-making body of the Syrian Ikhwan, was composed of five members coming from the cities of Damascus, Aleppo, Hama, Homs and Latakia respectively, the same organ became overwhelmingly dominated by Damascenes from the mid-1960s until the leadership crisis of 1969. Indeed, according to Muhammed Hawari, a leading figure of the "Damascus wing", when Issam al-Attar reshuffled the Executive Committee in October 1964, he nominated him as well as Muwafaq Da'abul and Teissir Ayti, all Damascenes, to the top decision-making body. Amin Yagan from Aleppo was then the only non-Damascene Ikhwani figure to reach a leadership position.[15]

"I have made some mistakes while being leader of the Ikhwan," Issam al-Attar acknowledged in an interview, "but never did I make a distinction between Syrian Brothers coming from Damascus or Aleppo."[16] In fact, when the 1969 leadership crisis broke out, a few prominent Ikhwani members who were not from the capital supported him, such as Hassan al-Houeidi from Deir ez-Zoor and Muhammed Riyad al-Shuqfah from Hama.[17] In addition, the geographic factionalism generally associated with the "Damascus wing's" leadership of the organization during the 1960s should perhaps be seen more as a result of than as a reason for the emergence of factionalism within the Muslim Brotherhood. The moment when Issam al-Attar reshuffled his Executive Committee in favour of the Damascene Brothers coincided with a period in which his leadership was already facing severe criticisms from many inside the movement. "In such circumstances, it was only natural for Issam al-Attar to rely on his Damascene colleagues, whom he knew best and trusted most,"[18] suggested Muhammed Hawari. So, if ideology, geographic factionalism and religious bias all seem to have been, to varying degrees, factors merely used in retrospect to legitimize the leadership crisis, what were its root causes?

The answer, as in every political formation composed of ambitious people who compete against each other for power, lies in a clash of personalities. This occurred in the Ikhwan during the mid-1960s and subsequently took on a regional and, at times, religious and ideological tone. The very character of Issam al-Attar seems to have played a role in his own marginalization from power in the late 1960s. A former secondary school teacher, he had quickly risen to prominence and had become, by the late 1950s, the preacher of the mosque at the University of Damascus Faculty of Islamic Law. As recognition for someone known as being intellectually gifted, this was a prestigious and influential position, for his Friday sermons were listened to by tens of thousands of pious Syrians. Issam al-Attar's passionate sermons are often given as the reason for joining the movement of the Muslim Brothers in late 1950s Syria.

However, despite the Damascene leader's ability to move the masses through brilliant speeches, criticism is often made of his lack of true leadership skills and political vision. In a statement echoed until today in Ikhwani circles, Umar Faruk Abd Allah went as far as asserting that Issam al-Attar "confused being a great speaker with being a great leader".[19] His style of leadership, which in the eyes of some was in substance more intellectual than political, was an aspect of al-Attar's handling of the organization that particularly irritated many outside Damascus who were prepared to challenge him. Others also claimed that the Damascene leader was simply an unskilled politician who did not give any direction to the Ikhwan at a time when strong leadership was needed. These critics quote Issam al-Attar's refusal to take up ministerial responsibilities in the successive governments that preceded the Ba'ath takeover in March 1963. The Damascene leader was also criticized when, in a tacit alliance with Syria's bourgeoisie, he delivered a series of key sermons denouncing the then prime minister, Bashir Al-Azmeh, for being "unworthy of the function" given "his strong left-wing inclination".[20] The sermons are believed to have led to mass student demonstrations eventually resulting in the prime minister's resignation a few months later, opening the door to political instability from which the Ba'ath Party would ultimately benefit the most.

Eventually, however, it was Issam al-Attar's exile from Syria that proved to be the most convenient pretext for asking him to renounce his leadership position. Ali Sadreddine al-Bayanouni, then a prominent member of the "Aleppo faction"—and therefore of the "northern axis"—

who was to rise to the leadership of the Ikhwan in the late 1990s, stated that the divergences within the organization, which had been growing since the early 1960s, eventually came to a head when the Damascene leader was forced into exile by the Ba'athist regime. "On the top of all, Issam al-Attar was now outside Syria at a time when we precisely needed a leader on the ground, based inside the country",[21] remembered Bayanouni. Many inside the organization came to resent the Damascene leader for being based abroad, some going as far as suggesting that he had abandoned his Ikhwani troops at a time of crisis.

Issam al-Attar's exile, however, was far from voluntary. He had been prevented from returning home when, on his return from a trip abroad in April 1964, the Ba'athist authorities refused to let him in on the grounds that the Muslim Brotherhood was supposedly behind the violent clashes at Hama a few weeks earlier between Islamist activists and the regime's security apparatus. "The regime blamed me for Marwan Hadid's activism,"[22] al-Attar explained. There is no evidence, however, that the violence at Hama at the time was supported by the Ikhwan's leadership. As a matter of fact, Muhammed Hawari, a close Damascene associate of Issam al-Attar, suggests quite the opposite. "While we were on a trip to Mecca, in Saudi Arabia, for a meeting of the International *tanzim* (organization) of the Muslim Brotherhood, Professor al-Attar and I learned through the radio about the violent clashes at Hama, before immediately and publicly denouncing the violence exercised on both parts."[23] It can only be inferred that, precisely at a time when the Ba'ath was desperately attempting to solidify its power, blaming the Ikhwan for the violence at Hama was a convenient way to weaken a potentially powerful political competitor. At any rate, al-Attar's exile proved detrimental not only to the Syrian Islamic movement, now led from abroad, but also to the leader himself, who came to increasingly rely on his Damascene followers in order to maintain his grip on the organization's leadership, thereby giving rise to the accusations of "regional factionalism".

The issue of al-Attar's exile became even more salient when, after being based in Arab states such as Lebanon for a time, then Jordan and Kuwait, the Damascene leader decided to travel all the way to Europe, first to Geneva and Brussels, before eventually settling down in Aachen in Germany, where he resides to this day. According to al-Attar, he moved to Europe in order to "avoid having the Syrian Ikhwan being used by Arab states as a bishop on the regional chessboard."[24] In any case, the European exile of the Muslim Brotherhood's leader made communication with the Ikhwan's base in Syria more difficult over the years and, eventually, greatly weakened his grip on a movement increasingly rebelling against its own leader. According to Issam al-Attar, the tipping point was reached in 1967–68 when he became physically unable to lead the organization for some time. "I fell gravely sick and, in a context of rising divergences amongst Ikhwani members, some took up this occasion to challenge my leadership."[25]

The "northern axis", which, for the overlapping reasons stated above challenged the leadership of the "Damascus wing", was led by Amin Yagan, a Brother from Aleppo who had also been al-Attar's deputy at the helm of the organization during the mid-1960s, before increasing divergences divided the two figures. Yagan was, by the admission of a leading member of the "Damascus wing", a very active and charismatic figure. He was supported by other prominent personalities within the movement, such as Adnan Sa'id from Latakia, Adnan Saadeddine and Said Hawwa from Hama and Sheikh Abdel Fatah Abu Ghuddah from Aleppo. This "northern axis" had the support of most members on the ground and opposed Issam al-Attar's numerically inferior "Damascus wing" which, despite its name, included not only prominent Damascene Brothers such as Muwaffaq Da'abul, Zuhair Shawish and Muhammed Hawari, but also a few other Ikhwani figures from elsewhere, such as Muhammed Riyad al-Shuqfah from Hama and Hassan Houeidi from Deir ez-Zoor, who both felt that Issam al-Attar should not be pushed out before his term as the Ikhwan's leader expired.[26]

Between 1969 and 1972, the Ikhwan were left with virtually no coherent leadership, the divergences and resentment between the two groups only growing over time before they effectively became separate entities. When new elections were organized, in a common effort to put differences aside by letting rank and file members decide who should be their leader, the candidate of the "northern axis", Sheikh Abdel Fatah Abu Ghuddah of Aleppo, emerged as the clear victor.[27] Because he was a respected religious scholar on whom all factions belonging to the "northern axis" could agree temporarily, it has been claimed that Abu Ghuddah merely served as a compromise figurehead. "Ambitious young members of the 'northern axis' instrumentalized Sheikh Abu Ghuddah's scientific and religious caution while he himself did not even have political ambitions",[28] a member of the "Damascus wing" claimed bitterly.

Despite official recognition of the new leadership by the international *tanzim* of the Muslim Brotherhood, Issam al-Attar's "Damascus wing", in its majority at least, never joined the whole group again. It was clear, according to the Damascene Muhammed Hawari, that the only reason why the international body of the Ikhwan eventually supported the "northern axis" stemmed from an old feud which, in the early 1960s, had been pitting the Egyptian Ikhwan against the "Damascus wing" of the Syrian branch. When the international *tanzim* of the Ikhwan met in 1963 to propose to the Syrian branch that it should integrate into the wider organization, political differences emerged between the Damascus and Aleppo wings of the movement on whether or not to accept the proposal. Traditionally, the *murshid*, or leader, of the international Muslim Brotherhood had always been Egyptian. This was because the original organization had been established in Egypt and because the Egyptian Ikhwan were the most influential branch within the international *tanzim*. While the "Damascus wing" wished to change this state of affairs, proposing that the *murshid* of the international Muslim Brotherhood could be of any nationality belonging to the *tanzim*, the "Aleppo faction" supported the Egyptian Ikhwan's claim to leadership and wished to see the Syrian branch integrate into the wider organization without any preconditions. Muhammed Hawari therefore suggests that, because the Egyptians never forgot this episode, one should view the support they granted to the "Aleppo faction" when it sought to challenge the "Damascus wing", via their influence in the international *tanzim*, through the lenses of this feud.[29]

At any rate, the victory of the "northern axis" following the leadership crisis of the late 1960s provoked the departure both from the Ikhwan and from Syria of many Damascene Brothers who had remained loyal to Issam al-Attar.[30] In the decades following his exile, and as Ba'athist repression of Islamic militants sharply increased, a core group gathered around the Islamic Centre of Brussels and then Aachen, where Issam al-Attar had launched his own movement, al-Tala'i ("The Vanguards", not to be confused with Marwan Hadid's al-Tali'a al-Muqatila, "The Fighting Vanguard"). In line with the legacy of the Salafiyya trend in Damascus, al-Tala'i was an intellectual network ideologically following in the footsteps of al-Tamaddun, advocating to Muslim elites in Europe a reform of Islam from within.

More generally, the Damascene Brothers who left Syria and the Ikhwan in the early 1970s concentrated on spreading *daw'a* (preaching) across the Arab world, many for instance taking up educational positions in Saudi Arabia and Jordan. This was the case, for instance, with Muhammed Surur Zein al-Abideen and Muhammed al-Abdeh who, having taught Islamic law in Saudi Arabia, left for the United Kingdom where they founded their own movements.[31] While working on magazines, Surur creating *al-Sunna* and Abdeh becoming an editor of *al-Bayan*, they both argued in favour of a more politically active and socially conservative brand of Salafism inspired by the Wahhabism they had experienced in Saudi Arabia. "What my father, who was a close associate of Muhammed Surur Zein al-Abideen, advocated was a blend of 'Salafiyya' creed with Ikhwani-style organization" explained Malik al-Abdeh, the son of Muhammed al-Abdeh and director of the London-based Barada TV. "In many ways, they were already advocating the birth of a sort of Hizb an-Nour [the Salafist party which emerged in post-revolutionary Egypt], an ideological platform with strong Salafi views, stressing their hostility to Shi'ism and their commitment to Sharia law, while at the same time wishing to engage in political activism and prepared to play the game of parliamentary democracy."[32]

Malik al-Abdeh, whose family stems from the "Damascus wing", created, together with his brother Anas, the Movement for Justice and Development (MJD), in late 2005, a Syrian opposition party based in London. The MJD seeks to emulate the blend of political liberalism and social conservatism put forward by the AKP Party in Turkey. Negatively perceived by an Ikhwani leadership which views it as a creation of the "Damascus wing", the MJD endorses the legacy of Issam al-Attar even if he does not wish to be too closely associated with it—al-Attar's associate, Muhammed Hawari, stressing that "both movements are from the same tree but bear different fruits".[33]

The radicalization of the Islamic movement

If the split in the "Damascus wing" had little to do with the moderate ideological inclination adopted by its members, the split of the early 1970s nonetheless ended up having profound doctrinal and political implications for the Islamic movement. Indeed, the departure of the Damascene members from the rest of the Muslim Brotherhood left an ideological vacuum which would eventually be exploited by more radical Islamic activists.

At first, however, the organization remained committed to the peaceful approach Issam al-Attar had charted for the Syrian Ikhwan. The Aleppine Abdel Fatah Abu Ghuddah, who had by then taken the reins of leadership, was a respected Islamic scholar who wished to focus the Brotherhood's efforts on preaching and education (*da'wa*). This also coincided with a period during which the Syrian Ba'ath, headed by Hafiz al-Assad, was striving to moderate the line it had inherited from his more radical "neo-Ba'ath" predecessors. At the time, the modest efforts undertaken by the Syrian President at opening up the country's political system were even tacitly supported by the Ikhwan. When local and legislative elections were organized by the regime, in 1972 and 1973 respectively, the Muslim Brotherhood, while not participating directly, supported conservative candidates in Aleppo and Damascus.[34] On the surface, therefore, the leadership crisis which had led to the departure of the moderate "Damascus wing" had not yet plunged the entire movement into radicalism.

Things were different on the ground, however, where at the grassroots level, resentment was growing against the seemingly passive stance the leadership had taken with respect to Ba'athist rule. Eventually, in 1975 Abdel Fatah Abu Ghuddah handed the organization's leadership to the more radical, Hama-born Adnan Saadeddine, in a move symbolizing the Ikhwan's progressive political and ideological radicalization. The new leader's rise to prominence at the helm of the Muslim Brotherhood gave way to the advent of what some refer to as the "Hama clan"—a group of younger Ikhwani activists whose more hard-line stance would eventually push the organization into an open confrontation with the Syrian Ba'ath. Key amongst them was Said Hawwa, a young Islamic scholar from Hama who is often considered the artisan of the Muslim Brotherhood's ideological radicalization from 1975 onwards. The main organizer of the January 1973 demonstrations against the "Godless" Ba'ath regime, which had just published a draft Constitution deemed "too secular", he quickly became the Ikhwan's main ideologue after Adnan Saadeddine's takeover of the organization's leadership. His hatred of the Ba'ath regime's secular face was coupled with a strong sectarian dimension. Whether in his most widely-read book, *Jund Allah* ("Army of God"), or in the numerous inflammatory public speeches he gave, Said Hawwa constantly denounced the "infidel Nusayri regime", unleashing by the same token a wave of Islamic radicalism with sectarian undertones which would significantly alter the nature of the once-peaceful Syrian Ikhwan.[35]

Itzchak Weismann, a researcher who studied the radical Islamic scholar's thought in depth, notes that "in defining his attitude toward the Alawis, Hawwa alludes to a *fatwa* of Ibn Taymiyya", and that,

According to this *fatwa*, jihad against this sect precedes jihad against polytheists (*mushrikun*) or against *ahl al-kitab* [the People of the Book, i.e. the Christian and Jewish communities] as it belongs to the category of jihad against *murtaddun* ["apostates" who have "left" Islam]. Thus, in Hawwa's view, Syria is a unique case of a Muslim state that is ruled by a heretical *halini* government, and in such case he sees no escape from a violent confrontation. The Sunni majority, led by the Islamic movement, must wage an uncompromising war against Assad's regime and against Alawi dominance in Syria.[36]

The popularity of Said Hawwa among the rank-and-file of the Brotherhood became such that, by the mid-1970s, books he had authored. such as *Jund Allah*, were distributed widely in mosques and underground religious bookshops.

Thus, while the Muslim Brotherhood's violent struggle against the Syrian Ba'ath would only be launched in late 1979, the process that led to its radicalization was well under way throughout the 1970s. In this respect, the Muslim Brotherhood's Hamawite leadership—formally in control of the organization from 1975 to 1980 and the main influence until 1982—seems to have been deeply influenced, both ideologically and tactically, by the growing strength of a particularly radical form of Islamic militancy which had emerged a decade earlier in Hama and was rapidly spreading throughout Syria.

In this bastion of religious conservatism, the rapidly growing popularity of a jihadist organization born on the fringes of the Ikhwan symbolized a radical trend which would mark the evolution of the Syrian Islamic movement. Early signs indicating the emergence of a jihadist current in Syria could be observed shortly after the Ba'ath regime's ascent to power. In April 1964, violent clashes erupted in Hama, pitting the authorities against a small group of radicalized Islamic activists who called for a violent overthrow of the "Godless" Ba'ath regime (see Chapter 3). They were led by Marwan Hadid, a charismatic figure whose daring outlook subsequently provided the jihadist literature with a mythology and a role model to look upon (see Appendices for an account of Hadid's "heroic" behaviour during and after the 1964 Hama riots, written by Sheikh Abdullah Azzam, a Jordanian Islamic scholar who was also the "godfather" of the 1980s international jihad in Afghanistan). Beyond his charismatic leadership, Hadid brought to the Islamic movement in Syria a vision and a doctrine for action. In the early 1960s, he went to Cairo to study agricultural engineering, and there he befriended Sayyid Qutb, a member of the Egyptian Muslim Brotherhood whose advocacy of the need to violently confront President Gamal Abdel Nasser seemed appealing to many Syrian Islamic activists disenchanted by the Ikhwani leadership's peaceful—some said passive— approach to the Ba'ath regime. Upon Marwan Hadid's return to Hama in 1963, and especially after the 1964 Hama riots which he directed, the "Qutbist ideology" started to spread with increasing pace across the country. But, in order to understand the extent to which Sayyid Qutb's theories made their way through the Islamic movement in Syria, a brief glance at the conceptual framework introduced by the Egyptian ideologue is needed.

When Qutb wrote his immensely influential *Ma'alim fi'l Tariq* ("Signposts"), in the mid-1960s, the Egyptian Ikhwan were undergoing a severe crisis of identity. While they found it difficult to cope with the ideological void following the death a decade earlier of their historic leader Hassan al-Banna, they were also having a hard time dealing with the increasingly heavy repression at the hands of Nasser's regime. In that context, the Egyptian ideologue brought crucial responses to the unanswered questions of many Muslim Brothers and Islamic youth who proved unable to come to terms with their organization's hardships. Sayyid Qutb explained the weak state of the Islamic movement by introducing the concept of *jahiliyya*, or "ignorance", which after characterizing the pre-Islamic era now seemed to again "contaminate" Muslim societies governed by rulers more inspired by foreign ideologies (socialism, nationalism, secularism) than by a commitment to *al-hakimiyya*—"God's sovereign rule on earth". An "Islamic renewal" would therefore entail a complete change in the attitude and thinking of Muslim societies that were now, in Qutb's opinion, not yet fully aware of the dangers to the *Umma* posed by left-wing, secular governments judged as "impious".

Besides offering a conceptual framework within which to analyse the growth of the Nasser regime and its consequences, the Egyptian ideologue also proposed a vision of what should be done to alter the situation. He argued that "our first task is to change society in deed, to alter the *jahiliyya* reality from top to bottom."[37] In his view, since the masses were blinded by ignorance, the restoration of divine law would only be achieved through the work of a vanguard *haraka* (movement)—a supposedly enlightened group tasked with carrying out the revolution. As to what method such a vanguard should employ, Sayyid Qutb left neither doubt nor ambiguity. "[Jihad] will not be achieved merely by teaching and preaching, for those who inflict the yoke on the necks of the people and who usurp the authority of God on earth will not concede their position through such explanation and sermonising,"[38] he stated. "The battle is constant and the sacred combat lasts until Judgment Day."[39] Sayyid Qutb's advocacy of the use of violence to overthrow Arab regimes judged as "impious" would have far-reaching implications for Egypt's Muslim Brotherhood, an organization long committed to preaching and political activism. Gilles Kepel, an expert on radical Islam, explained how, "for the author of *Signposts*, the propagation of Islam now required a shift of both field and instrument [...] The Book was no longer indicated: it was time for the sword. [The Nasserist state] was a *jahiliyya* regime, which had to be fought the way pagans were fought."[40] Notwithstanding the official rejection of Qutbist thought by the Egyptian Ikhwani leadership—whose leader in the 1960s, Hassan al-Hudaybi, criticized it in a book entitled *Preachers, not Judges* that he published shortly afterwards—the radical ideologue managed to influence a whole generation of militants until well after his death in 1966.

The Syrian Marwan Hadid was one of them. His return to Syria in 1963 marked the spill-over of the debate on the immediacy of armed struggle in Syrian Islamic circles. According to Umar Faruk Abdallah, the author of a book on the Syrian Islamic movement, "Hadid came to hold that there must above all be no compromise between Islam and non-Islamic or anti-Islamic systems of government and he also became convinced that the anti-Islamic systems represented by [Nasser] and the Syrian Ba'ath could only be dislodged by armed resistance." He also contended that "Like Qutb, Hadid was convinced that the Islamic movements would be quashed whether or not they took up arms and that their only hope for survival was to heed the Islamic call of jihad as long as some strength and capacity to fight still remained."[41]

The success of the Qutbist ideology beyond Egypt's borders resided in the universal message it carried to committed Muslims across the Arab world. Its meaning had particular relevance in Syria, dominated since March 1963 by a Ba'ath Party heavily populated by religious minorities. There, the *jahiliyya* dimension of secular Ba'athist rule seemed to be quickly converging with the growing sectarian aspect assumed by the struggle against the regime. Syrian activists inspired by Sayyid Qutb revived Ibn Taymiyya's legacy of anti-Alawism, declaring the sect as *takfir* (to be excommunicated) and promising to fight what they referred to as "Nusayri dogs" until the very last.

However, as Marwan Hadid started to call publicly for immediate jihad against the regime in his home town of Hama, he was quickly sidelined by the "Damascus wing" then in control of the Brotherhood's leadership, which categorically rejected his ideas and did not wish to be associated with him. The split came to the fore when the Syrian jihadist emerged as a charismatic and popular figure in the anti-regime riots of Hama in 1964, as a result of which the Ba'athist rulers forced the Brotherhood's leader, Issam al-Attar, into exile for not being able to control his troops. Even though Marwan Hadid could count on the tacit support of the prominent Ikhwani members Adnan Saadeddine and Said Hawwa from Hama, the Brotherhood's leadership—under both the Damascene al-Attar and the Aleppine Abu Ghuddah—was not prepared to endorse his actions, out of fear of further Ba'athist retaliation and their own lack of consensus. The group which Marwan Hadid developed in Hama throughout the 1960s and early 1970s therefore became a "fringe movement on the periphery of the Brotherhood"[42]—even though the full extent to which "Marwan Hadid's group", as it was then known, was close to the Ikhwan's local leadership in Hama remains unknown.[43]

Birth of an extremist organization: the Fighting Vanguard

In the late 1960s, Marwan Hadid and his followers went to the Palestinian *fedayeen* camps scattered throughout Jordan for military training. When they were forced out of the country after King Hussein destroyed many such camps during the "Black September" of 1970, they returned to Syria with crucial skills and an unyielding determination to fight against the Ba'ath. An al-Qaeda document found during the American raid on Usama Bin Laden's home in Abbottabad, Pakistan, retraces parts of this little-known episode of Marwan Hadid's story. "Whatever military experience Hadid had learned in Jordan made him feel confident about himself. Hadid wanted to use his training to do something for his religion. He decided that he could no longer live under the Syrian apostate regime […] and he was able to recruit a number of people so he could begin his work against the Syrian regime", the document stated, while also pointing out that "Hadid did not want to wait for the right time."[44]

Following the constitutional crisis of 1973, which seemed to confirm the secular orientation of the regime (see Chapters 3 and 4), Marwan Hadid's views in Islamic circles close to the Brotherhood became influential, to the extent that he managed to gather a sufficient number of committed followers to carry out the targeted killings of prominent members of the Ba'ath security apparatus, not only in Hama but also in Damascus where he had gone into hiding. "By 1974, Marwan Hadid had at his disposal a large number of trained armed cells ready to do anything asked of them,"[45] reported Ayman al-Shorbaji, the organization's field commander in Damascus. Hadid's "Qutbist" ambition was clear and well summed up in the name eventually given to his group, al-Tali'a al-Muqatila lil-Mujahidin (The Fighting Vanguard of the Mujahidin). By taking the initiative to kill prominent representatives of the regime, he hoped to trigger government retaliation that would ultimately convince the Brotherhood's leadership of the inevitability of armed struggle. Muhammed Riyadh al-Shuqfah, an active Brotherhood member in Hama who was to rise to the leadership of the Ikhwan in 2010, recalled his "friendship" with "Sheikh Marwan" and gave more details on the jihadist figure: "he was a brave Islamic militant; he had the temper of a true leader and had much influence on Hama's youth." However, "while he had always been part of the local Muslim Brotherhood circle in Hama, he strongly disagreed with the peaceful policy we followed at the time." "Sheikh Marwan was an enthusiastic member of the Ikhwan but he was not very respectful of the organization's rules; he wanted the Brotherhood to think less and act more," he added. "In other words, he ambitioned to revolutionize our organization."[46]

With the help of commando training received from the Palestinian group Fatah in its Jordanian and Lebanese camps, "Marwan Hadid's group"—as it was known before assuming the name of the Fighting Vanguard (al Tali'a al-Muqatila)—soon became so efficient that the Ba'ath regime concentrated its resources on tracking down its leader, who was arrested in Damascus in June 1975.[47] His subsequent death in prison one year later, allegedly due to poisoning, provoked a cry of outrage so loud that it was heard not only from Hadid's admirers but also from many within the Brotherhood, who admired his courage and lonely struggle and sought revenge for his slaying. Already a myth during his lifetime, Marwan Hadid had become upon his death a true legend for all jihadists, both in Syria and abroad (see Appendices for Abdullah Azzam's account of the "heroic" way in which the jihadist figure was forced to give up arms). According to Husni Abu, an Islamic militant from Aleppo, it was upon Marwan Hadid's death that many radicals who had been sensitive to his call for armed struggle but were spread out throughout Syria decided to set up a more coordinated, nationwide organization tasked with carrying on his enterprise.[48] From Hama, the militant Abd-us-Sattar az-Za'im took on this task, bringing together the various armed cells which had also sprung up throughout Aleppo and Damascus. The organization soon became highly effective, assassinating Major Muhammad Gharrah in early 1976, the chief of the Hama branch of General Intelligence, most certainly in an act of retaliation for the torture which Marwan Hadid was rumoured to have undergone while in prison.[49]

According to Abu Mus'ab al-Suri, a member of The Fighting Vanguard who would become al-Qaeda's main ideologue in the early 2000s, the period ranging from 1976 to 1980 proved to be the "Golden Age" of Syria's jihadist current. "Due to its small size and secrecy, the Fighting Vanguard was able to retain the initiative until 1980,"[50] he explained. Ayman al-Shorbaji detailed in his memoirs the impressive list of actions carried out by the organization during this period. Following Hafiz al-Assad's re-election as Syrian President on 8 February 1977, explosive charges were simultaneously detonated at headquarters of the Ba'ath Party and the National Progressive Front (a coalition of pro-regime political groups) and at the People's Assembly. The Fighting Vanguard's field commander for the region of Damascus also recounted how, shortly afterwards, Abd-us-Sattar az-Za'im ordered the assassination of Ibrahim al-Nasiri who, besides being Hafiz al-Assad's nephew, was also a prominent member of the Ba'ath Party and the chairman of the Syrian-Soviet Friendship Association. "When he got out of his Peugeot 504 and walked towards the entrance of the building, one Brother followed him and called five steady shots in the head from a gun equipped with a silencer before withdrawing quietly,"[51] Shorbaji recounted. Prominent security officers, Ba'athist politicians, university professors affiliated with the ruling party, high-ranking civil servants of the regime: virtually all the personalities representing Ba'athist rule in Syria became targets of the Fighting Vanguard, whether they were of Alawi, Christian or Sunni faith.

All of these actions represented major successes for the Fighting Vanguard as they proved to the regime that the jihadist organization had managed to outlive its charismatic leader's death. In Islamic circles, Abd-us-Sattar az-Za'im is often praised as the man who gave the Fighting Vanguard its "organizational foundations" and "disciplined military character". In addition, Marwan Hadid's successor was keen on maintaining strong co-ordination between all local cells while leaving each regional commander with a degree of autonomy. This allowed the organization to increase the efficiency of its attacks while decreasing the risk of a total destruction of the group in case the attackers were caught. Under his leadership, the Fighting Vanguard also managed to penetrate the Syrian armed forces, having convinced a few high-ranking Sunni officers of the need to overthrow the "impious" regime—even though their attempted coup d'état, named the "Decisive Plan",[52] eventually failed. Overall, while upon Marwan Hadid's death Abd-us-Sattar az-Zaim had taken over a loose group of jihadist fighters spread throughout Syria, he had by the late 1970s managed to transform the Fighting Vanguard into a terrorist organization of a professional dimension. Its fighters were carefully selected and so well-trained that those who survived the state repression would later rise to prominence in other organizations such as al-Qaeda (see Appendices for an account of the type of training followed by the Fighting Vanguard fighters).

Operating in secrecy and without publicizing its exploits, the jihadist activists of al-Tali'a did not draw the attention of a regime which thought, at first, that the terrorist attacks were carried out by its Iraqi neighbour and rival. When it became clear, however, that the violent campaign was being led by the former companions of Marwan Hadid, the Ba'athist authorities dramatically increased their surveillance and repression of the movement. Sometime in mid 1979, Abd-us-Sattar az-Za'im was tracked down and killed. His death would have far-reaching consequences on the evolution of the Fighting Vanguard, for his immediate successors—Hisham Jumbaz, Tamim al-Shuqraqi and Umar Jawad—were not as gifted and eventually failed to contain rising divergences within the movement. By 1979, there were increasing tensions inside the Fighting Vanguard between jihadist fighters from Hama and Aleppo, who both wished to sharply step up violence against the regime, and the more cautious Damascene members who were "careful not to do more harm than good"[53] to the organization. One figure was particularly keen on accelerating, at any price, the pace of jihad against the Syrian Ba'ath: Adnan Uqlah from Aleppo.

Those who have known Adnan Uqlah, whether critics or admirers, all refer to his deeply entrenched and uncompromising character. Zealous and charismatic for some, over-ambitious and self-centered for others, Adnan Uqlah's persona quickly grew to mythical proportions in Syrian Islamic circles. In June 1979, he took the initiative—alongside a small group of fighters aided by the Ba'athist Ibrahim Youssef—of launching an attack against the Aleppo Artillery School, slaughtering eighty-three Alawi cadets and wounding many others. The attack was significant in the meaning it conveyed. From assassinating personalities affiliated with the Ba'ath regime, the Fighting Vanguard had transformed into an overtly sectarian terrorist organization willing to go as far as resorting to indiscriminate mass killings. According to the converging accounts of militants then close to Fighting Vanguard circles, Adnan Uqlah, who was only the head of a local commando group when he executed the operation, carried it out without consulting either Hisham Jumbaz, then the organization's leader, or Husni Abu, its field commander for the region of Aleppo, who both "would never have agreed to it".[54] The violent campaign led by the Fighting Vanguard soon escalated in both intensity and scale as the organization became in effect directed by Adnan Uqlah from the time of the June 1979 Aleppo massacre until his capture by the Syrian security services in late 1982.[55] At the height of the regime, the state of paranoia became such that, while the Syrian president is reported to have surrounded himself with a personal guard of several thousand elite troops, the three generals heading the security services constantly had sixty soldiers at their disposal tasked with protecting them.[56] In June 1980, Hafiz al-Assad himself miraculously survived an assassination attempt.

However, if Adnan Uqlah proved to be an effective commando leader, the grand ambitions he charted for the Fighting Vanguard soon came to provoke a harsh backlash on his organization. Abu Mus'ab al-Suri for instance suggested that, instead of leading to victory against the Ba'ath, Uqlah's decision to widely increase the number of Fighting Vanguard recruits throughout the country marked the slow demise of the jihadist movement. "Within [a] few months hundreds of youth joined in, the organization expanded beyond its financial capabilities, they were unable to train properly or arm sufficiently, things got out of control, the influx created a fishing ground for moles and spies, and even though they were few—caught and executed in accordance with the Islamic rules of the organization—they caused a lot of harm." He concluded that, eventually, "a series of confessions and arrests led to exposing the entire hierarchy of al-Talia and to its destruction."[57]

In addition, since the big increase in numbers of Fighting Vanguard recruits could not be properly balanced by an equal increase in the organization's financial and material resources, the new fighters proved to be less prepared for jihad—both ideologically and physically—and therefore less committed to it than the generation of jihadists that had emerged under the leadership of Marwan Hadid and Abd-us-Sattar az-Za'im. "The base membership became a group of enthusiastic youth who lacked ideological strength; with the passing of every day their enthusiasm cooled down and many of them lost their connection to the cause",[58] al-Suri remembered. Their young age did not help matters as they did not seem to display the same level of educational preparedness for jihad as their elders. Obeida Nahas, a Syrian Brother living in London, thus recounted that "within al-Tali'a a new generation of jihadists started to emerge who had not gone through the proper educational process"; "Drawn to the organization by Adnan Uqlah's charisma, they were usually recruited just out of the mosques, universities and even high schools".[59] An analysis of the social base of the Fighting Vanguard, on the basis of the memoirs written by Ayman al-Shorbaji, confirms that most of the fighters were indeed barely twenty years old when recruited into the jihadist organization. Hanna Batatu has confirmed that pattern in his study of the background of those who were arrested by the Ba'athist authorities in the period ranging from 1976 until 1981, pointing out that the student body was by far the social group most represented in Syrian jails at the time—totalling at least three times that of schoolteachers and professionals.[60]

However, if the exponential growth and ever-younger outlook of the Fighting Vanguard's fighters were the products of decisions taken by Adnan Uqlah, these were not properly approved by the jihadist organization's consultative body. Such a state of affairs symbolized the Fighting Vanguard's increasingly personal dimension centered on the persona of its "Caliph", as Uqlah was reported to enjoy being called.[61] Abu Mus'ab al-Suri described the situation and analysed the consequences of the "one-man rule" which came to characterize the Fighting Vanguard from 1979 until 1982. "Adnan Uqlah, in spite of his consultations with the [consultative] council, decided and ruled independently, and thus rendered that council obsolete."[62] In al-Suri's view, the Fighting Vanguard's "Caliph" was of course a gifted military leader whose charisma had drawn enthusiasm from the Sunni crowds in Syria: "Adnan Uqlah was a role model for a leader: he was daring, sacrificing, fundamentalist, revolutionary, and persistent in his principles and path, steadfast in his resolve, his virtues were attested to by his enemies before his friends, he had a history of exemplary jihad and seniority in preaching the doctrine." Yet the problem with Uqlah, al-Suri suggests, lay in the shortcomings which emerged from those traits. His style of management could be best described as filled with "extremism, excessive emotionalism and inflexibility even on the slightest of matters". In addition, he lacked the "judiciousness and political savvy" needed in an effective leader. The analysis of the personality of the Fighting Vanguard's "Caliph" offered by a member of Syria's Muslim Brotherhood to Abu Mus'ab al-Suri sums it up quite well. "I do not doubt Adnan Uqlah's loyalty and integrity as a leader, nor do I doubt his courage. I also have no doubt that he lacks the wisdom to benefit from those two characteristics,"[63] the Syrian Brother was reported to have told him. With time, the pre-eminence of the "Caliph" over the whole of the Fighting Vanguard became the organization's Achilles heel. "Al-Talia revolved around the persona of Adnan Uqlah, which led to its fragmentation and demise." "Those were the negative results of the one man rule," concluded al-Suri. Because the "Caliph" became the "sole decision-maker on all matters," "when he was captured and imprisoned the entire organization collapsed and ceased to exist."[64]

6

ENDORSING JIHAD AGAINST THE BA'ATH
(1980–1982)

The Syrian Ba'ath was quick to blame all of the Fighting Vanguard's attacks on the Muslim Brotherhood. For a time, this attempt at discrediting its most serious political competitor proved fruitless as, despite the links existing between both groups, the two remained for the large part organizationally and ideologically distinct. A dose of competition and, to a certain degree, bitterness at one another even came to characterize the relationship between the Fighting Vanguard and the Syrian Brotherhood. By late 1979, however, and particularly following the June 1979 Aleppo Artillery School massacre, state repression had become such that the Ikhwani leadership decided it was time to respond to Ba'athist provocations by raising the banner of jihad itself. The subsequent alliance it made with the jihadist forces of the Fighting Vanguard and Issam al-Attar's more moderate "Damascus wing" in late 1980 would provide the regime with the pretext it had long been seeking to brutally crush the Islamic movement. Under the cover of a "war against terrorism", Ba'athist officers came to kill and torture thousands of members of the Syrian opposition as well as their relatives.

The Muslim Brotherhood had been trapped: by resorting to violence and allying with the jihadists, it had played to regime propaganda which claimed that it was "terrorist". The brutality of state repression, as illustrated by the February 1982 Hama massacre, was then such that the

Islamic organization would never truly get back on its feet. Its public image, long shaped entirely by the Syrian Ba'ath's rhetoric, became for decades associated with radicalism and violence. How was the Muslim Brotherhood lured into such a trap? Why exactly did the organization start out on a path it knew was potentially self-destructive? Such questions are not only relevant for those experts and scholars who seek to better understand the exact flow of events and the dynamics leading to the tragic confrontation between government forces and the Islamic opposition at Hama in 1982, but also for those Syrians who, today more than ever, look into their past to learn more from the crucial 1980–82 period. This chapter presents an attempt at uncovering the complex dynamics which, in relation both to how the Brotherhood dealt with the regime and to how internal Ikhwani politics came to influence the policies it carried out, led to the eventual disaster of February 1982.

State repression

By mid-1979, the ideological shift within Muslim Brotherhood ranks had finally come to a head. At a meeting of the Ikhwan's consultative body (*Majlis al-Shura*) held in October of that year in Amman, the leaders of the organization officially endorsed the use of violence as a legitimate means to fight the Ba'ath regime.[1] Shortly thereafter, it was decided that the Muslim Brotherhood would set up a "military branch" and would enter into a partnership with the forces of the Fighting Vanguard. But, for all the regime's attempts at describing such a radical turn as reflecting the Brotherhood's supposedly inherent violent doctrine, the endorsement of violence should be viewed as an exception in the movement's history, to be seen through the lens of the increased repression it suffered at the hands of the regime. Until today, official Muslim Brotherhood statements relating to the use of violence at the time are unsurprisingly filled with references to "self-defence" and "option of last resort".[2] For instance, in an April 1980 issue of *An-Nadhir*, an information letter published outside Syria by the Muslim Brotherhood, Ikhwani leaders stressed that "we did not begin our jihad until the oppressors had begun to exterminate Islam and until after having received the broken bodies of our brothers who had died under torture."[3] In fact, it is unquestionable that increased state repression did have a polarizing effect on the political situation in Syria. This is even recognized retrospectively by the country's former Vice President, Abdel Halim Khaddam, who recalled, "the regime made a mistake by increasing the repression after the Aleppo Artillery incident [of June 1979], as it only further radicalized many Brothers who came to feel they had no option but to use violence."[4]

To this day, many Muslim Brotherhood members hold the view that the June 1979 Aleppo massacre represented an opportunity long awaited by the regime to blame the violence on the Ikhwan and portray it as "terrorist"—despite the publication by the then leader, Adnan Saadeddine, of an official communiqué denying the organization's responsibility shortly afterwards. In fact, there is evidence that the regime knew that the Muslim Brotherhood was not responsible for the attacks yet maintained its claim to legitimize its repression of the movement. Yahya Bedin, a member of the Ikhwan living in Turkey, thus recounted how the Interior Ministry published a list of seventeen names accused of being behind the massacre of the eighty-three Alawi cadets—they were all Muslim Brotherhood members and none, it was reported, belonged to the Fighting Vanguard:

My name was on the list even though I was a student in Riyadh during the summer of 1979! I left Syria for Saudi Arabia on April 26th, 1979, and still have the certificate of passport registration stamped at the Syrian Embassy in Riyadh during the summer of 1979 […] the regime accused me of having participated into the attack because I was a known Muslim Brotherhood member as it wanted to involve the Ikhwan into the story! When, after having fled for Turkey, I went to the Syrian Embassy in Ankara in order to show the official stamped documents proving I was not in Aleppo at the time, Syrian officials warned me to neither come again nor to talk with the media. The sixteen other people who were on the list have all been killed.[5]

This version of events was not only voiced by Brotherhood members but also supported by former members of the Fighting Vanguard who went on to work with al-Qaeda when the Syrian jihad came to an end. In a document found by American forces during the Abbottabad raid on Bin Laden's home, it is confirmed that, at the time, "the Syrian regime treated the Brotherhood as if it was the one who assassinated its officials" even though "the regime knew that it was not the case". "The Syrian government saw this as an opportunity to demolish the Muslim Brotherhood, and forever,"[6] concluded the anonymous al-Qaeda document. Significantly enough, the regime's narrative of the June 1979

Aleppo massacre has continued to dominate not only the official Ba'athist discourse but also much of the work of scholars of Syria who, out of ideological bias or lack of detailed information, have rarely questioned the Muslim Brotherhood's alleged involvement in the incident.[7]

Refusing to draw a distinction between the Fighting Vanguard and the Brotherhood, the regime greatly heightened its repression against the Islamic movement. "The situation became untenable", a prominent Syrian Brother, in Aleppo at the time, describes it today. "The leadership of the movement was shocked: we did not know who the perpetrators [of the Aleppo Artillery School attack] were, a crisis was unfolding and we could feel it."[8] After officials in the Interior Ministry vowed to "exterminate" the Ikhwan, over six thousand Syrians were arrested across the country.[9] Walid Safour, a London-based human rights activist who was living in Homs at the time, recalled that the June 1979 attack indeed marked a turning point in the intensity of the repression suffered by those accused of belonging to the Muslim Brotherhood. "From then on, life became a hell: I was arrested several times between June 1979 and October 1980 and tortured so severely by the Military Intelligence that I would later need to undergo three surgeries, leaving my back disabled until today."[10]

Methods employed by the Syrian security services to "treat" alleged Muslim Brothers followed a ritual process, exposed by a team of human rights activists who carried out an investigation into the repression of the late 1970s and early 1980s:

Interrogation sometimes begins immediately after arrest, but prisoners may be held in these centers for days—even weeks—before their interrogation commences. Severe mistreatment usually begins during this time to break the prisoners' spirit and will to resist. Guards may prevent captives from sleeping, force them to stand on one leg or to crawl on the floor, and pour boiling or freezing water on their naked bodies. Sounds of torture of other prisoners echo through the halls. Prisoners' fear builds and their physical strength ebbs as food is withheld and guards assault them with curses and threats.[11]

The most common technique used by the security services to torture alleged Muslim Brothers was the *dullab* ("tyre"). Walid Safour recounted how, after refusing to sign an official document confessing that he was a Muslim Brother, he underwent the *dullab*. "[Military intelligence officers] squeezed me into a painful position inside a tire so that my feet could touch my eyes. Unable to move and to properly breathe, I was flogged and boxed by the group of men for two to three hours every day for 21 consecutive days." "Sometimes they beat me with their Kalashnikov, sometimes with electric wire,"[12] he recalled. Syrian intelligence officers were known for their sinister inventiveness. Beyond the *dullab*, they practiced the *farraj* ("chicken") whereby the victim is tied to a rotating bar resembling a roasting spit while being exposed to severe beatings; exposed prisoners to the *ghassala* ("washing machine"), a spinning drum into which the individual must put their arms before having fingers and forearms crushed; and asked their victims to sit on the *kursi al-Alman* ("the German chair"), a metal chair with hinges on the back which, when lowered backwards, causes unbearable pain in the spine, neck and legs.[13]

The Muslim Brotherhood's political leadership also became a key target of the Syrian *mukhabarat*. An intimidation campaign was undertaken by the Ba'athist authorities aimed at deterring any prominent Muslim Brothers from engaging in opposition activities. If they did participate in the opposition, the most sacred of all boundaries would be crossed: their own families would become targets of the state's security apparatus. Ali Sadreddine al-Bayanouni thus recalled that, while he was at an opposition conference in Europe, the Syrian security services raided his home in Aleppo and seized both his son and his son-in-law as hostages. "My son was later released but my son-in-law was killed in prison—although he was not a member of the Ikhwan,"[14] al-Bayanouni recalled. The family of Issam al-Attar, who had then resumed his political activities from Aachen in Germany, met a similar tragic fate. His daughter recalled how, on 17 March, 1981, a team of three men entered the family house and savagely slaughtered her mother. Issam al-Attar's presence in Aachen continued to be considered by the German government as a serious threat to the security of the surrounding residents until well after the murder of his wife. According to his own account, the German security services even banned him from public speaking and ordered him to change residence on a regular basis, in neighbourhoods as remote as possible from important residential areas.[15] Exiled leaders of the Muslim Brotherhood came to be constantly harassed. The message sent to them by the Syrian *mukhabarat* was very clear: no protection, even from abroad, would ever shield them and their families from the wrath of the regime were it to find out that opposition activities were being carried out or planned.

The regime's uncompromising stance towards the Muslim Brotherhood seems to have been primarily—but not chiefly—guided by the Syrian President's own brother, Rif'at al-Assad, who at the Ba'ath Party's 7th Congress called for a "national purge" and the setting up of "labour and re-education camps in the desert." When an attempt on Hafiz al-Assad's life nearly succeeded, in June 1980, hardline elements in the regime are reported to have ordered a reprisal against the inmates of a prison where many Islamic militants were held, located in the desert surrounding Palmyra—though the full extent of the involvement of the Syrian President and his family is not clear to this day. At any rate, commandos from the aforementioned and much feared Defence Brigades were taken on helicopters to Palmyra where they landed the morning after and carried out the massacre of so many jailed prisoners that the approximate number of deaths can only be estimated, ranging between 500 and 1,000.[16] One of the soldiers later described what happened at the Palmyra prison.

They opened the door of a communal cell for us—that is about sixty or seventy people. Personally, I must have machine-gunned fifteen or so. Altogether, we must have killed about five hundred and fifty of those nasty Muslim Brothers; the Defence Brigades had one dead and two wounded. We left again. Lieutenant Ra'if Abdullah went off to wash his hands and feet, which were covered with blood… The operation lasted about half an hour. During it, there was a terrible tumult, with exploding grenades and cries of 'Allah Akbar!' Finally, we got back in the helicopters… At Mezze, a Major welcomed us and thanked us for our efforts.[17]

Whatever the degree of the Assad regime's actual involvement in the Palmyra massacre, the President's brother seemed emboldened enough to publicly assert, barely a week later, that "if necessary we are ready to engage in a hundred battles, destroy a thousand citadels and sacrifice a million martyrs to bring back peace and love, the glory of the country and the honour of the citizen."[18] But, for all of Rif'at's particularly strong hand in dealing with the Islamic militants, his opinions on the methods used seem to have been shared by most other senior Ba'athist figures at the time. This refutes the long-standing idea that such policies reflected the winning hand of the regime's "hawks" against supposed "doves". "The atmosphere was very tense both at the security and political level," recounted ex-Vice President Abdel Halim Khaddam. "Blood was spilling in every province, the climate was not one in which conciliatory measures could have been put forward."[19] If Rif'at was therefore subsequently "blamed" by Hafiz al-Assad for all the bloodshed, it was because of the bitter rivalry which emerged between the two brothers and led to the younger fleeing to exile in 1984, according to Mohammed Aldik, a former Ba'athist official who was on intimate terms with both Assads. "If Rif'at was blamed for Palmyra and for Hama, it's because Hafiz wanted his son Basil to succeed him after his death and was ready to do anything to decredibilize his own younger brother Rif'at!" he asserted. "Having acted as a main confident to Hafiz al-Assad, I can today assert having witnessed a lot of cynicism and a certain cowardice in the way the President lay all the blame on the advisors he was politically fearing the most."[20]

At any rate, Syria's security officers were soon given the legal tool to implement the harsh policies they wished to pursue. On 7 July 1980, the notorious "Law No. 49" was promulgated by the Parliament, with Article 1 stipulating that "each and every one belonging to the Muslim Brethren organization is considered a criminal who will receive a death punishment."[21] An exiled Syrian Brother summed up the situation: "We were being tracked by the security services; and if they found us we faced four options: prison, torture, death, or one after the other."[22] In such circumstances, the leadership of the Syrian Ikhwan soon became overwhelmed by increasingly loud demands from rank-and-file members to act more violently against the regime.

The Muslim Brotherhood's jihad

"We had no other option but to defend ourselves,"[23] Ali Sadreddine al-Bayanouni now argues. At a meeting of the Muslim Brotherhood's Consultative Council in October 1979, it was decided that the organization would set up a "military branch". The Syrian Brother Adnan Sheikhouney was chosen as its first leader, but when he was murdered by the regime a few months later, Ali Sadreddine al-Bayanouni took over as "military commander" of the Brotherhood, though he insists that such description of his role is "not the most suitable"—preferring instead "coordinator of the communication between the membership inside Syria and the leadership established outside the borders".[24] By the end of the 1970s, increased state repression had forced most of the leadership of the Muslim Brotherhood to seek exile in Jordan and, to a lesser extent, in Iraq, Saudi Arabia and Turkey. For their part, however, most members on the ground had not been able to flee the daily harassment and torture they were suffering at the hands of the security forces. Hence the idea of creating a "military branch" with a leader outside Syria who would give orders and provide weapons to a small group of Ikhwani fighters inside the country so that they could carry out "protection operations". "Such operations were always characterized by their defensive nature," claimed Muhammed Riyadh al-Shuqfah, a Hama-based Syrian Brother who also came to hold responsibilities in the "military branch". "Our mission was to set up a group of fighters and train them so that they could exfiltrate outside of the country those accused of belonging to the Muslim Brotherhood who were tracked down by the Syrian intelligence services," he explained. "Since the Law No. 49 was punishing by death anyone proved to be an Ikhwani sympathizer, we advised people inside Syria to not surrender to the authorities." "In the end, we managed to safely exfiltrate thousands of Brothers,"[25] al-Shuqfah asserted.

His proud assessment of the Muslim Brotherhood's military achievements was not, however, shared by everyone—certainly not by Fighting Vanguard members, who spoke of the amateurism displayed by the Brotherhood's "military branch". Abu Mus'ab al-Suri thus wrote that if "the Muslim Brotherhood claimed to have created a special independent institution dedicated to waging military operations" it was "dead on arrival". "Just like all their other institutions, it was run by incapable elders lacking the determination and qualifications to bring this idea into fruition." The Brotherhood's "military branch", just like the Ikhwani organization itself, was thoroughly structured into committees and subcommittees, leading al-Suri to mock its "open ended useless meetings" which gave the impression that it was "closer to a board of directors for a financial institution than a leadership council for gang warfare."[26] Eventually, al-Suri suggested, "the very little military operations they initiated ended up in dismal failure".[27] His negative views of the military jihad waged by the Brotherhood against the regime also seem to have been shared by other Syrian jihadists who would rise to prominence inside al-Qaeda decades later. A document found by American forces at Abbottabad indeed stated that, when the Brotherhood decided to go to war, "it lost big". "The Brotherhood became serious and it called for the removal of the regime and to create an Islamic government," the document stated, before stressing that "the [Ikhwan] never bothered to calculate, however, what it needed to accomplish all of that." "The Brotherhood's calculations were unrealistic: it even thought that, after it was able to topple the regime, it would take on Israel. But the Brotherhood did not have enough personnel who had the expertise or prudence to lead their military operations,"[28] the document critically concluded. But if the Muslim Brotherhood's own military activities therefore seem to have had little impact on the security situation on the ground, why does it keep being held responsible for the violence which shook many of Syria's cities at the time?

Here, at least two factors seem to have been at play—beyond the regime's interest in blaming the violence on its Islamic competitor. First, while the Ikhwani leaders are today keen on arguing that they never resorted to armed violence against targets inside Syria, at the time they seem on the contrary to have displayed a particular willingness to suggest their own involvement in such attacks, as a way to increase their popularity inside Syria. Abu Mus'ab al-Suri thus fiercely criticized the fact that the Muslim Brotherhood, "through the use of its media outlets," "resorted to taking credit for the military activities of the mujahedeen [of the Fighting Vanguard], claiming them as its own, bragging and exaggerating." "They used the blood of our martyrs to claim fictitious glory and collect donations in their name,"[29] he bitterly summed up.

Second, the violent image still associated with the Syrian Ikhwan stems from the short-lived yet highly significant alliance they entered when, in December 1980, they temporarily joined forces with Issam al-Attar's "Damascus wing" and, more importantly, the jihadist fighters of Adnan Uqlah. "At this point in time, we faced two options", explained a prominent Syrian Brother. "Either the organization would distance itself from those who were fighting the Ba'ath or, on the contrary, it could decide to side with them and support their struggle." He admitted, "We decided to choose the latter option even if, in retrospect, the Ikhwan should have opted for more democratic means than the use of violence."[30]

To this day, it remains unclear exactly to what extent the collective body formed by the three wings of the Islamic movement, also referred to as the "Joint Command" (*wifaq*), carried out violent activities as a coherent unit against the Ba'athist state. Muhammed Hawari, a longtime member of the "Damascus wing", claimed that Issam al-Attar's faction made its adherence to the "Joint Command" dependent on the Fighting Vanguard and the Ikhwan agreeing not to use arms against the regime. "If we, the Damascene Brothers, accepted to integrate the 'Joint Command', it was because we wanted to lead the anti-regime campaign in a peaceful way and to bring the militant youth back into the right path,"[31] he explained. Issam al-Attar had been in touch for some time with Adnan Uqlah who had for long been an admirer of the Damascene leader's religious credentials. "Adnan was writing me from Syria," the head of the "Damascus wing" acknowledged, continuing, "He wanted me to become the leader of the violent struggle against the Ba'ath but I always refused and instead attempted to convince him that another path of resistance was possible. When Adnan came to visit me in Aachen, we had a long discussion and I came to the realization that he would never change his mind and turn his back on armed struggle."[32] It is certain, indeed, that Adnan Uqlah's Fighting Vanguard did not cease its violent activities in the framework of the "Joint Command". The Brotherhood, for its part, maintains that it kept carrying out "defensive actions" throughout the early 1980s.

At any rate, the setting up of a "Joint Command" stemmed from a common realization on the part of the three wings that, despite the significant ideological differences setting them all apart, harmony and unity were needed if the Islamic movement was to effectively topple the Assad regime. An executive team of twelve men, four representing each faction, was set up under the command of Hassan al-Houeidi, a Brother from Deir ez-Zoor affiliated with the "Damascus wing". His actual influence at the helm of the "Joint Command" is still debated as several analyses suggest that the Muslim Brotherhood's Adnan Saadeddine was in fact the true power broker in the coalition. "The title of leader was given to the weak Hassan al-Houeidi yet Adnan Saadeddine was able to run things his own way,"[33] the jihadist Abu Mus'ab al-Suri recalled. Such comments also reflect the way in which the Muslim Brotherhood took on a most prominent role inside the "Joint Command"—fuelling resentment against it on the part of the two other wings which gradually grew frustrated with the alliance.

At first, the coalition nonetheless held as all three parties expressed an interest in joining forces. Indeed, while the setting up of the "Joint Command" marked the return of the "Damascus wing" to the political chessboard of the Syrian Islamic movement, the Fighting Vanguard could benefit from the Muslim Brotherhood's financial and material capabilities in its pursuit of jihad against the Ba'ath. The Ikhwan, for their part, felt that the exile of most of their senior members had greatly weakened the organization's grip on its political base inside the country, to the advantage of the Fighting Vanguard. In this respect, Adnan Uqlah's jihadist organization had grown to such popularity that, by 1980, it had gained the title of the "Internal Muslim Brotherhood"[34]—a reflection both of the prominent influence it had come to wield over the Syrian Islamic movement and of the marginalization of the traditional Ikhwani leaders in exile. Membership of the Muslim Brotherhood was about to decline as many of its activists were joining the Fighting Vanguard instead. A cable from the US Defense Intelligence Agency, which at the time closely monitored the unfolding of the protests in Syria, stated that while it was estimated that the Fighting Vanguard counted, in the late 1970s, only a few hundred members, by the early 1980s it had reached over 1,000 jihadist militants.[35] In the words of a Syrian Brother, the Ikhwan were therefore in the midst of a "struggle for control,"[36] doing their utmost to prevent their influence on the ground from declining further. By declaring jihad against the Ba'ath and joining forces with the Fighting Vanguard, the exiled leadership of the Syrian Ikhwan was therefore trying to reassert its political position inside Syria and regain some of the popularity which it had lost after it had to leave the country. The Muslim Brotherhood's leadership also certainly wished to "retain control"[37] of Adnan Uqlah after his Aleppo Artillery School massacre had backfired on the whole of the Islamic movement. After the "Joint Command" was set up, the Muslim Brotherhood exfiltrated the Fighting Vanguard's "Caliph" to Amman where he remained with the Ikhwani leadership for some time. As months passed by, however, the underlying divergences which had always existed within the "Joint Command" started to manifest themselves with more acuity, hindering the collective nature of its work and eventually leading to its demise.

Ideologically, much was dividing the three factions. While both the Muslim Brotherhood's leadership and Issam al-Attar's "Damascus wing" believed that an alliance with anti-regime secular parties would help sustain the momentum leading to the possible downfall of the Assad regime, this was an option which Adnan Uqlah's organization ruled out completely. Committed to a literal interpretation of the "Qutbist ideology" whereby *al-hakimiyya* (God's sovereignty on earth) would characterize a post-Assad Syria, the forces of the Fighting Vanguard expressed a particular scorn for democracy and political pluralism. "For us, men don't have a right to govern by themselves, they must be governed through God,"[38] a close associate of Adnan Uqlah proclaimed. Another member of the Fighting Vanguard made that approach clear when he asserted: "I do not know why and on what religious ground should reform be achieved through the democratic process."[39] Such statements were hardly compatible with the principles set out in the Charter of the Islamic Front, a statement of purpose signed by prominent *ulama* and Muslim Brothers (Said Hawwa, Adnan Saadeddine, Ali Sadreddine al-Bayanouni amongst others) spread throughout Syria in January 1981. It stressed that if the Islamic movement ever managed to topple the Ba'athist regime, the transition towards democracy would be based on principles such as respect for the rights of religious minorities, the independence of the judiciary, free elections and the separation of powers.[40]

The wide ideological gap dividing the Fighting Vanguard from much of the Muslim Brotherhood was coupled with mutual mistrust and resentment. This had always been the case. Although many scholars and authors of Syrian politics have for long confused the Fighting Vanguard and the Syrian Brotherhood—suggesting for instance that the latter was behind the 1979 Aleppo massacre—the relationship between the two organizations was much more complex as, in fact, there was more rivalry than complementarity. As an example, Muhammed Hawari, the "Damascus wing's" representative in Syria during the time of al-Attar's exile, recalled receiving a visit in the Syrian capital from Abd-us-Sattar az-Za'im, Marwan Hadid's successor at the helm of the Fighting Vanguard, in 1976 suggesting that they join forces in order to better counterbalance the Brotherhood's leadership.[41] This example is quite telling as it shows the extent to which the Fighting Vanguard and the Brotherhood were competitors: the jihadist organization was prepared to go as far as striking an alliance with the more moderate Damascene Brothers, who had by then left the main organization, in order to counterbalance the Ikhwani leadership.

Tensions between the Ikhwani leadership and Adnan Uqlah's Fighting Vanguard came to a head with the collapse of the "Joint Command" some time in late 1981. The "Caliph" seems to have been at the origin of the split. After almost a year of cooperating with the Muslim Brotherhood's leadership in Amman, Adnan Uqlah and his troops had grown frustrated with the Ikhwan's "old-fashioned mentality".[42] While they had wished to act as the vanguard of the Ikhwan, and were therefore, at first, proud to associate themselves with the organization, the members of the Fighting Vanguard eventually became the organization's fiercest critics. Adnan Uqlah himself grew so frustrated with the Muslim Brotherhood's leadership that a Syrian Islamic scholar who knew him well reported that the "Caliph" came to him to enquire whether he could issue a *fatwa*, or religious ruling, allowing the kidnapping and imprisonment of Ikhwani leaders.[43] Abu Mus'ab al-Suri's memoirs are also filled with negative references to the Muslim Brotherhood's leadership. Accordingly, the organization's "no war no peace" mentality would allow its most prominent members to "live a peaceful civilian and secure life while claiming they are at war."[44] "They were not able to set a good example in daring, sacrifices and perseverance, and neither did their family members, those family members were placed farthest from the frontlines and encouraged to get on with their personal lives, continue their education and get married," he asserted bitterly. "They were enjoying the easy life while their parents in the leadership were planning to send hundreds of other people's kids to war."[45]

In addition, the members of the Fighting Vanguard were always very critical of the competing individuals whose political ambitions underpinned the sometimes chaotic work of the Muslim Brotherhood's leadership—in their eyes to the detriment of true ideological and military opposition to the Ba'ath. Such a perception of the Ikhwan's state of affairs had already been a main rationale behind their creation of the Fighting Vanguard. "The people trying to initiate true reform realized that they cannot succeed in such an atmosphere and that their only hope is to choose a different path,"[46] explained al-Suri. The following sentences describe the extent to which this former Fighting Vanguard member despised the Ikhwani culture, reflecting the profound divergences which ultimately set the Islamic movement's "jihadist wing" apart from its "political leadership":

[In the Brotherhood's leadership,] axis of power was formed not based on political philosophy or ideology but rather on the persona of leadership, power and responsibilities were concentrated in the hands of few traditional personalities. Loyalty and access to those few leaders played a big role in assigning mid-level positions. Tasks that required a dedicated system of many specialists were often assigned to a single individual not because of his qualifications but because of his loyalty or connections to the traditional leadership—[leading] to an excessive situation of cronyism and nepotism I'd rather not get into.[47]

Abu Musab al Suri concluded: "[the leadership of the Muslim Brotherhood] was side-tracked by marginal conflicts and spent a lot of time and effort jockeying for positions instead of concentrating all their resources and efforts on winning the battle."[48]

Frustrated by what they saw as a passive stance displayed by the Muslim Brotherhood's leadership, the members of the Fighting Vanguard, who inside Syria were coming under increasing pressure in their stronghold of Hama, started to express impatience. As the occupation of the city by governmental forces intensified throughout early 1982, a group of fighters belonging both to the Muslim Brotherhood and to the Fighting Vanguard started distributing weapons to the city's inhabitants and called for the uprisings which, in February 1982, would lead to the fiercest governmental retaliation ever experienced in the history of the country.

A last stand: the Hama uprising

It has for long been a thorny issue to understand the complex dynamics which led the Muslim Brotherhood to enter into what all members of the organization admit today as having been "a tragic confrontation". Until recently, the leaders of the Ikhwan were still reluctant to address the reasons which led the organization to call for an all-out uprising against the Ba'ath in Hama on 8 February 1982. Discussing with Syrian Brothers the exact flow of events remains contentious to this day—not least because the happenings underline the profound rift which then emerged among the organization's ranks and has plagued the collective nature of its work ever since. Two overlapping factors seem, in particular, to have led the Muslim Brotherhood's leadership to endorse an immediate full-scale *jihad* against the Ba'ath in Hama. On the one hand, divisions within the organization led the more hard-line Hamawite members to take over its leadership. On the other hand, these Hama-born Ikhwanis entertained a particularly complex yet clearly close relationship with the Fighting Vanguard, which led them to embrace the jihadist organization's call for immediate uprisings in their home town in early 1982.

If the leadership of the "Joint Command" regulating the alliance between al-Tali'a, the Ikhwan and the "Damascus wing" formally lay in the hands of Hassan al-Houeidi, it is widely believed, as noted earlier, that the hard-line Adnan Saadeddine was the true power broker inside the coalition. In 1975, he had taken over the Muslim Brotherhood's leadership and had given rise to the so-called "Hama clan", a group of more radical Ikhwani militants who mostly originated from that conservative city. "When Adnan Saadeddine became leader, he imposed his views on the movement and applied Hama's tribal structure to the leadership of the Ikhwan,"[49] Zouheir Salem, a Brother from Aleppo, bluntly asserted. In Hama, it seemed as if personal friendships sometimes superseded political loyalty. The "Hama clan" is thus reported to have been bound by a particular form of solidarity and kinship which was the product of the city's peculiar socioeconomic structure, very distinct from the more business-oriented and open way in which the Aleppines are said to have operated inside the organization. Much of the blame for the violent confrontation which ensued is placed on this "Hama clan".

Shortly after the debacle of February 1982, the Muslim Brotherhood's consultative body asked that a "Truth-Seeking Committee" be set up in order to shed light on the way in which the organization was lured into a battle resulting in its immediate military and political demise. In it, Adnan Saadeddine and his right-hand man, Said Hawwa, were heavily criticized for the significant role they were reported to have played in the events leading to the Hama massacre.[50] The former Syrian jihadist Abu Mus'ab al-Suri, originally from Aleppo, also pointed out the special responsibility of the "Hama clan" in the unfolding of events. "Adnan Saadeddine took control, made all the decisions and was directly responsible for what ensued […] including the tragedy of Hama,"[51] he claimed in his memoirs. The ambiguous relationship Saadeddine and Hawwa seem to have entertained with members of the Fighting Vanguard in the city came under particular scrutiny.

A local leader of the Ikhwan in Aleppo explained the different ways in which the militants of the Fighting Vanguard were treated by the Ikhwan in Hama and in the rest of the country in the years preceding the advent of the "Joint Command". "Between the 1960s and the end of the 1970s, the Muslim Brotherhood's official policy was to withdraw the membership of any Brothers known to also belong to the Fighting Vanguard. In Aleppo for instance, when we learnt that Husni Abu, Zouheir Zaqruta and Adnan Uqlah, at first all members of the Brotherhood, followed regularly the circles of Marwan Hadid, we immediately fired them from the Ikhwan." "However, in Hama, things were blurred as the local leadership there was much more open to dual memberships".[52] This is confirmed by a prominent Syrian Brother, at the time a local leader of the organization in Hama, who said there might indeed have existed "members who belonged to both organizations between the mid-1970s and the early 1980s."[53] For example, it is widely maintained that Umar Jawad, the commander of the Fighting Vanguard for the region of Hama, also belonged to the local section of the Muslim Brotherhood.[54]

In another instance reflecting the divergent perceptions of Ikhwani members from Hama and those from the rest of the country, it is difficult to know exactly how long the Hama-based Marwan Hadid, the hero of the jihadists, remained an actual member of the Muslim Brotherhood. While the Hamawite Brothers generally assert that he remained a Syrian Brother all through his life, Damascene and Aleppine Brothers instead insist that Hadid's membership was withdrawn after his involvement in the violent April 1964 Hama riots.[55] It is quite obvious that the Hamawite members of the Ikhwan entertained close relations with the jihadists of the Fighting Vanguard originating from Hama. "Abd-us-Sattar az-Za'im, then leader of the Fighting Vanguard, was my friend", Muhammed Riyadh al-Shuqfah, thus recalled. "The local Brotherhood was active in providing money and funds to the Fighting Vanguard which, in turn, benefited the families of those in Hama who had died fighting the Ba'ath regime," he explained, while nonetheless insisting that "not one penny was at that time spent to help the Fighting Vanguard in its military fight" and that "personal friendships"[56] did not mean an actual merger of the two groups.

Whether this was truly accurate or not, it appears that the persona of the Hama-born Adnan Saadeddine, then leader of the organization, was deeply involved in trying to set up informal cooperation between the Fighting Vanguard and the Brotherhood between 1977 and 1980. Ali Sadreddine al-Bayanouni, at that time a prominent Aleppine member of the Ikhwan acknowledged that "Adnan Saadeddine met with Abd-us-Sattar az-Za'im in Beirut during January 1977." But he also insisted on adding that the meeting of the then Ikhwani leader with the head of the Fighting Vanguard "was an individual act which did not result from a collective decision made by the leadership," emphasizing that "it is worth noticing that both az-Za'im and Saadeddine were from Hama."[57] The alleged secret co-operation between al-Tali'a and the then leader of the Ikhwan was reported to have been put on hold for a few months when the person who acted as intermediary between the two men, Riyath Jamour, was caught by the regime in early 1979, ushering in several months of dysfunctional coordination between the two groups. This seems to suggest that Adnan Saadeddine did not have prior knowledge of the Aleppo Artillery School massacre before it happened, in June 1979, although at least one source has disputed this.[58] But what was the degree of involvement on the part of the Hamawite leaders of the Ikhwan in the debacle of February 1982?

The year 1981, during which the repression of the Islamic movement in Hama sharply increased, saw the convergence of two trends which, when they intersected, put the Ikhwani leadership onto a self-destructive path. On the one hand, the already existing rift between the Hamawite and Aleppine members of the Ikhwan, which until then was mainly of a clan-based nature, took on a quasi-ideological dimension. "Hamawite members of the Muslim Brotherhood perceived the situation differently than [Aleppine Ikhwanis] did, they had a different thinking,"[59] Ali Saddreddine al-Bayanouni explains today. While those originating from Hama expressed an eagerness to do whatever it took to defend their home town from Ba'athist tanks, those from Aleppo seemed more cautious not to provoke the regime into a last-ditch battle before the Ikhwan were certain they had chances of winning it. Ultimately, however, the former prevailed over the latter. Said Hawwa, an influential young radical ideologue who also acted as Adnan Saadeddine's right hand man, was reported to have successfully threatened Ali Saddredine al-Bayanouni that, if he did not pass on his job as "military commander" of the Brotherhood, he would resign from the organization. While still open to debate, the role played by Said Hawwa in the subsequent unfolding of events seems to have been crucial. Having taken over as head of the "military branch" of the Ikhwan in January 1982, a few weeks before the violent Hama uprising, he appears to have pushed the Brotherhood into a doomed confrontation with the regime.

In parallel, Adnan Uqlah was recalled to Hama by the commander of the Fighting Vanguard, Umar Jawad, who wished to brief the "Caliph" on the tough security situation experienced by the Hamawites on the ground. Without consulting the Muslim Brotherhood's leadership, Adnan Uqlah left Amman for Hama where he remained throughout December 1981. There, he apparently became convinced of the necessity to go beyond the sporadic attacks undertaken by the Fighting Vanguard and the Brotherhood in order to open in that bastion of Islamic militancy an all-out frontal attack against the Ba'ath which, if successful, would then spread throughout Syria to eventually topple the regime. During his stay in Hama, he was reported to have told the city's inhabitants that the time would soon come for the city to rise as a single man against the Syrian Ba'ath and that, with the expected help of the Muslim Brotherhood, and despite wranglings between some factions, the planned uprisings would have the effect of a bomb and destroy the remnants of the regime. For the Hamawites to know exactly when would be the best time to rise up, he told his local companions that he would send a code word which would be broadcast from a radio station based in Iraq.

When the collective leadership of the Ikhwan was told that Adnan Uqlah had visited Hama and planned an all-out uprising against the Ba'ath there "with the blessing of the Muslim Brotherhood," it immediately summoned the "Caliph" of al-Tali'a back to Amman for consultations. Members of the Brotherhood's Executive Committee did not object to Adnan Uqlah's broad intentions. They in fact agreed with him that the best way to topple the Assad regime would be to foment a full-scale revolt in the city of Hama, the bastion of Islamic activism in Syria, which, it was hoped, would trigger a series of similar uprisings in Aleppo, Damascus and other major cities alongside general strikes to paralyze the country and ultimately bring the regime to the verge of collapse.[60] But some within the Brotherhood's decision-making body, and in particular most of its Aleppine members, disagreed with Adnan Uqlah on his plea for the unleashing of an immediate all-out rebellion in Hama. Organizing uprisings against the regime would take time as well as careful preparation and any attempt to rush the process could potentially be catastrophic for the Islamic movement. According to al-Shuqfah, who was present in Amman when the events occurred, the Ikhwan's Executive Committee, then headed by Hassan al-Houeidi, asked Said Hawwa to send a letter to the Fighting Vanguard's leader in Hama, Umar Jawad, instructing him to not follow Adnan Uqlah's orders. The message, however, never reached Umar Jawad, who called upon the whole city to rise when he received Adnan Uqlah's orders soon after an abortive government raid on the group's weapons cache on 2 February 1982.[61] The outcome is known: having distributed weapons to the inhabitants of Hama, the local Ikhwani and Fighting Vanguard militants slaughtered dozens of Ba'athist officials and led violent street riots which, in turn, would draw the government troops into bloody acts of revenge against the city's inhabitants (see appendices for Abu Mus'ab al-Suri's detailed account of the battle of Hama). When the uprising spread throughout the city, the Brotherhood's whole leadership based in Amman was left with no other choice than supporting the rebellion—whatever its fate.

There is still considerable controversy inside the movement as to how the message for Umar Jawad became "lost" between Amman and Hama, underlining the still-existing mistrust and, to a certain extent, tension pitting Ikhwanis from Hama against those from Aleppo. Muhammed Riyadh al-Shuqfah, a long-time member of the "Hama clan", asserts that his colleague Said Hawwa did send the message to Umar Jawad and that the messenger, a trusted driver, should therefore be blamed for having "lost" it.[62] Others belonging to the "Aleppo faction" suggest that given Said Hawwa's particularly hard-line stance against the Ba'ath, he might not have wished to follow the Executive Committee's orders and instead went his own way, tacitly supporting Adnan Uqlah's jihadist effort.[63] In addition, when asked why Said Hawwa subsequently resigned from the Brotherhood's Executive Committee in 1983, Ali Saddredine al-Bayanouni, a member of the Aleppo faction, explained that the radical Ikhwani ideologue might have felt a "special responsibility"[64] for the tragic way the Hama uprisings ended—tragic not only for the Islamic movement but also for the Hamawite population irrespective of its political affiliation.

At first, though, it seemed as if Adnan Uqlah's call to arms had a chance to succeed in toppling the Ba'ath's authority over Hama. The estimated 400 rebel Islamic fighters were joined by two thousand citizens who came to take control of the old city for a few days. According to a cable from the US Defense Intelligence Agency (DIA), which at the time closely monitored the unfolding of the rebellion in Hama, loudspeakers on top of mosque minarets started calling on the people to begin their jihad against the government and to pick up weapons, which were available at specific mosques. Soon, fighting teams affiliated with the Fighting Vanguard and the Muslim Brotherhood, some even wearing army uniforms, moved to attack preselected government targets in the city. "One of the teams attacked the Office of Civil Registry and destroyed residency records for the city of Hama and the surrounding province. These records were a primary tool of Syrian intelligence in maintaining population control," the DIA cable noted. "At the same time, other elements attacked police stations, security offices, Ba'ath Party headquarters and army units, forcing them to withdraw from the city after several days of intense fighting."[65] Government troops, however, soon regained the initiative as the regime's most ruthless and reliable combat units were called in. Shafiq Fayad's 3rd Armoured Division (responsible for the repression of demonstrations in Aleppo throughout March 1980) and the feared Defence Brigades (which participated, among other deeds, in the Palmyra Prison events of July 1980) joined forces to oust the rebels, house by house and district by district. Street battles lasted for several days before the security forces spent weeks shelling whole quarters of the city. The following sentences describe the humanitarian situation endured by Hamawites during Syria's bloodiest three weeks, which would durably put an end to any political contestation to the regime for more than three decades.

"Hama endured a collective punishment" was the conclusion of a team of human rights activists who undertook a study of the Ba'ath regime's violations of humanitarian law throughout the years:

For three days, security forces killed hundreds of people in a series of mass executions near the municipal stadium and at other sites. Troops pillaged stores and homes and fired weapons indiscriminately, treating all citizens as responsible for the insurrection. Army sappers blew up many of the buildings that still stood, sometimes with tens of people inside. Some reports say that security forces used cyanide gas to kill people inside structures […]. Commandos seasoned by the battlefields of Lebanon blasted the city with helicopter-launched bombs and rockets, artillery and tank fire.

For three consecutive weeks, the shelling of the city was so intense that entire neighbourhoods were flattened and became unrecognizable. "North of the Orontes River, the dense, ancient neighbourhoods had been reduced to rubble. Old quarters south of the river lay in ruins. Army bulldozers arrived to flatten the smoking shells of buildings […]. Tens of thousands fled the city, homeless and traumatized. Thousands of others, attempting to flee, were caught in the security ring and arrested."[66] Estimates of the number of dead range between 10,000 and 40,000, but it has never been possible to come up with a precise number of people killed at Hama in February 1982.

ENDORSING JIHAD AGAINST THE BA'ATH (1980–1982)

A "Camp David conspiracy"?

Surprised by the strength and resilience of the movement encountered at Hama, the regime launched a massive investigation which led to the discovery of over 15,000 machine guns allegedly belonging to armed members of the Islamist opposition.[67] Their provenance left the regime in no doubt about their origins, as their serial numbers referred to weapons having transited through Iraq, Saudi Arabia and Jordan, all of whom had differing interests in further polarization of the Syrian political scene.

Of these countries, Iraq was the most prominent provider of training, money and weaponry to the Syrian Islamists. At first glance, this can be seen as surprising, given the shared ideological features of the Syrian and Iraqi Ba'ath regimes. However, by 1966 the Ba'ath Party had separated into two competing branches, a left-wing Syrian "neo-Ba'ath" and a more centrist Iraqi Ba'ath which welcomed Syrian dissidents belonging to the "old guard" such as Michel Aflaq and Salah al-Din al-Bitar.[68] According to one author, Syria and Iraq were thus ruled by "two mutually antagonistic elites, each claiming to be the sole representative of the true Ba'ath Party."[69] Perhaps most important, the two countries shared a history of rivalry in the struggle for regional primacy. Relations between Baghdad and Damascus reached a historic low when Hafiz al-Assad supported the Ayatollahs in Tehran upon Saddam Hussein's invasion of Iran in September 1980. According to the former Ba'athist Vice President Abdel Halim Khaddam, this was the proof that interests have always trumped ideology in Syrian-Iraqi relations. According to him, "despite our common 'Ba'athist' nomination, the Iraqi security services became actively involved in supporting the Islamist movement in Syria while [the Syrian government was] financing rebel Iraqi Islamists."[70] The estrangement between the two governments was such that, in 1981, Saddam Hussein went as far as publicly welcoming a delegation of prominent leaders of the Syrian Muslim Brotherhood in Baghdad, promising them "full support and money".[71] Although the Syrian Ikhwan have historically been reluctant to recognize the Iraqi Ba'athist provenance of the bulk of their external help, many inside the Brotherhood retrospectively recognize that Baghdad might have, at the very least, "logistically facilitated"[72] their struggle against the Syrian regime.

The Iraqi capital thus quickly became a safe haven for Syrian Islamist activists who could undergo military training in any of the numerous camps set up at their disposal by the Iraqi Ba'ath's security apparatus. Adnan Saadeddine in particular and his Hamawite followers in general seem to have enjoyed a special relationship with Saddam Hussein, this becoming obvious throughout the late 1980s and early 1990s (see Chapter 8). For quite some time, Iraq remained a strong and steady provider of arms, funds and security to Islamic militants from Syria. "For once in our lives, we were prized by the Ba'athists!" Muhammed Riyadh al-Shuqfah—who himself found refuge in Baghdad after fleeing Hama in the late 1970s—claimed with irony. He remembered the extent of the Iraqi regime's help to the Islamic movement at such a crucial moment of Syrian history:

The Iraqis were of a highly significant help […] Saddam Hussein appointed his Vice President, Taha Yassine al-Ramadan, to be in direct liaison, he was tasked with being constantly in touch with us in Baghdad. […] But beyond money and weapons, we were also provided with security help. Safe houses were at our disposal in the Iraqi capital and the local *mukhabarat* [intelligence services] strove to foil any assassination attempts aimed at us. On a personal level, out of four assassination attempts I suffered at the hands of the Syrian security services, three were foiled by the Iraqi *mukhabarat*.[73]

On the security front, Adnan Saadeddine was in constant contact with Colonel Mohammed Salmani who was then heading the "Syria Desk" of the Iraqi secret services.[74] Iraqi help to the Syrian Islamists was such that it came close to provoking an all-out war between the two neighbours. While the Syrian government expelled the Iraqi Ambassador from Damascus alongside his staff in August 1980, events accelerated after the Hama uprising which the regime was quick to blame on Baghdad. Shortly thereafter, Syria closed its border with Iraq, and following its shutdown of the Kirkuk-Banyas pipeline transporting Iraqi oil to the Mediterranean, it broke off all diplomatic relations in April 1982. It remains until today a delicate subject to discuss the Iraqi provenance of much of the external help which the Muslim Brotherhood received at such a crucial stage of its history. One can understand the embarrassment of Muslim Brotherhood leaders, who found in the Iraqi Ba'ath a pragmatic ally willing to back-up their struggle while the one country from which they could have theoretically expected help given its ideological proximity, the Iran of the Islamic Revolution, had joined Hafiz al-Assad in accusing the Ikhwan of being "a gang carrying out the Camp David conspiracy against Syria."[75]

The reference to the Camp David Accords which formalized peace between Egypt and Israel in 1979 was far from neutral. Beyond the bitterness in Syrian-Iraqi relations lay a more regional, strategic game for influence in the Arab world. Pressure was mounting on the shoulders of the Syrian regime which felt increasingly isolated by Egypt's geopolitical realignment. Although Nasserism and Ba'athism shared a common ideological background embedded in a declared commitment to secularism and socialism, bitter rivalry between Damascus and Cairo had emerged after Nasser tried to use the short-lived union between the two countries to advance Egypt's influence in the Near East. By 1979, the struggle for regional primacy between the two countries had transformed into a strategic challenge for both in a reshaped Middle East. The peace accords signed that year by Egypt with Israel had decisively put Cairo behind an axis supported by the United States which seemed to threaten Syria's interests in the region—focusing by then on the situation in Lebanon. For Cairo and Damascus, much was at stake. While it became in Egypt's interest to pursue an agenda favouring peace in the region so as to decrease the isolation it had suffered since its signing of the agreement with Israel, Syria was for its part opposed to any compromise with the Jewish state, as the struggle against Israel had become a main source of legitimacy at a time of domestic unrest. Tensions rose between the two countries as, by then, the Egyptian President Anwar al-Sadat was reported to be organizing clandestine security training programmes destined to increase the Syrian Islamic movement's military capabilities. According to Brynjar Lia, who wrote a biography of the former Fighting Vanguard member Abu Mus'ab al-Suri, a team of Egyptian officers had been tasked with assisting the paramilitary instruction of Syria's jihadist fighters. The six-week training course followed by Syrian activists was reported to be so good that al-Suri would even praise its efficiency in teaching how to carry out "guerrilla warfare techniques, security affairs and external terrorist operations."[76] However, as the Egyptian President himself quickly became the target of Islamic militants in his own country, he drastically reduced the assistance brought to Syrian activists loosely linked with Egypt's Muslim Brotherhood.[77]

By the late 1970s, Damascus was closely watching the strategic realignments taking place in the Middle East. Chief among Assad's worries was that countries other than Egypt might follow through and sign peace agreements with Israel, transforming Syria's frontal opposition to

Tel Aviv from a majority opinion into a minority position in the region. Jordan, a longtime strategic rival to its Syrian neighbour, was widely suspected by the Ba'ath regime in Damascus of being on the verge of signing an agreement with Israel. In parallel, King Hussein of Jordan had become by the late 1970s a major host for exiled leaders of the Syrian Ikhwan whom he welcomed throughout their stay in Amman. Training camps were set up in the Jordanian desert and the Syrian Ikhwan regularly held their Shura Council meetings in Amman where most of the leadership resided until the late 1990s. Therefore, while the Jordanian security services did not seem to have been as widely involved in the active training of the Syrian jihadist fighters as their Iraqi and Egyptian counterparts, they nonetheless displayed a benign neglect judged as suspicious by Damascus. According to Brynjar Lia, the Syrian Muslim Brotherhood thus operated in Amman "relatively secretly albeit with the knowledge and tolerance of the Jordanian government."[78] In turn, in February 1981 Hafiz al-Assad allegedly sent an assassination squad to eliminate Mudar Badran, the Jordanian Prime Minister, who, when the attempt on his life failed, had to resign in a tacit acknowledgement by the Jordanian regime that it had gone too far in supporting the Syrian Islamist movement.[79] Damascus would nonetheless have to wait until King Hussein's death and King Abdullah's accession to witness the departure of prominent Syrian Brothers, such as Ali Sadreddine al-Bayanouni, from Amman.

In order to compensate for the regional realignment taking place in the Middle East, Hafiz al-Assad strengthened Syria's ties with the USSR, a move initiated by the Syrian President's approval of the Soviet invasion of Afghanistan in December 1979 and finalized by the signing of a Pact of Friendship in October 1980. In the framework of the Cold War, this could only have infuriated the American government. Given the Syrian Ikhwan's strong anti-communist outlook, visible not only in their programme but, through their sporadic attacks on USSR missions inside Syria, a tacit alliance between them and the US was conceivable. However, allegations that the leader of the Syrian Brotherhood, Adnan Saadeddine, met a senior American diplomat in Amman in 1982 cannot be confirmed, despite the numerous interviews carried out in research for this work. Nevertheless, it is clear that a significant amount of the external help received by the Brotherhood was coming from Saudi Arabia, a pillar of United States strategy in the region, although the Saudi aid is said to have been provided on a more "cautious basis"[80] than its Iraqi counterpart. The Saudi government welcomed exiled leaders of the Brotherhood, such as Abdel Fattah Abu Ghuddah, and allowed Ikhwani fundraising activities in the Kingdom to gather financial support for the organization. This was coupled with the significant backing of Saudi Arabia's Grand Mufti who, conveying his dislike of Alawi rule in Damascus, granted his "full support to the Syrian Mujahidin's struggle against the heretical and secular Ba'ath regime."[81] Whether these were in fact individual acts not sanctioned by the Saudi government remains unclear, but the very fact that such moral and financial support could be gathered in a Kingdom characterized by its authoritarian rule sent an unmistakable signal to Damascus.

In retrospect, many members of the Syrian Islamic movement who once benefitted from Arab states' help provided in their struggle against the Ba'ath later voiced strong criticisms of the way they felt instrumentalized in the regional game for strategic primacy. For them, it seemed as if the cause they defended—the toppling of the Syrian Ba'ath and its replacement by an Islamic state—had too often been claimed by states ultimately interested in advancing their own interests, abroad but also at home. In this respect, Abu Mus'ab al-Suri's memoirs provide a fascinating insight into the way in which Fighting Vanguard militants were provided with help and training by states for purposes other than what they thought at the time. The former al-Qaeda ideologue suspected Jordan, Iraq and, to a lesser extent, Saudi Arabia of having all helped Syria's jihadist fighters solely with the goal of improving their knowledge of Islamic networks so as to better fight them at home. "By studying our organization, they were able to wage effective campaigns against similar Islamic groups in [their countries],"[82] he claimed. The extent to which host regimes controlled the networks developed by Syrian activists remains unknown but, for that former Fighting Vanguard member, it is quite clear that they came to possess intimate knowledge of the functioning and methods employed by Islamic activists. "The host regimes infiltrated our organizations, monitored all our activities, restricted and checked us, and in some cases arrested or killed our members and representatives."[83] Drawing a lesson from this, al-Suri concluded: "A neighbouring regime or a regime antagonistic to the one we are fighting may step in and offer arms and financing unconditionally. We should never be dependent on such sources because their own hidden agenda will be aimed at controlling the revolution and using it to serve their own interest."[84]

PART IV

ASHES OF HAMA

THE SYRIAN ISLAMIST MOVEMENT SINCE 1982

7

MILITANT ISLAM AFTER HAMA

The massacre of thousands of Syrian citizens in February 1982 was Hafiz al-Assad's own way to send an unmistakable message to the Islamic opposition which had been challenging Ba'athist rule ever since 1963. Any attempt to resist the Syrian President's grip on power would be met with a disproportionately harsh response: these were his "Hama rules".[1] The Syrian Brotherhood was seriously weakened—left for decades with neither a base inside the country nor a coherent organization abroad (see Chapter 8). The Brotherhood's long exile, however, did not mean that all forms of political Islam were suppressed, for two powerful dynamics emerged out of the ashes of Hama.

On the one hand, the Islamic rebellion had shown to the Syrian rulers that they had to take into account the growing popularity of political Islam, something the Ba'athists were keen to do by striving to co-opt religious scholars and to accommodate Syria's increasingly vocal conservative constituencies. It is in this light that one should see their efforts to adopt foreign and domestic policies more in line with popular sentiment than ever before. The fierce anti-American stance taken by the regime at the dawn of the 2003 war in Iraq also enabled the Syrian Ba'ath to encourage the departure for Baghdad of radical Islamists who wished to raise the banner of jihad there. By doing so, however, the security services were playing with fire as the secular and minority-dominated Ba'ath regime was bound to be the ultimate target of those Syrians who, after waging jihad in Iraq, would be prepared to come back and fight for an Islamic state at home. As the Syrian uprisings continue to unfold, that trend is likely to merge with another dynamic linked to the history of radical Islam in Syria: the fate of the 1970s Syrian jihadists.

The exile of the members of the Fighting Vanguard who had managed to survive the Ba'athist repression of the late 1970s and early 1980s only heightened their radicalism and bitterness at the regime. After a failed attempt at reviving jihad against the Ba'ath, they concentrated all their resources on bringing in the ideological, material and organizational *acquis* of the Syrian Islamic struggle to the more global jihadist movement—while keeping in sight the changes in the situation at home and preparing to return when the time was right.[2] By doing so, they would participate in the rise of a particularly violent form of political Islam most explicitly expressed through the birth of al-Qaeda a decade after the Hama massacre. "There is an organic connection between the Syrian jihad and the birth of al-Qaeda,"[3] confirmed a former senior British intelligence official with deep knowledge of such matters. How could that possibly be explained?

Al-Qaeda: the Syrian connection

Although the battle of Hama did not crush the totality of the forces loyal to the Fighting Vanguard and the Brotherhood—many of whom were already in exile in neighbouring Iraq and Jordan—it nonetheless seriously weakened the Islamic movement, leaving it with virtually no base inside Syria. In this desperate situation, the leadership of the Muslim Brotherhood decided to join as early as March 1982 the National Alliance for the Liberation of Syria, a Baghdad-based group already comprising dissident Ba'athist figures such as Amin al-Hafiz and other secular left-wing groups opposed to the Syrian regime, most notably Akram al-Hawrani's Arab Socialist Party.[4] The Ikhwan's move, however, infuriated Adnan Uqlah's Fighting Vanguard, which found it outrageous that the Muslim Brotherhood teamed up with secular parties not sharing its goal of ultimately establishing an Islamic state in Syria.

Relations between the Fighting Vanguard's jihadists and the Ikhwan's political leadership had already been damaged in December 1981—following Adnan Uqlah's visit to Hama—and had further deteriorated after the massacre of February 1982, blamed on the activism of the Fighting

Vanguard. Relations between the two groups were definitely broken off when the Ikhwan entered into a coalition with secular forces in March 1982. Expressing the bitterness which came to characterize the Fighting Vanguard perception of the Ikhwan, Adnan Uqlah was then reported to have declared that "the Muslim Brotherhood and anyone who agrees with or supports the alliance [with secular parties], or anyone who is aware of this alliance yet remains loyal to those leaders and organizations, is a heretic, blasphemer and infidel!"[5] Besides denouncing the "religious illegitimacy" of the alliance, the members of the Fighting Vanguard criticized the Brothers for having turned their backs on the "Caliph" and his organization. "The Muslim Brotherhood traded a good son for someone pretending to be friendly,"[6] one member commented.

At the time, the Ikhwani leadership was also fiercely criticized by some of its more hardline militants for having abandoned the military struggle against the Ba'ath too soon after the Hama massacre—thereby playing into Hafiz al-Assad's argument that any attempt to resist his rule would be crushed and silenced for ever. In fact, a source close to the Islamic movement reported that the Syrian Brotherhood's leadership had called for a *nafeer* (general mobilization) in mid-February 1982 and had managed, as a result, to gather a few thousand Syrian fighters who had left their jobs in Europe or in the Gulf to join a military training camp in Baghdad, from where they would prepare to join for the last battle in Syria. On 16 February, Said Hawwa, a Syrian Brother from Hama who was the head of the organization's "military branch", called on Islamist militants scattered throughout the world to join the Brotherhood and the Fighting Vanguard in Iraq and carry out their religious duty against the regime in Damascus. "The Jihad in confronting the tyrant is now a duty of all those capable of carrying arms,"[7] he declared on Baghdad's Voice of Arab Syria radio channel. But, once thousands of militants were gathered in military camps surrounding Baghdad, the Ikhwani leadership's call for a military march towards Hama never came. Owing to the sensitive nature of this episode, seemingly haunting the Brotherhood's leaders until today and still plaguing their relations with other groups inside the Islamic movement, the reason which led the Brotherhood to hold back from sending this fighting force to Hama to help the local population fighting the Ba'ath regime remains obscure at the very least.

"The call for *nafeer* aimed to prepare for a general confrontation in order to face the consequences of the events at Hama and its developments, if chance permitted," explained Ali Sadreddine al-Bayanouni, who held important responsibilities in the Brotherhood's leadership at the time. "But, in the end, it proved that there would have been no use for such an intervention. As a result, it was cancelled and members of the Brotherhood returned to their places of residence."[8] But did the Brotherhood's inaction really reflect its leaders' strong political sense that the battle for Hama would have been a vain gesture which would only have led to more human casualties without a chance of success? Or was the organization's leadership temporarily paralyzed by the aforementioned tensions between its "Hama clan" and its "Aleppo faction"? Or, after all, were the Syrian Brotherhood's plans for the attack on Hama suddenly shut down by its Iraqi patron whose leader, Saddam Hussein, had an interest in weakening Syria by supporting the Ikhwan without provoking an all-out war between Damascus and Baghdad? "The thousands of fighters gathered in Baghdad by the Brotherhood's leadership expected to go and fight for the liberation of Syria," the source close to the Islamic movement remembered with still apparent bitterness, "but instead the *nafeer* came to nothing, Hama was destroyed and the Muslim Brotherhood's leadership lost credibility with its own members."[9] At the time, some inside the organization who were disappointed by the leadership's handling of the situation left the Ikhwan for good and joined the remnants of the Fighting Vanguard.

Despite the heavy losses suffered at Hama in February 1982, Adnan Uqlah had indeed decided, for his part, to not give up the military struggle against the Syrian Ba'ath. From Amman, he had managed to gather several groups of jihadists who had fled Syria and were preparing for the right time to go back inside the country to resort to arms again. A source close to the "Caliph" remembered the tragic way in which Adnan Uqlah's jihad against the regime ultimately ended. In late 1982, he fell prey to a Syrian *mukhabarat* sting operation:

An agent posing as someone from Jisr al-Shughur, in Idlib, who was known by his *nom de guerre* as Abu Abdallah al-Jisri had arrived in Jordan [where Adnan Uqlah resided] claiming to have escaped for his life. The irony was that the Muslim Brotherhood suspected that he was an agent and kept well away from him, but Uqlah did not suspect him. Through an elaborate scheme he was able to lure Uqlah into Syria where he was arrested and believed to have been executed.[10]

Adnan Uqlah's disappearance would have disastrous consequences for the jihadist struggle against the Ba'ath. A group gathering fighters scattered between Baghdad and Amman was organized in 1984 as there were still men who wanted to take revenge for the Hama massacre. Their attempt, however, failed utterly as it became clear that, without its "Caliph", the Fighting Vanguard had lost all sense of direction and zeal to fight the powerful Ba'ath regime. "When [Adnan Uqlah] was captured and imprisoned, the entire organization collapsed and seized to exist,"[11] a former member of the Fighting Vanguard confirmed.

As hopes soon withered of raising the banner of jihad again in Syria, the fate of many members of the Fighting Vanguard fighters diverged. After a "special pardon" granted to them by Hafiz al-Assad through the intermediary of Ali Duba, head of Syria's Military Intelligence, a few leading jihadists surrendered and simply returned home. A former fighter of thus recalled: "When the majority of al-Tali'a's forces were defeated and after Adnan Uqlah was arrested, few members of the leadership decided on their own to pursue a peace treaty with the Syrian regime; this caused a lot of division and friction among the remaining members—who were still shocked and had not gotten over the arrest of their leader."[12]

Other Fighting Vanguard members, for their part, decided to temporarily give up their fight against the Ba'ath and leave for Afghanistan where, in the early 1980s, their skills were prized by the "Arab Afghans" striving to fight the Soviet occupation. Their decision did not mean that they suddenly had a change of heart. Rather, it was the result of a strategic calculation. By continuing their fight in Afghanistan, they would maintain networks and skills which could well be used when the opportunity of turning the jihad against the Syrian regime would rise again. It was precisely this generation of experienced Syrian jihadists that would bring the skills and learned lessons needed to build a more global jihadist movement giving rise, a few years later, to the birth of al-Qaeda.

Ideologically, the Syrian jihadists' flight to the Afghan theatre was deeply influenced by Abdullah Azzam, often mentioned as the "Godfather" of the jihad in Afghanistan. A Palestinian religious scholar long resident in Jordan, he had been crucial in the 1969 establishment of the "Sheikh's Camp", a military training centre aimed at gathering all jihadist fighters wishing to combat Israel without being associated with the "secular" PLO. In other words, the Camp was destined for "those who preferred to see Muhammed instead of Che Guevara as a reference for the Palestinian resistance,"[13] a source close to Abdullah Azzam explained.

Marwan Hadid and his Syrian followers, it was reported, spent some time training there before bringing their skills back to Syria where their jihadist enterprise was building up. Links between Abdullah Azzam and the Syrian jihadists became even clearer when, in the late 1970s, many of them found refuge at his home in Jordan.[14] When the Palestinian sheikh left Jordan in the early 1980s for Peshawar in Pakistan, from where he aimed to organize the resistance against the Soviet invasion of Afghanistan, a few prominent figures in the Fighting Vanguard followed him. Abdullah Azzam is often credited by radical Islamists with having given the Afghan fight against the Soviet occupiers a transnational religious dimension which would fill the ranks of the resistance. He called on his fellow Muslims throughout the world to "join the caravan"[15] and wage jihad against the atheist Communist occupiers.

Ideologically, Azzam's thought became significant as it brought an international taste to jihad—a concept which had been revived only two decades earlier by Sayyid Qutb. Until then, the Islamic struggle against secular Arab governments had been limited to Egypt's and Syria's borders but, in the early 1980s, the fight against the Soviet presence in Afghanistan internationalized the notion of jihad. Abdullah Anas, an Algerian jihadist fighter who married Abdullah Azzam's daughter, claimed that his father-in-law's greatest merit was to have "brought the flag of jihad universal."[16] He held that Muslims worldwide should unite into a "pioneering vanguard" dedicated to fulfilling the "forgotten obligation" of Islam through waging jihad against the foreign occupation of Muslim lands. This found a practical application when, in the early 1980s, Abdullah Azzam set up the paramilitary structures which enabled thousands of "Arab Afghans" to travel to Pakistan to train and fight the Soviet occupation on the other side of the border. In 1984, he set up the "Services Bureau" (*maktab al-khadamat*) tasked with organizing the hosting of Arab volunteers into several "guesthouses" (*madafat*) and their training at the *al-sada* ("the echo") paramilitary camp. Barely a year after its creation, the camp was reported to comprise over 400 Arab fighters prepared to cross the border at any time to fulfil their jihad obligation.[17]

The connection between Azzam's legacy and the birth of al-Qaeda has long been debated. For Abdullah Anas, there are no generic links between the two: "For him, jihad was a worship and a journey bound by strict rules which he clearly set out, it had nothing to do with al-Qaeda's killing of civilians [...] The place to wage jihad, in Azzam's view, was on the frontline and in the trenches, not in restaurants or in airports." Yet Azzam's "Services Bureau" was to be used as a base for the recruitment of future al-Qaeda leaders who would pride themselves on representing Abdullah Azzam's legacy when the Palestinian sheikh was later murdered, in November 1989. In addition, there is no dispute about the fact that he did set out the ideological and semantical basis behind the birth of al-Qaeda when he stated that "the vanguard constitutes the solid base [*qaeda* in Arabic] for the hoped for society [...]; we shall continue the jihad no matter how long the way until the last breath or the last beat of pulse."[18]

Meanwhile, although the Syrian contingent in Afghanistan remained modest for some time, the situation experienced by Sunni Muslims at the hands of Hafiz al-Assad fuelled the rage of "Arab Afghans" whose desire to wage jihad against the Soviet occupation of Afghan lands also turned to fighting regimes associated with the USSR such as the Syrian Ba'ath. In March 1982, the local branch in Peshawar of the Union of Muslim Students, closely associated with Abdullah Azzam, declared the Hama massacre the "tragedy of the century".[19] The Syrians Marwan Hadid and Adnan Uqlah—together with the Egyptian Sayyid Qutb— were the references of the Arab jihadists then arriving *en masse* in Peshawar. The number of Syrians who actually joined the struggle against the Soviet occupation of Afghanistan seems to have been relatively small. Abdullah Anas, Azzam's son-in-law and a prominent commander in the "Arab-Afghan" resistance, recalled that the Syrian contingent was originally small with only three nationals forming part of Abdullah Azzam's first training camp in 1984. "Abu Talha, Abu Baker and Abu Hussain, all former members of al-Tali'a, joined 'the caravan' very early on but, eventually, the overall number of Syrian jihadists must not have exceeded twenty or thirty,"[20] he remembered. According to Brynjar Lia, however, "even if they were numerically few, they still played an important role."[21] The military skills of the Syrian jihadists were indeed prized by the Arab resistance in Peshawar. Abdullah Azzam was even reported to have flattered former members of the Fighting Vanguard, such as Abu Mus'ab al-Suri, with the ultimate goal of incorporating them into his nascent paramilitary body. "Azzam exhorted al-Suri and his friends to fight for the Afghan cause, flattering them about their possession of significant military skills, which, after all, were in great shortage in the Arab-Afghan movement at that point in time,"[22] Lia wrote.

Abu Mus'ab al-Suri, who had joined the Fighting Vanguard in June 1980 and had participated into the few attempts to revive the jihad after Adnan Uqlah's capture in late 1982, travelled to Afghanistan with some of his friends in the mid-1980s and joined the Arab camps in Peshawar. He later recalled that "we left the Syrian cause because there existed no opportunity to revive it and we turned to the Afghan cause instead [...] We could not do anything [else] so we entered the framework of contributing to the international jihad."[23] According to his biographer, this period marked the time when "the global character of the duty of jihad and the global nature of the Muslim causes became apparent to him in earnest."[24] The former jihadist fighter of the Fighting Vanguard was to take part in the creation of al-Qaeda, later becoming one of its most efficient ideological advocates and propagandists.

In 1987, Abu Mus'ab al-Suri had been among the first to leave Abdullah Azzam's "Services Bureau" to join Usama Bin Laden in the new guesthouse which the Saudi jihadist had just set up with the Wahhabi Afghan leader Abdul Rasul Sayyaf. Upon Abdullah Azzam's death in November 1989, many of the Palestinian sheikh's Arab followers joined Bin Laden's training camp networks. Whereas Azzam had tried to temper his followers' tendency to "excommunicate" (*takfir*) non-Islamic Arab regimes, his death led to the growth of Salafi-jihadism. The emergence of this doctrine—whose insistence on implementing the absolute rule of God on earth boiled down to military combat against the non-Islamic Arab regimes and foreign powers such as the United States—would mark the ideological birth of al-Qaeda.

Abu Mus'ab al-Suri's contribution to the advent of al-Qaeda on the global stage was not limited to the military skills he crucially brought to the nascent organization in the training camps of the Afghan-Pakistan border zone. In the early 1990s he was a prominent lecturer on politics, strategy and guerrilla warfare in the organization's Pakistani camps, devoting much of his time to intellectual matters. He was particularly interested in further developing a jihadist theory building upon the ideological legacy of Abdullah Azzam and Sayyid Qutb, and drawing crucial lessons from the failed experience of the Syrian jihad. One of the things he had learned from his jihadist experience in Syria was that the forces of the Fighting Vanguard had not prepared well enough for the struggle against the Ba'ath on both strategic and ideological levels. The failure of the campaign against the Ba'ath was also due, in his eyes, to a lack of media efforts and thorough planning as well as a lack of unified ideology binding together the broad Islamic movement. The lessons he drew from his Syrian experience, laid out in a booklet he published in May 1991, would serve as one of the bases upon which al-Qaeda would build its organizational and doctrinal capacity. Abu Mus'ab al-Suri would, however, have to wait fifteen years to be celebrated as a true ideologue when he published a 1,600-page tome entitled "The Global Islamic Resistance Call". In it, the jihadist ideologue called for a decentralized "global jihad" which would be carried out "without any *tanzim* [organization]". His slogan, "*nizam la tanzim* [system, not organization],"[25] was meant to encourage individual jihadist actions within the framework of a broader struggle, and would find its expression after the US intervention in Iraq in March 2003.

In the early 1990s, al-Suri travelled back to Europe where he had already spent some time directly after February 1982, and settled down in Spain for a few years. From there, he remained involved with the al-Qaeda network and convinced a few Syrian veterans of the jihad against Hafiz al-Assad to join his new global struggle. A cable from the US Embassy in Madrid recounted the significance which Syrian expatriates in Spain saw in the emergence of terror cells scattered inside the country and throughout Europe:

The first Islamic terrorist organizations were formed by Syrian members of the Muslim Brotherhood [and al-Tali'a al-Muqatila] who had fled repression by the Asad regime and settled in Spain in the late 1980s. Police believes Palestinian radical Anwar Adnan Mohamed Salah, also known as 'Chej Salah', and Syrian al-Qaeda member and propagandist Mustafa Setmarian, also known as 'Abu Mus'ab al-Suri', played a critical role in organizing Syrian exiles in Spain to support the international jihadist movement.[26]

Upon Abu Mus'ab al-Suri's departure in 1994 for London, where he wished to work more closely with the Algerian Groupe Islamique Armé (GIA), and Salah's exile to Pakistan where he went to work with al-Qaeda's leadership, a Madrid-based Syrian named Imad Eddine Barakat Yarkas led the jihadist group in the Spanish capital—giving rise to what has become known as the "Barakat Yarkas network", allegedly responsible for the 2004 bombings in Madrid. "From 1995 until his 2001 arrest, Imad Eddin Barakat Yarkas led the Syrian group in Spain, during which period this cell expanded its activities and aided the development of other Islamist extremist groups," the US Embassy cable read. "Yarkas and many of the other Syrian extremists were relatively educated, prosperous and projected the appearance of being well established in Spain." The twenty-four men allegedly involved in the "Barakat Yarkas network" had, according to the US Embassy, "direct links to al-Qaeda".[27]

Abu Mus'ab al-Suri's increasingly global outlook did not mean, however, that he and his Syrian jihadist friends had lost interest in the situation in their home country. On the contrary, it seems as if they temporarily took on the flag of "global jihad" while waiting for the right time and opportunity to return to Syria in order to fight the Ba'ath regime to the finish. It is believed that, in the 1990s, Usama Bin Laden entrusted Abu Mus'ab al-Suri with a jihadist project, and that Al-Suri's organization, Jama'at e Jihad al-Suri, drew resources from the "Barakat Yarkas" network in Spain and from other Syrian exiles such as Abu Dahda and Riyad al-Uqlah, but that his attempt to build a Syrian branch of al-Qaeda on the model of Abu Mus'ab al-Zarqawi's Iraqi group eventually failed.[28] Shortly after the death of Hafiz al-Assad in June 2000, al-Suri published a text in which he branded the Syrian jihad of the late 1970s and early 1980s as the starting point of the global jihadist movement and encouraged his fellow Sunnis residing in the country to finish the job started then or face the threat of eternal domination by the Alawi minority. In the text, he asked the Sunnis of Syria who had remained in the country after February 1982: "have you acquiesced to trade, to [university] degrees, to menial jobs, or to farming and the tending of cows, have you acquiesced to food, drink, travels and picnics, have you acquiesced to restaurants and resorts[...]?"[29] The ideologue of al-Qaeda advised his fellow Sunni Syrians that the easiest path to repentance was to wage jihad against the regime. In al-Suri's eyes, jihad against the Ba'ath was also an imperative if the Sunni community was to survive: "A threat that places us [Sunnis] in Greater Syria before a fact in which [...] we either remain or disappear: do we and the [Sunnis] in Greater Syria remain as guardians of the religion of Allah in the blessed Greater Syria or shall the heretical sects, comprising the Jews, the Crusaders, the Alawi-Nusayris and the other deviating sects, remain in it?"[30]

Abu Mus'ab al-Suri's overtly sectarian tone is representative of most Syrian jihadists who fled the country in the early 1980s while not giving up on their struggle against the Syrian Ba'ath. Amongst those is Abu Baseer al-Tartousi, a London-based jihadist scholar originally from the coastal town of Tartous, situated in the Latakia region from which many

Alawis belonging to the Syrian regime also originate. It is clear to see that his view of the minority community is filled with sectarian bias. Beyond castigating the Alawis as being a sect situated outside the "realm of Islam" and the "glory of Arabism", he adds that "[the Nusayri-Alawi sect] can never be patriotic or safeguard the safety and power of the realm of Muslims [...] for I am one of those who has lived among and interacted with the Nusayris in their mountains and plains, and learned their secrets and their dangerous esoteric doctrines... the [loyalty] of the Nusayri is merely to his lusts and cravings and he has no other [loyalty] but to that [...]"[31] Ever since the uprisings started in Syria, this prominent jihadist figure has been active in trying to recruit fellow Arab jihadists across the Muslim world to launch a renewed jihad against the Syrian Ba'ath.[32]

It is clear that the sectarian dimension of Hafiz and then Bashar al-Assad's rule on Syria has acted as a great source of motivation for contemporary jihadists. In their eyes, not only is Syria ruled by the secular Ba'ath Party, it is also heavily dominated by religious minorities. After decades of inactivity on the part of anti-regime jihadist circles inside Syria, a new group was formed on 27 May 2007, called "The group for monotheism and jihad in Greater Syria" (Jama'at al-Tawhid wel Jihad fi Bilad al-Sham). Its leader, Abu Jandal, declared shortly thereafter that "we are Muslim mujahedin from the blessed Greater Syria who are pained by the conditions of our *Umma* [Islamic community] that has languished under the Nusayri occupation for tens of years and the Nusayris—who resent the Sunnis—are creative in desecrating the sanctities and honor of the Muslims under the cruel guidelines set down by the Nusayri [Hafiz al-Assad]."[33] Such radical jihadist groups are bound to flourish throughout the country as the anti-regime struggle of the Syrian opposition threatens to drag on for some time to come.

The Syrian mukhabarat *and radical Islam: a blowback?*

In retrospect, the Iraq War launched by the United States in 2003 can be seen as a turning point for the global jihadist movement. In Abu Mus'ab al-Suri's eyes, the event was so significant that he compared it, in importance with the 1980s jihad against the Soviet invasion of Afghanistan—which subsequently saw the advent of a well-trained generation of jihadists. Accordingly, the young Arabs who went to join the

Iraqi insurgency *en masse* would come to be recognized, in due course, as the "Arab Iraqis" who fought in the same vein as their "Arab Afghan" predecessors. For the Syrian ideologue of al-Qaeda, this "third generation" of jihadists learned during the street battles they fought in many Iraqi cities skills that would inevitably become crucial when, on their return to their respective countries, they would decide to wage jihad against their own non-Islamic governments.[34]

In theory, the potential development of such a trend should have alarmed the Syrian security services, as concurring reports point out that, in addition to Syrian nationals representing the third largest contingent of foreign jihadist fighters and providing the highest number of jihadist detainees at the Iraqi Camp Bucca jail, the country also served as the entry point for 90 per cent of all foreign insurgents going to Iraq as of December 2008.[35] Although terrorist attacks have touched Syrian territory on a sporadic basis since 2004, it nonetheless seems as if the Syrian *mukhabarat*, the country's powerful security services, tolerated the flow of jihadist fighters going to Iraq from 2003 onwards—or, according to certain analysts, even encouraged it for dubious reasons. Paradoxically, the regime thus indirectly participated in the revival of a jihadist current within and surrounding its own borders, with potential disastrous security consequences for its survival. According to the analyst Michael Rubin, "this Syrian blind eye should raise concerns about the country's future stability as it suggests a vulnerability to blowback should these same Islamist terrorists decide to return to Syria to take on the Assad regime."[36]

The Syrian Ba'ath has a long history of supporting groups with ties to political violence. It has actively helped the Popular Front for the Liberation of Palestine (PFLP), the FPLP-General Command [in English], Palestinian Islamic Jihad, Hizbullah and Hamas by providing a safe haven and, in some cases, material and financial support for their leaders. This policy saw the country put on the list of states sponsoring terrorism by the US State Department as early as 1979—a designation with significant commercial and political implications for US-Syrian relations. There were more accusations that the Syrian government was using groups involved in political violence to serve its interests after the US intervention in Iraq. For various reasons, ranging from the intensity of the regional climate to a willingness to safeguard its security interests in a post-Saddam Iraq, the Syrian regime indeed appeared to have been particularly interested in keeping its hand in the flow of jihadist fighters crossing its territory to go to fight the US invaders in Baghdad.

At first glance, it seems as if the regime was only guilty of displaying some kind of benign neglect towards the array of foreign insurgents crossing the Syrian-Iraqi border for attacks on American and British troops. As a former senior British Intelligence official put it, "Let's say that the Syrian security forces could have controlled the border and did not!"[37] This is confirmed by several media reports detailing jihadist fighters who crossed the Syrian-Iraqi border without being checked by local security forces. A Syrian radical interviewed in 2005 by *The Guardian* goes as far as stating that "the call to jihad was encouraged by the Syrian government." "It arranged for buses to ferry fighters, speeded up the issuing of documentation and even gave prospective jihadis a discount on passport fees," and recalled that he had witnessed "Syrian border police waving to the jihadi buses as they crossed into Iraq."[38] In several reported instances, US troops have also captured foreign fighters carrying Syrian passports including entry permits and stamped with the mention "volunteer for jihad" or "join the Arab volunteers".[39]

The Syrian regime's deliberately passive stance on its border with Iraq was explicitly demonstrated when, as a retaliation for an American Special Forces raid into Syria—with the aim of killing al-Qaeda operatives smuggling fighters into Iraq—the local security forces withdrew from their posts, thus leaving the border open for jihadists to pass safely. At the time, the US Embassy in Damascus stated in a cable that "the Syrian government can do more to interdict known terrorist networks and foreign fighter facilitators operating within its borders." It went on, "Syria's ability to turn the flow of fighters off and on for political reasons was apparent in the wake of the alleged 26 October [US] military incursion into Syria when the Syrian government's self-described response was to remove border guards from key border checkpoints along the Iraqi-Syrian border."[40]

Such reports also suggest that Syrian involvement went a step further than benign neglect. Indeed, a close look at concurring sources hints at the possibility that the Syrian *mukhabarat* might have played a much more active role than is generally accepted in the smuggling and help of foreign insurgents going to Iraq. According to some sources, the Syrian regime might even have been actively involved in the financing of groups directly linked to the Iraqi insurgency. In January 2005

Muayed al-Nasseri, then the commander of the "Army of Muhammed"—
a paramilitary organization set up by Saddam Hussein in the wake of
the US invasion to resist the foreign occupation—confessed on Iraqi
television the clandestine links connecting the insurgency to the Syrian
security services:

> Cooperation with Syria began in October 2003, when a Syrian intelligence
> officer contacted me. Sa'ad Hamad Hisham [the first commander of the Army
> of Muhammed] and later Saddam Hussein himself authorized me to go to
> Syria. So I was sent to Syria. I crossed the border illegally, then I went to
> Damascus and met with an intelligence officer, Lieutenant Colonel "Abu Naji"
> through a mediator called "Abu Saud" [...]. They organized a meeting for me
> with a man named Fawzi al-Rawi, who is a member of the national leadership
> [of the Ba'ath Party] and an important figure in Syria. The Syrian government
> authorized him to meet with me. We met twice. In the first meeting, I explained
> to him what the Army of Muhammed is, what kind of operations we carry out
> and many other things. In the second meeting, he told me that Syrian govern-
> ment officials were very pleased with our first meeting. He informed me that
> the Army of Muhammed would receive material aid.

"The Syrian government was fully aware of this and the Syrian intelligence cooperated fully",[41] he concluded.

In addition, there is an increasing amount of evidence that the regime
in Damascus also tacitly—if not actively—encouraged, through proxies,
members of the Iraqi insurgency explicitly linked to al-Qaeda to carry
out terrorist attacks on Iraqi soil. Such accusations were voiced time and
again in an increasingly assertive fashion by Iraqi intelligence officers
who told American diplomats about "Syrian support for Iraqi Ba'athists
[linked with the former regime]," in turn suspected of having cooperated with al-Qaeda in Iraq—though these were said to have done so by
"disguising their Ba'athist sympathies".[42] The US Embassy in Damascus
designated "several Iraqis and Iraqi-owned entities residing in Syria
which provided financial, material and technical support for acts of
violence that threatened the peace and stability of Iraq."[43] In 2007, the
US Treasury Department gave a specific list of seven individuals who
brought significant help to the Iraqi insurgency—six of them former
Iraqi Ba'athist officials now all based in Syria.[44] It is widely suspected
that former elements of Saddam Hussein's regime residing in Damascus
have provided the al-Qaeda insurgency in Iraq with financial help, material aid and media support. In a thinly veiled accusation aimed at
Damascus, the Iraqi Foreign Minister Hoshyar Zebari stated in the

aftermath of an August 2009 bombing in Baghdad that "one or more of the neighbouring countries have conspired with al-Qaeda."[45]

The Syrian regime's proximity to the al-Qaeda networks in Iraq does not seem to have been solely the work of former Iraqi Ba'athists supported by Damascus. Instead, there seems to have been a direct link between the regime and Syrian militants known for their close connection to radical Islamic insurgents in Iraq. Prominent al-Qaeda facilitator Suleyman Khalid Darwish, *aka* Abu Ghadiya, has safely operated for years on Syrian territory—in a country known for the high level of surveillance provided by its powerful security services. As his contribution to the smuggling of jihadist fighters into Iraq was prominent, it is doubtful that the Syrian *mukhabarat* was not aware of their presence. Over the years, the Syrian regime also strengthened its own ties with prominent Syrian Islamic radicals with the ultimate goal of better controlling the flow of jihadist fighters leaving for Baghdad as well as obtaining a renewed insight into the growth of jihadist networks on Syrian soil. "We are practical, not theoretical," Ali Mamlouk, Syria's head of General Intelligence, explained in a meeting with his US counterpart. "In principle we don't attack or kill immediately; instead we embed ourselves in them and only at the opportune moment do we move."[46] In this respect, the figure of most interest is Abu al-Qaqaa. A radical Salafi cleric preaching at the popular al-Sahrour mosque in Aleppo, he had by the early 2000s become a loud advocate of anti-Americanism, attracting to his cause over 1,000 men—most of them wearing camouflage military trousers and highly trained in martial arts.[47] In his influential sermons, al-Qaqaa encouraged young Syrians to go to Iraq to fight the foreign occupiers. "Our hearts are filled with joy when we hear about any resistance operations in Iraq against the American invaders. We ask people to keep praying to God to help achieve victory for Iraq against the US,"[48] the radical Aleppine cleric used to preach. It is also reported that Abu al-Qaqaa himself was involved in providing material and financial help to the Iraqi insurgency.[49]

Some of his radical followers, however, soon started to suspect that their leader might be a stooge for Syrian intelligence when, in the face of mounting criticisms, he maintained his support for the regime. One of his former disciples stated in retrospect that "in the 1980s, thousands of Muslim men died in Syria for much less than we were saying." "We asked the sheikh why we weren't being arrested. He would tell us it was because we weren't saying anything against the government, that we were focusing on the common enemy, America and Israel [...]. We thought 'Oh, how strong our sheikh is that they do not touch us'. How stupid we were [...]"[50] In 2006, Abu al-Qaqaa was nominated head of the Khosrowiyya, Aleppo's most prestigious school of Islamic law, as well as the lead preacher at a large mosque of the Halab al-Jadida in the city's most bourgeois district. Arnaud Lenfant, a specialist of Salafism in Syria, believes that "such career evolution would probably not have been feasible without the excellent relations entertained by [al-Qaqaa] with the security services."[51]

There was always a risk that the Syrian security services' tacit support for certain radical Islamic activists could backfire. After all, perhaps that was even an effect sought to a certain degree by the regime. Despite maintaining his support for the Syrian Ba'ath, Abu al-Qaqaa called in his sermons for the advent of an Islamic state—the antithesis of the established Ba'ath Party ideology. "Yes, I would like to see an Islamic state in Syria and that's what we are working for,"[52] he declared in October 2003, while also attacking the "atheist dogs"[53] in his sermons. Yet, while al-Qaqaa had personally pledged allegiance to the Syrian Ba'ath out of pragmatism, his disciples might not have shared his willingness to be on intimate terms with the regime. Some of them might even have been so convinced by the immediate need to establish an Islamic state in Syria that they took matters into their hands and started to aim at regime's symbols. In June 2006, the Syrian State TV and radio headquarters became the targets of a jihadist suicide attack. This seems to have been partly inspired by Abu al-Qaqaa's followers. While the US Embassy in Damascus suggested at the time that the suspects had been trained in martial arts in the way al-Qaqaa's followers were, other reports pointed out that CDs containing sermons of the radical Aleppine cleric had been found by security officers on the attack scene.[54] Shortly afterwards al-Qaqaa appeared before journalists and denied all responsibility for the attacks. The Aleppine preacher was shot dead in September 2007 by an unknown gunman—most probably an Islamist dissident who viewed al-Qaqaa as a traitor and spy working for the *mukhabarat*.[55]

Other terrorist incidents involving jihadist networks struck Syrian territory throughout the decade. In April 2004, a UN building was the target of an attack by radical Islamic militants leading to a shootout with the security forces in the Mezze neighbourhood of the capital, and in July 2005 there was a gun battle between jihadist activists and the police

on Mount Qassioun, overlooking Damascus. More crucially, it is suspected that it was terrorists affiliated to Fatah al-Islam, a Sunni Lebanese
jihadist organization formerly alleged to be linked with Syrian Intelligence, who carried the battle against the Syrian Ba'ath to one of the
places most symbolic of the regime's might when the headquarters of
Military Intelligence were bombed on 27 September 2008. A cable sent
afterwards by the US Embassy in Damascus reported on the incident:

The Syrian government, using tightly controlled press outlets, was quick to
blame a Lebanese-based, al-Qaeda affiliated group, Fatah al-Islam; for this
attack. Syrian TV broadcast a November 7th programme featuring the confessions of some 20 Fatah al-Islam members, including the daughter and son-in-
law of Fatah al-Islam leader Shakr al-Absy, of their involvement in the attack
against the prominent military intelligence installation. Syrian and other commentators have noted that the Syrian government allegedly had maintained
ties to Shakr al-Absy [...]. It remains unclear why this group would have
launched an attack against Syrian security elements [...]. Since the attack, the
regime has attempted to portray Syria as a victim of terrorism rather than a
purveyor of it.[56]

Indeed, since the 9/11 attacks and, most significantly, since the beginning of the Iraq war, the Syrian regime had striven to portray itself as also
targeted by terrorism. Little is known about whether this was the result
of a true blowback against the *mukhabarat*'s longstanding relations with
Islamist insurgents in Iraq, local radical Islamic activists or al-Qaeda-
affiliated groups such as Fatah al-Islam, or reflected the regime's interest
in acting as a victim of Islamic violence in the framework of the US-led
"War on Terror". At any rate, the regime did its utmost to benefit from
the situation by taking the opportunity to seemingly lend a hand to the
US on matters related to security co-operation. The minutes of a long
meeting held in Damascus by US security officials with their Syrian
counterparts, represented by the General Intelligence director, Ali Mamlouk, are in this respect revealing of the Ba'ath regime's willingness to use
its newfound image as a victim of terrorism as a bargaining chip in its
relations with America: "Mamlouk pointed to Syria's 30 years of experience in battling radical groups such as the Muslim Brotherhood as evidence of Syria's commitment to the fight against terrorism." Alluding to
the "wealth of information" Syria had obtained over the past years while
penetrating terrorist groups, Mamlouk declared that "we have a lot of
experience and know these groups, this is our area and we know it; we

are on the ground and so we should take the lead [in the fight against terrorism]," before concluding "by all means we will continue to do all this but if we start cooperation with you it will lead to better results and we can better protect our interests."[57]

The Syrian regime's apparent willingness to cooperate with the United States on the security front reflected its longstanding desire to kick-start relations with America. This was made clear during the above-mentioned meeting when a Syrian official declared that "politics are an integral part of combating terrorism" and warned that "listing Syria as a state sponsor of terrorism and including Syria on the list of 14 countries for enhanced screening by the Transportation Security Administration (TSA) creates a 'contradiction' when the US subsequently requested cooperation with Syria against terrorism." Ali Mamlouk concluded the meeting by informing his American counterpart that "in summary, President Assad wants cooperation, we [the security services] should take the lead on that cooperation, and don't put us on your lists [of states sponsoring terrorism]."[58]

Taming political Islam

While the potential rise of radical Islam in Syria—alongside its violent consequences—may therefore have partially served the regime's interest in portraying itself as being at the forefront of the "War on Terror", the Syrian Ba'ath was also quick to realize that its long-term survival paradoxically lay in the encouragement of a more moderate form of political Islam at home. This did not come as a self-evident development since the ideological substance of the Ba'ath came from secularism and, in the early 1980s, the Syrian regime had just come out of a lone struggle against Islamic forces which resulted in the disappearance of virtually all expressions of political Islam for years. Drawing lessons from the bloody struggle, Hafiz al-Assad came to terms with the reality that, whatever the scale of repression, it would never be possible to stifle completely the increasing desire of conservative sections of Syrian society to display their Muslim faith. The Syrian President as well as his successor, Bashar al-Assad, therefore resorted to carrying out policies which, instead of brutally suppressing all expression of political Islam, encouraged the emergence of institutions and personalities which, under the watchful eye of the regime, called for the advent of a "moderate Islam".

A few co-opted Sunni Muslim religious scholars, or *ulama*, were granted privileged access to the regime as a way to make sure that their political loyalty lay on the side of the Syrian Ba'ath. This policy was initiated by Hafiz al-Assad when he built up his ties with Ahmad Kuftaro, a prominent Kurdish *alim* appointed Great Mufti of Syria in 1964. This long-time supporter of Assad—a self-professed admirer of his "personality and characteristics, his dedication and his steadfastness on the principle of faith"[59]—was known for his pro-regime statements, granting a stamp of approval to many of its policies. Kuftaro would for instance, go as far as stating that "Islam and the regime's power to enforce the law are twin brothers"[…] "it is impossible to think of one without the other, Islam is the base and the regime's power of rule is the protector; after all a thing without a base is destined to collapse and fail, and a thing without a protector will end in extinction."[60] In exchange for his loyalty, Kuftaro was able to run things his own way until his death in 2005, establishing in 1974 the Abu al-Noor centre which quickly became the country's leading teaching centre for Arabic language and higher Islamic studies. The centre was taken over by his son Salah Kuftaro, who has enjoyed the same level of access to state-controlled media as his father, despite his repeated assertions that secular Arab governments have failed and that an "Islamic democracy" should instead be implemented in Syria.[61]

But even more representative of the pro-regime religious scholars who have been co-opted by the Ba'ath is Ahmad Hassoun who, two years after being promoted by presidential decree to the post of Grand Mufti, replacing Ahmad Kuftaro, declared that Bashar al-Assad's election for a second term was comparable to a "*bai'a* [oath of allegiance] similar to that of the Prophet."[62] Another prominent cleric is Said Ramadan al-Buti, a Kurdish scholar of Damascene extraction who has been a constant source of support for the Syrian Ba'ath since the late 1970s when he sharply attacked the Muslim Brotherhood and the Fighting Vanguard for having acted "in contradiction with the principles of Islam" and having brought *fitna*, or civil war, to Syria. Ever since, he has backed the regime's ban on the establishment of political parties carrying a religious agenda, backing up the regime's security argument by stating that "there is always the fear that extreme elements will infiltrate such a party and turn it into a tool for sowing dissension and violence in society."[63] In an interview, Salah Kuftaro backed this argument by adding that "our religious community in Syria is always under surveillance by the government and I support that so no extremist[s] sneak in among us."[64]

While the drive behind the regime's support for institutions and personalities encouraging a "moderate Islam" initially came from Hafiz al-Assad, who in addition to supporting moderate, pro-regime clerics oversaw a great increase in the number of mosques built and gave his name to institutes dedicated to memorization of the Quran, it was his son Bashar who, upon succeeding his father in June 2000, brought further momentum to a policy eventually aimed at containing radical expressions of political Islam. One of his first steps as the new President of Syria was to allow female students to wear the *hijab*, or headscarf, in school.[65] Early on in his presidency, he strove to project the image of a leader faithful to Islam and a guardian of the Muslim religion in Syria. The state-controlled media thus regularly reported on his participation in religious holiday prayers in mosques throughout the country. In December 2002, the young President made news when he took part in the service for the last Friday of the month of Ramadan at the Umar Ibn al-Khatab Mosque in Hama.[66] Since the city had been the focal point of the Islamic insurrections of the late 1970s and early 1980s, the message conveyed, almost twenty years later to the day, by Bashar al-Assad, was power. Not only was the regime willing to turn a page in the story of its troubled relations with political Islam, it also seemed ready to open a new chapter by embracing parts of the ideology and the sought-after policies of those it had been fighting decades earlier.

In the first ten years of Bashar al-Assad's rule, the regime did more to accommodate conservative Syrian Muslims than at any point before. A religious scholar—not a secular Ba'athist—was appointed as head of the Minister of *Awqaf* (religious endowments), religious activities could take place in the stadium of Damascus University, soldiers were allowed to pray in their barracks, charitable Islamic foundations such as *Zayd* were allowed to operate again after years of prohibition, the state sponsored the emergence of a number of institutes dedicated to Islamic studies, and the banking sector was reformed in order to encourage the emergence of Islamic banks. "Before, religion for the regime was like a ball of fire, now they deal with it like it could be a ball of life,"[67] a Syrian professor of Islamic studies summed up in 2006. The opinion of the country's most prominent religious scholar was taken into account more seriously than ever before. In the same year, while the government was on the verge of reorganizing religious education so that students who wished to enter a school of Islamic studies should have at least gone through the basic phase of obligatory teaching, the anger of the clerics was swiftly heard and the regime backed down. In a show of their new-found influence, when Bashar al-Assad received a letter signed by influential religious figures such as Said Ramadan al-Buti, Salah Kuftaro, Mohammed al-Khatib and Osama al-Rifa'i among others, he immediately promised to solve the problem and the reform was aborted.[68]

Some analysts suggest that, if the political discourse and practical policies of the Syrian Ba'ath progressively moved in a mildly Islamic direction, it was because, at the time, the regime was faced with mounting internal and external pressures. Externally, Bashar al-Assad's grip on power threatened to erode in view of warnings from the US that Syria could very well be next on the list after Iraq was invaded in March 2003. Shortly thereafter, the security services' powerful interests in neighbouring Lebanon partially collapsed with the passing of the Franco-American UN Security Council Resolution no. 1559 which, following the assassination of the Lebanese Prime Minister Rafiq Hariri, requested that Syria swiftly withdraw its troops from Beirut. The security apparatus also felt directly targeted by the newly-installed Special Tribunal for Lebanon which increasingly seemed to take aim at prominent Syrian figures suspected of involvement in the assassination. Domestically, it took a few years for Bashar al-Assad to impose his own authority not only over the country but also over his own regime. Having succeeded his father as President at barely thirty-five years of age, he was the target of some within the regime who, like former Vice President Abdel Halim Khaddam, resented the hereditary dimension of continued Ba'athist rule under the Assads. The short-lived timid liberalization process which led to the so-called "Damascus Spring" in the early 2000s did not help matters as the regime itself became the main target of the Syrian opposition. In January 2005, Khaddam himself defected from the regime and joined the ranks of the opposition, leaving the regime as if it was about to collapse (see Chapter 8). This is the context in which Bashar al-Assad's willingness to court religious conservatives throughout the early reign of his rule should be seen.

In turn, many of the country's religious men brought their loyalty to the regime. For instance, Muhammad al-Habasch, a leading member of Parliament with a strong religious inclination, supported the regime's clampdown on opposition leaders participating in conferences in Washington or Paris by stating that "it's not a suitable time to allow people to travel abroad to participate in opposition conferences, we have to be real." He also added that he was satisfied to see regime officials moving towards an accommodation with religious forces inside the country, saying, "they realize we need Islamic power, especially at this time."[69] The regime, long secular out of ideology and interest, now seemed to move in a mildly Islamic direction on the model of the ruling AKP in Turkey, a close partner of Bashar al-Assad in his first ten years in power. An Egyptian journalist reported in 2010 on that paradox by observing that "some months ago, a closed seminar on secularism at Damascus University attended by no more than 100 people from the ranks of progressives and democrats was banned by the authorities, while two weeks ago a conservative cleric was allowed to preach in Aleppo, in the north of the country, in a sermon attended by 6,000 people."[70]

The regime's softer policies towards renewed expressions of faith by Syria's Sunni Muslim citizens were made even more apparent by its silence regarding the exponential growth of the Qubaysiyat, a secretive religious movement emphasizing women's role in Islamic life, whose name comes from its founder Munira al-Qubaysi. Since the 1970s, more than 120 religious education institutes and 600 higher institutes for religious learning have opened, which are affiliated with many of the country's 9,000 mosques. There are no official statistics on the degree of infiltration of the Qubaysiyat but estimates suggest that, in Damascus alone, these conservative female preachers control eighty religious schools.[71] Hence they have been able to oversee the education of many young female students and have subsequently acted in the social sphere in a way that has seen their popularity grow quickly over recent years. Analysing the reason behind their success, the journalist Ibrahim Hamidi explained that beyond "supervising the teaching of hundreds of thousands of school children from an early age and in a conservative manner," the Qubaysis then "take care of them through charity and people's contributions, offering some medical services in the Salamah Hospital, which is affiliated with it." In addition, "The Qubaysis also provide some books on their thought in bookshops they own such as the al-Salam bookshop in the al-Baramikah neighbourhood in the centre of Damascus." There are also rumours that the wives and daughters of some influential members of Damascene society have been converted to the Qubaysiyat movement. One can therefore assume that the regime is aware of the movement yet does not move against it for fear of alienating a potentially powerful constituency. Such a passive stance is also due to the fact that, according to Muhammed al-Habasch, the most prominent characteristic of this women's Islamic society has since the 1970s been "their keeping away from politics whether in support of or against the regime." The group, he says, "has not been involved in any act against the country," and "the Qubaysis have no political project"[72] and instead focus on achieving Islamic unity through enhancing the role of women in Islamic life. According to Thomas Pierret, the women's Islamic society, long operating in secrecy so as not to upset the security services, was in 2006 allowed to gather in mosques—once again, probably in order to court the conservative religious constituency in the context of a regional crisis.[73]

During that year, Syria was coming again under intense regional and international pressure because of its long-time backing of the Shiite Lebanese militia Hizbullah which embodied the resistance to the Israeli invasion of Lebanon in July 2006. Then, as during its opposition to the 1979 Egypt-Israel Treaty, the 1994 Oslo peace process and Israel's incursions into Palestinian territories as in January 2009, the Syrian regime was always careful to employ a distinctively pro-Palestinian rhetoric, most often couched in Islamic terms. Practically, this policy meant that Damascus had to reach out to Islamic groups throughout the region which were at the forefront of the anti-Israel struggle. Over the past forty years, the Syrian regime has brought key support to explicitly religious Shiite Lebanese militias such as Amal and Hizbullah—most often for strategic reasons linked to the Syrian Ba'ath's lack of good relations with the PLO. Mohammad Hussein Fadlallah, Hizbullah's spiritual leader, and Hassan Nasrallah, the organization's secretary general, have long been regular visitors to the Syrian capital.

Over the past decade, however, and at least until the Arab uprisings reached Syria in March 2011, the regime has striven to broaden the sectarian scope of its regional partnerships by increasingly supporting Sunni militant groups which, despite their instinctive distaste for the Alawi-dominated Syrian Ba'ath, have shared its anti-Israeli agenda with fervour. The Palestinian Islamic movement has been particularly welcome in Damascus where Islamic Jihad has established its headquarters and Hamas found a safe haven for its most wanted members. The Jordanian Islamic Action Front has also been vocal in its support for the anti-Israel stance of the Syrian Ba'ath. This was particularly paradoxical given the Islamic Action Front's own affiliation with the Muslim Brotherhood movement whose local branch in Syria was so severely crushed by the Ba'ath regime in the late 1970s and early 1980s. But it also reflected the Syrian Ikhwan's great difficulty, at the time, in convincing their regional partners of the need to support attempts to topple the Ba'ath regime. Reflecting the complex situation into which the regime's increasingly Islamic discourse and policies had put the Syrian Ikhwan, members of the local branch of the organization were severely criticized at an international Muslim Brotherhood conference in the late 1990s. One of the Jordanian participants in the meeting was reported to have accused them by saying that "Syria is the only Arab state standing up to Israel and granting support to every opposition to the Zionist occupation!" and that accordingly "it is impossible for an Arab or a Muslim to attack it and try to harm it and its leadership."[74] This trend would dramatically change with the advent of the Arab uprisings in Syria after the head of Hamas, Khaled Meshaal, decided to leave Damascus in the wake of Bashar al-Assad's bloody crackdown on the protesters.

8

STRUGGLING FOR RELEVANCE

THE MUSLIM BROTHERHOOD'S EXILE

"The Muslim Brotherhood has changed,"[1] argued a secular left-wing opposition activist, after dismissing a question on whether he feared a takeover by the Syrian Brothers should the Assad regime be toppled. The violent and sectarian image long associated with the Syrian Ikhwan had mainly been due to the radical path pursued by the organization in the late 1970s and early 1980s. But, for all the regime's attempts at making such picture endure throughout the years, most analysts and militants agreed that, by the late 1990s and early 2000s, the period of the Brotherhood's radicalization had passed and that the time had come to give the organization a second chance. It is against that backdrop that, just about a decade before the "Arab Spring" started to shake Damascus, the Ikhwan regained their influence as a powerful component of the Syrian opposition—battling the regime from abroad, this time, and with words rather than swords.

The Brotherhood's comeback on the Syrian political chessboard was not, however, an obvious development as the state repression of the early 1980s, culminating with the Hama massacre of February 1982, had dealt it a near-fatal blow. As a result, the organization had been left for decades with neither a base inside the country nor the credibility it once enjoyed. Forced into exile, and with members scattered throughout the world, the organization temporarily lost relevance. The disastrous state of the Brotherhood unleashed a blame game amidst its ranks, trapping the group in a cycle of internal bickering and political dramas which greatly fragmented its work for decades and left scars still visible today. The regime's hand was never far from any of these happenings. Still watchful of the Brotherhood's each and every move, it became skilled in putting forward policies which only heightened the Ikhwan's successive crises of identity.

So how did the organization, against all these odds, eventually manage to get back on its feet and regain its former position as Syria's most influential opposition group? The answer lies partly in the ability of the Syrian Brotherhood's leadership to review its past policies and undergo a profound ideological evolution. In many ways, however, telling the story of the Brotherhood's evolution boils down to recounting how the Ikhwan's "Aleppo faction" took up the leadership and trod a different path to that of the more hard-line "Hama clan".[2]

Divided between the "Hama clan" and the "Aleppo faction"

Divisions have long plagued the Muslim Brotherhood's ranks, but all its members agree on one thing: the February 1982 uprisings at Hama, which the group eventually supported (see Chapter 7), came to have disastrous consequences for the whole of the Islamic movement. The blame game which ensued would have far-reaching implications as the two competing leaderships which then emerged from inside the Ikhwan projected seemingly irreconcilable visions of the organization's future. "Hama was like an earthquake for the Muslim Brotherhood," a former Ikhwani leader recognized in retrospect. "The differences among us surfaced and some of us started looking for scapegoats".[3] In the eyes of many inside the organization, the "Hama clan", in charge of the organization from 1975 to 1980—but in fact chiefly influential until February 1982—was responsible for the dynamics which led the Ikhwan to enter into a fatal partnership with its radical offshoot, the Fighting Vanguard. Many Hamawite members of the Muslim Brotherhood had also belonged to the Fighting Vanguard, and this helped to blur the lines between the two organizations and thereby played into the regime's argument that it was unnecessary to distinguish one from the other.

For their part, the Hamawite members of the Ikhwan have shunned all responsibility for the bloody events of the late 1970s and early 1980s, instead blaming the Fighting Vanguard and its "Caliph" for the violent dimension the struggle then assumed. Shortly after the crackdown in Hama, Adnan Saadeddine declared that "all of Adnan Uqlah's actions proceeded from want of prudence, undue haste or sheer recklessness," stressing that the leader of the Fighting Vanguard had provoked "considerable damage" to the Islamic movement by the way he "conducted the fighting in Aleppo" and "drew the mujahidin into the ill-timed confrontation at Hama."[4] This is also the reading of events provided to this day by most prominent members of the "Hama clan". For Muhammed Riyadh al-Shuqfah for instance, now the leader of the organization, the once-political struggle between the Muslim Brotherhood and the Ba'ath turned into a doomed military fight, pitting the most irreconcilable Ba'athist figure, Rif'at al-Assad, against the zealous "Caliph" of the Fighting Vanguard, Adnan Uqlah, hence its tragic outcome.[5] To the present day, many Hamawites still hold Adnan Uqlah's troops responsible for the violence which descended on Hama in early February 1982—though it is worth bearing in mind that the distinction between many of Uqlah's men and Ikhwani Hamawites was not always clear-cut. However, the sense of lasting bitterness still found among Ikhwani ranks at the evocation of the events of 1982 has been less between members of the Muslim Brotherhood and the activists of the Fighting Vanguard than between Ikhwanis from Aleppo and those from Hama. Eventually, the former accused the latter of having been the real driving force behind the movement's radicalization at the time.

The blame game was eventually settled as the Muslim Brotherhood's consultative body (*Majlis al-Shura*), decided to set up a special committee headed by the Syrian Brother Muhammed Ali Ashmi, tasked with investigating what had gone wrong inside the movement. Perhaps unsurprisingly, Adnan Saadeddine and Said Hawwa were very uneasy about the idea of having such a "truth-seeking committee" set up.[6] Because of their fierce opposition, the evaluation report was never made publicly available and its content remains, to this very day, a closely guarded secret. According to Alison Pargeter, it is reported to have placed much of the blame on Adnan Saadeddine, accused of having set up a special committee tasked with secretly coordinating actions with the Fighting Vanguard in 1977—something the former Ikhwani leader has denied in a booklet defending his record.[7] At any rate, the accusation exacerbated the already existing tensions between the "Aleppo faction" and the

"Hama clan". The first group, principally based in Amman, had by the mid-1980s regrouped around Sheikh Abdel Fattah Abu Ghuddah while the other, led by Adnan Saadeddine, had settled in Iraq.

From their respective exiles, the two groups started to put forward seemingly irreconcilable visions of the way in which the Muslim Brotherhood, defeated and based abroad, should now best deal with the Ba'ath regime. The "Aleppo faction" quickly realized that the Hama massacre had been such a great loss of human life that it was impossible to bear any more. If some within the group, such as Zouheir Salem, had always criticized the Ikhwan's violent policy of 1980–82, others, such as Abdel Fatah Abu Ghuddah and Ali Sadreddine al-Bayanouni, reversed their formerly radical positions and came to hold a compromising stance towards the Syrian Ba'ath. For the Hamawite Brothers, however, the issue was more than merely political or strategic: it was emotional. Many had lost one or several relatives in the bloody governmental retaliation of February 1982. Still bitter at the destruction of their home town by the Ba'athist troops, the "Hama clan" carried on its radical policy by continuing to advocate armed struggle against the regime. From Baghdad, the group managed to gather sufficient material and financial resources to continue its violent endeavours. Upon Said Hawwa's resignation from the Muslim Brotherhood's Executive Council, in 1983, it is reported that the Hamawite Farouk Tayfour took over the group's "military branch" and led sporadic attacks inside Syria until the late 1980s. In its violent endeavour, the "Hama clan" could benefit from Adnan Saadeddine's excellent relations with the Iraqi ruler who provided it with weapons, money and training. In turn, as a show of his loyalty to Saddam Hussein, the leader of the "Hama clan" would go as far as stating that members of the Iraqi Ba'ath are "true Muslims" and that "their leadership is devout"—whatever the contradiction in terms. He would also turn his back on al-Tali'a whose "Caliph" was unsuccessfully required to ask forgiveness for having accused the Iraqi Ba'ath of "blasphemy".[8]

For a time, it seemed as if the Syrian regime hesitated as to which policy it should pursue in order to definitively crush the remnants of the exiled Muslim Brotherhood. At first, an assassination campaign was carried out in order to deter any further political and military activity against the Syrian Ba'ath. As quoted before (Chapter 7), the regime was eventually successful in infiltrating the remnants of the Fighting Vanguard, regrouped in Amman, and through an elaborate scheme, lured Adnan Uqlah back to Syria where he is believed to have been immediately arrested and killed. The current leader of the Ikhwan, Muhammed Riyadh al-Shuqfah, remembered having suffered four assassination attempts after fleeing Hama for Baghdad in the early 1980s, three of them foiled by Iraqi Intelligence, which underlines the extent to which Saddam Hussein's security apparatus was active in protecting members of the "Hama group" living on its territory.[9] Whether the leaders of the Islamic movement were based in Aachen, Amman or Baghdad, the message sent to them by the Syrian *mukhabarat* became as clear as it could get: all attempts to resume opposition activities would be met with a disproportionate response against both them and their families.

In parallel to the regime's willingness to maintain its repression against known Muslim Brotherhood leaders, however, there co-existed another policy, in appearance more conciliatory, but in reality as cynical as the former. In late 1984, Ali Duba, Hafiz al-Assad's head of Military Intelligence, made it known to the Muslim Brotherhood's leadership based in Amman and Baghdad that the regime would be prepared to engage in negotiations with the ultimate goal of achieving a compromise acceptable to all parties. While the Hamawite members of the Ikhwan were deeply reluctant to participate, they were nonetheless convinced by the rest of the organization that a dialogue with the regime, at such a catastrophic stage for the Islamic movement, was the only way forward. Several thousand members of the Muslim Brotherhood had been forced to flee the repression they suffered in Syria, many of them finding refuge in Jordan, Iraq and, to a lesser extent, Saudi Arabia and Turkey. "In exile, our situation was desperate," remembered Walid Safour, who fled to Jordan in 1979 before settling in London where he set up a human rights group. "The organization did whatever it could to support us, providing a monthly assistance of around 30 dinars to each refugee, but this was hardly enough in a country where 5 dinars a day are needed to survive."[10]

Keen to seize every possible opportunity to have its members safely return to Syria, the Muslim Brotherhood agreed to meet Ali Duba to start negotiations with the Ba'athist regime. These took place in December 1984 in a hotel in Bonn, in Germany, where Ali Duba and two aides, Hisham Bukhtiar and Hassan Khalil, met the leader of the Syrian Ikhwan, Hassan al-Houeidi, assisted by Munir al-Ghadban and

Muhammed Riyadh al-Shuqfah. According to the latter, it quickly became clear that the regime's real aim was to provoke divisions within the Muslim Brotherhood by sowing confusion in its ranks. Thus, it was reported, while Ali Duba and Hassan al-Houeidi isolated themselves in a separate room—suggesting that progress was made towards a negotiated settlement—Hassan Khalil came to Muhammed Riyadh al-Shuqfah and expressed, for his part, a clear lack of willingness to proceed with the negotiations. Confused and exhausted after a day of talks and countertalks, hope and disappointment, both camps agreed to take some rest before carrying on with the next round of negotiations. "A few hours later, Ali Duba called Hassan al-Houeidi: the Syrian intelligence officers were on a train back to Berlin before taking off for Damascus, they had fooled us,"[11] al-Shuqfah commented.

By holding out the prospect of settling the dispute with the Ikhwan, the regime had managed to achieve two goals. While its offer had exacerbated the tensions between the Brotherhood's two wings as to whether a conciliatory approach should be adopted or not, it had also had a glimpse into how fractured and weak the Brotherhood had become in exile. "There never was any serious intent on the part of the regime to actually settle the dispute with the Muslim Brotherhood, these negotiations were doomed in advance," confessed Abdel Halim Khaddam. "The delegation led by Ali Duba suggested to the Ikhwan that they could be allowed to return to Syria but only under the condition that they do so as individuals and refrain from any political activity…In reality, the regime did not wish to see any form of agreement being reached with the Muslim Brotherhood."[12]

If the regime's real intention was to sow division among Ikhwani ranks, it was successful. The frictions between the "Hama clan" and the "Aleppo faction", already present in 1982 and 1983, came to a head with the failure of the 1984 negotiations. Back in Baghdad, the "Hama clan" led by Adnan Saadeddine continued to plan attacks against Ba'athist installations inside Syria. Members of the "Aleppo faction", for their part, persisted in believing that negotiations with the regime were still the only way forward, despite the failure of the earlier attempt. It is against this ideological backdrop, of dispute between those favourable to armed struggle and those privileging negotiations, that the 1986 leadership crisis emerged. "Tensions [which] had been simmering since the Hama massacre, became evident with the failure of the 1984 negotiations and emerged publicly with the advent of the 1986 leadership cri-sis,"[13] confirmed a source close to the Syrian Ikhwan. The struggle was between the moderate Aleppine scholar Sheikh Abdel Fatah Abu Ghud-dah, who favoured talks with the regime, and the more hard-line Hama-wite Adnan Saadeddine, for whom there was "nothing to discuss with these criminals; they are not a government, they are a mafia."[14] But, while the leadership crisis was depicted as an ideological struggle between the organization's moderates and hard-line members, more profound underlying factors were separating the "Hama clan" and the "Aleppo faction".

"The debate on armed struggle was a façade," Muhammed Riyadh al-Shuqfah, a long-time member of the "Hama clan", admitted. "It provided a useful pretext to decide who should be the next leader and, in my opinion, Adnan Saadeddine was by far the best."[15] It is quite clear that a clash over ideology was only one of the many elements that led to the split between the two wings of the Muslim Brotherhood. Promi-nent among other factors was the clash of personalities and very distinct styles of leadership that the two leaders were known for. "While Abu Ghuddah was a respected conciliatory figure whose academic back-ground gave him a broad outlook, Saadeddine was on the contrary an impulsive and individualistic character who had a narrow view of the situation,"[16] explained a leading member of the "Aleppo faction". To a certain extent, such criticisms might also have reflected cultural differ-ences between members of the Ikhwan from Hama and those from Aleppo. Indeed, in recurring conversations with members of both the "Hama clan" and the "Aleppo faction", mention was made of regional differences, emphasizing a strong cultural component that might account for much of the still-existant tensions between the two wings. It was suggested that Hama's tribal structure and harsh socio-geograph-ical surroundings bind its inhabitants together with a sense of inner solidarity and these self-described "men of action" instinctively favour tough, conservative policies, while the inhabitants of Aleppo, a sizeable commercial city with a large variety of religious and ethnic groups and socioeconomic classes, are more moderate and prone to dialogue; Alep-pines are said to engage in politics in a business-like manner, favouring pragmatic compromises to rigid ideology. Thus, if the 1986 struggle between Abu Ghuddah and Saadeddine took on a strong personal dimension, it might well be because their diverging outlooks and visions reflected the traditional regional divide between Hamawite and Aleppine Ikhwanis inside the organization.

Between 1984 and 1985, elections contested by the two figures were held inside the movement, and since Abu Ghuddah's declared victory was not recognized by Saadeddine, an interim leadership was created, putting Adeeb Jajeh and then Munir al-Ghdaban at the helm of the organization for six consecutive months each. Ultimately, however, Adnan Saadeddine unilaterally declared that he was taking up the leadership position, exacerbating the rift of mistrust to an extent still felt until today in relations between Ikhwani members from Aleppo and those from Hama, who then largely rallied behind their chief.

By 1986, the personal, ideological and cultural differences setting the "Aleppo faction" apart from the "Hama clan" had effectively fractured the Islamic movement into two clearly distinct organizations. The first, led by Sheikh Abu Ghuddah, was recognized by the international body of the Muslim Brotherhood as the legitimate representative of the Syrian Ikhwan. It also adopted a more conciliatory stance towards the Ba'athist regime. A new round of negotiations between this organization and Ali Duba was carried out in Frankfurt throughout September 1987, though with no more success than the preceding talks. It has been reported that, when Hassan al-Houeidi met Ali Duba for the second time and asked that the security services release the thousands of Muslim Brothers still imprisoned inside Syria as a gesture of goodwill, Hafiz al-Assad's chief of Military Intelligence replied arrogantly, "But, you want the end of the regime!"[17] The Syrian Ba'ath, aware of the existing divisions separating the two wings of the Ikhwan, certainly intended to use the 1987 negotiations as a way to further exacerbate tensions within the Islamic movement. In retrospect, those inside the "Aleppo faction" who were responsible for the 1987 negotiations acknowledged they were aware of the risk that the regime might instrumentalize the talks to the detriment of the Ikhwan. "We knew that the regime wanted to play a game with us but we still thought that we should take up every opportunity to negotiate and give dialogue a try, believing that by reaching out we would all move forward and that, in the end, progress would be made in the interest of all,"[18] Ali Sadreddine al-Bayanouni explained in an interview.

By tantalizing the Muslim Brotherhood's moderates with the prospect of a settlement, Hafiz al-Assad was successful in exploiting the Islamic movement's ideological contradictions. From Baghdad, Adnan Saadeddine's dissident Ikhwani organization fiercely criticized the "Aleppo faction" for being lured into the regime's negotiations trap again. His "Hama clan" continued to be financially and materially supported by an Iraqi Ba'ath regime keen, for its part, to benefit from Adnan Saadeddine's presence in Baghdad to present itself with Islamic credentials. "For once in our lives, we were prized by the Ba'athists!"[19] a leading member of Saadeddine's group remembered with irony. In turn, the "Hama clan" strove to support Saddam Hussein in the battles he fought in the regional and international arenas. While throughout the 1980s Adnan Saadeddine repeatedly blamed the "evil" Iranian regime for its war with Iraq, he also became, in the early 1990s, Saddam Hussein's personal envoy to the Islamic world.

In his memoirs, Saadeddine even devoted a whole chapter to relations with Saddam's Iraq in which he explained how close he and his "Hama clan" were to the regime in Baghdad over several years. Even though he stated that Iraq's invasion of Kuwait had been a mistake, he explained how, when Baghdad became targeted by UN sanctions, he mounted public relations activities to persuade Islamic countries in South East Asia to support an isolated Saddam Hussein. At that point, Adnan Saadeddine's plea in that corner of the world might even have exceeded the role of Iraqi embassies. "We arrived in the Malaysian capital at the beginning of the new year," the leader of the "Hama clan" recounted. "Hotels were full of visitors celebrating the new year and the Iraqi Embassy envoy left us and did not accompany us to the hotel […]. We did not find anyone from the Iraqi Embassy staff to help us as they were indulging in Christmas celebrations and not feeling the stringing crisis through which their country was passing […] We made our affliction obvious but they couldn't care less."[20] In exchange for loyalty and support in times of crisis, the Iraqi regime continued to lend its crucial support to the "Hama clan" which, in turn, enabled the group to continue its armed campaign against the Syrian Ba'ath until well after the 1986 split.[21]

By 1990, the leadership of the officially-recognized branch of the Syrian Ikhwan had switched back again from Sheikh Abu Ghuddah, who at seventy years old had no more political ambitions, to Hassan al-Houeidi. Under the new leadership, efforts were made at reconciling the "Aleppo faction" with the "Hama clan". Eventually, much of the

"Hama clan" agreed to progressively rejoin the main organization throughout 1991 and 1992, aware that armed action against the regime had not led anywhere and the alliance with Iraq had somewhat constrained its autonomy. However, their historic leader, Adnan Saadeddine, was not allowed back into the wider organization. His membership of the movement had been "suspended" by the internationally-recognized faction after he had unilaterally proclaimed himself leader of the movement in 1986, and it was not restored until 2008, shortly before he died in 2010. According to Zouheir Salem, a prominent member of the "Aleppo faction", much of the "Hama clan" agreed to rejoin the main organization in the early 1990s because they realized that the tensions inside the movement were not between Hama and Aleppo but, in reality, between the antagonistic personality of Adnan Saadeddine and the rest of the Ikhwan. "They eventually came to the realization that the problem came from within Hama,"[22] he concluded.

Back to basics: the ideological evolution

Since the early 1990s, the history of the Ikhwan has essentially been marked by the moderate ideological footprint left upon it by the "Aleppo faction", which stipulated that the "Hama clan" renounce the use of violence against the regime as a precondition for the 1991–92 regrouping. In that regard, the personal evolution in the views of the Ikhwan's leader throughout the late 1990s and 2000s, Ali Sadreddine al-Bayanouni from Aleppo, is revealing of the movement's progressive doctrinal moderation. Once a radical member of the "Aleppo faction" and one of the first "military commanders" of the Muslim Brotherhood, he had by the early 2000s made his newfound commitment to non-violence, the protection of minorities and the promotion of democracy, the cornerstone of Ikhwani discourse in exile. Far from being an impediment, his background as a Muslim Brotherhood hard-liner in the late 1970s in fact proved crucial in winning over the broader membership to ideas of reform and peaceful resistance. "Without Bayanouni, there would never have been a review of the Syrian Brotherhood's policies," a figure long close to the Ikhwani leadership argued. "He was able to carry out the reforms because he had the legitimacy of armed struggle behind him."[23] As leader (1996–2010), Ali Sadreddine al-Bayanouni's first steps were to soften the image of an organization tainted by its links to the violence of the early 1980s.

In 2001, Ali Sadreddine al-Bayanouni pushed Ikhwani members to adopt a National Honour Charter which condemned in unequivocal terms the use of violence against one's own government. In addition, the document also signalled the Brotherhood's willingness to turn the page for good in its relations with the Syrian Ba'ath. "The confrontation between Islam and Arabism is a feature of a long-gone phase and an era buried in history which resulted essentially from emotional spillage as well as misinterpretation and misunderstanding,"[24] it read. Such efforts at conciliation culminated with the publication of the Muslim Brotherhood's political project in 2004, which represented a partial attempt at acknowledging part of the Ikhwan's responsibility for the bloody events of the late 1970s and early 1980s (see appendices for the full text).

The document stressed that "the Muslim Brotherhood in Syria has carried out a thorough review of its policies." It acknowledged that "we, together with large numbers of Syrian citizens, found ourselves forced to resort to self-defence in a situation of spiralling violence."[25] According to Zouheir Salem, often considered as the chief ideologue of today's Syrian Ikhwan, the organization learned from the failure of armed struggle. "Today, we believe that the only way forward is to oppose the regime through peaceful means on the model of the organization's historical leaders, Mustapha al-Sibai and Issam al-Attar,"[26] he asserted. The Muslim Brotherhood's discourse emphasized a willingness to return to its basics and stress the extent to which its radical and sectarian tone throughout the late 1970s should be considered as an exception instead of the rule. "Mustapha al-Sibai, Muhammed al-Mubarak, Issam al-Attar, Abdel Fatah Abu Ghuddah, Muhammed al-Hamid and many other leading Islamic figures [...] presented their views in reply to other views [...] but when they were met with harm and oppression, they reacted with patience and forbearance, committing themselves always to remain within the law and advocating free and fair elections,"[27] an official Brotherhood document read in reference to the moderate spirit of the organization's founders.

The reference to "free and fair elections" is not an innovation in Syrian Ikhwani thought. As noted earlier (see Chapter 2), the organization became involved from the outset in parliamentary politics. Despite the political instability characterizing Syrian politics from 1946 to 1963, the Muslim Brotherhood's political platform played an active and constructive role.[28] However, the violence of the late 1970s and early 1980s, when the country became dominated by authoritarian rulers of Alawi Ba'athist extraction, greatly damaged the Syrian Ikhwan's image. Ideologically, the Muslim Brotherhood's short-lived alliance with the jihadist forces of the Fighting Vanguard led the Ikhwan to temporarily radicalize its discourse. While Ali Sadreddine al-Bayanouni for instance started questioning whether Marxist groupings should be allowed at all to form political parties, the radical Said Hawwa stressed for his part that "in Islam the sources of the law cannot be interpreted"[29]—thereby suggesting that political Islam and democracy might in fact not be so compatible.

The confusion over the Syrian Ikhwan's commitment to democracy, aroused after the radicalism of the late 1970s and early 1980s, started casting doubts over the sincerity of the various statements of support for democracy by the organization during the 1990s and early 2000s. Such concerns were voiced by Hans Günter Lobmeyer. "After the failure of its religious strategy in the 1960s and the anti-Alawi strategy in the 1970s and 1980s, [the Syrian Brotherhood] is trying the democratic option in the 1990s," he said, adding that "it is beyond the question that democracy is not the Brotherhood's political aim but a means to another end: the assumption of power."[30] It is clear, however, that Said Hawwa, a radical Ikhwani ideologue of the 1970s, is no longer popular amongst many members of the Muslim Brotherhood. "The views of Said Hawwa do not represent the current strategy and ideology of the Ikhwan,"[31] asserted the organization's current ideologue, Zouheir Salem.

Today, there is little doubt left about the organization's commitment to ideas and concepts such as democracy and political pluralism. "Basic freedoms and political and civil rights are no longer a matter of debate,"[32] a recent official Brotherhood document stated. In that document, there is little insistence on the need for an Islamic state in Syria. Instead, the Ikhwan stress that they are committed to participating in the emergence of what they call a "modern state" partly inspired by Western norms of democracy. The "modern state" is "one which is built upon a contractual basis in which the contract stems from an aware and free will between the ruler and the people," "one where the respect and recognition of international charters and mandates on Human Rights form a primary backbone to acknowledging basic rights and freedoms for individual as well as societies," "one where Emergency Laws do not substitute normal civil conditions" and "one where alternation of government prevails and where free and fair elections determine the manner in which this alternation amongst all the people culminates." Above all, the document concludes, "the modern state is a plural state where arrays of views exist."[33] Recognizing "the other"—"religiously, politically, intellectually and culturally"[34]—is a key part of the Brotherhood's ideological discourse as it seeks to distance itself from the "discourse of crisis" of the late 1970s when its sometimes sectarian overtones frightened more than one member of Syria's religious minorities. In an effort to make this more concrete, the Ikhwan's leader throughout the 2000s even went as far as pledging that the organization would respect election results even if a woman or a Christian were chosen as President of Syria.[35]

While formally democratic, the Syrian Ikhwan's doctrine remains deeply embedded in the ideological substance of political Islam. This means that, to this day, it rejects the notion of secularism, associated in many Ikhwani members' minds with an attempt to counter forces linked to religion. In return, the organization does not call for the advent of a theocracy but rather for the emergence of an "Islamic civil state"—a system in which civil laws prevail in a state characterized by its Islamic culture. Zouheir Salem, the Muslim Brotherhood's ideologue, explained the difference between "Western democracies" and the organization's sought after "Islamic civil state". "The emphasis put by Western democracies on the notion of secularism is natural as it results from a long struggle between society and the Church," explained Zouheir Salem. "Since we never had such kind of struggle in Syria where Islamic law has long prevailed, we do not see any need to actively separate religion from politics." However, he concluded, "we are keen to insist that the Islamic nature of any future state in Syria would not deprive any religious minorities from their rights as the political system and laws would remain civil and members of such communities would therefore be treated as any other equal citizen."[36] The Syrian Brotherhood's ideological moderation is best reflected in its rejection of the Iranian theocracy and its adoption of the policies implemented by the AKP, a mildly Islamic party which has won a series of elections over the past decade in Turkey. "The AKP is neutral in the area of religion—neither does it impose religion upon Turkish citizens nor does it seek to fight religion— and for this reason we find it to be an excellent model," explained Ali Sadreddine al-Bayanouni. "We cannot impose any particular way of dressing on citizens. We do call for and encourage women to wear the *hijab* [Islamic veil] and to follow Islamic behaviour and action but individuals must be free to choose what they want."[37]

Women's rights, however, are one of the areas in which there remains a degree of ambiguity in Ikhwani discourse. While stressing women's "freedom of choice" and the importance of them being granted "equal rights", the Brotherhood's political project emphasized at the same time that "appropriate values must be put in place to ensure that men and women continue to fulfil the mutually complementary roles God has assigned to them"[38]—leaving the reader free to interpret what such "appropriate values" may be.

While coming from a moderate background, the Ikhwan's current ideologue, Zouheir Salem, also strikes ambiguous chords when detailing his thoughts on the relationship between God's sovereignty on Earth (*al-hakimiyya*) and the people's own sovereignty. "There is a shared sovereignty between these two components," he explained. "For us, God is sovereign on Earth and if we reach power we will therefore strive to implement His willingness, the Islamic law, as a working foundation for the Syrian state." The Ikhwan's ideologue, however, also stressed the primary importance of people's sovereignty. "We cannot enforce Islamic law […] it would have to be chosen in a referendum, thereby testing people's will." But there remained an ambiguity. What if a freely elected assembly chose to pass a law permitting something strictly prohibited by Islamic law, such as gambling or prostitution? "The details will come later but there are certain things we cannot legislate on and these are indeed two examples of it!" he replied, while stressing that "in Western democracy there also are red lines defined by a set of principles" and that, in the Muslim Brotherhood's case, "respect for Islamic values is our core basis."[39] Such remaining ambiguities over certain aspects of the Ikhwan's ideology might reflect the way in which the organization remains trapped by its long-time confrontation with the Syrian Ba'ath—devoting much energy and time to voicing its commitment to democracy, non-violence and dialogue while leaving key parts of its ideological programme unachieved.

Engaging with the Syrian opposition

The Muslim Brotherhood's doctrinal moderation should also be seen against the backdrop of the evolution of its relations with the Syrian Ba'ath. The organization's official rejection of violence voiced in the 2001 National Honour Charter reflected the possibility that, with the accession of Bashar al-Assad to power in June 2000, a new page in the bloody chapter of the Ikhwan's relations with the Ba'ath could be turned. In the late 1980s, already barely a decade after the Hama massacre, hope had been raised that a settlement of the dispute with the regime be in sight. A cable from the American Embassy in Damascus in February 1985 reported that a few hundred members of the Fighting Vanguard had returned to Syria after the regime negotiated with them through the mediation of Sa'id Shaban, a prominent Sunni Lebanese activist.[40] Throughout the 1990s, Hafiz al-Assad also proceeded to release prisoners who had been accused of belonging to the banned organization, most of them in jail since the late 1970s. Out of the estimated 10,000 political prisoners, the Syrian President released 2,864 inmates in December 1991, 600 in March 1992, 554 in November 1993, 1,200 in November 1995, 250 in 1998 and 600 in November 2000.[41] Relations also seemed to be markedly improving between the Syrian Ikhwan's leadership and the Ba'athist regime. In December 1995, the Syrian authorities allowed the former Ikhwani leader Sheikh Abdel Fatah Abu Ghuddah to return to Aleppo, his city of birth, on the condition that he occupied himself only with religious and educational work while giving up all political activities. Two years later, in February 1997, upon learning that Abu Ghuddah had just passed away, Hafiz al-Assad himself sent his condolences to the Islamic scholar's family, praising "a man who inspired respect during his lifetime,"[42] in return earning the gratitude of the bereaved family.

In this context, new mediation efforts between the Syrian Ba'ath and the Muslim Brotherhood's leadership were initiated. They were carried out through the intermediary of Amin Yagan, a former prominent Ikhwan member who had distanced himself from the organization at the height of the violent confrontation. The negotiations, however, soon proved fruitless as they came to reflect the regime's continued willingness to accentuate divisions within the Islamic movement, according to Muhammed Riyadh al-Shuqfah. When Amin Yagan was assassinated in ambiguous circumstances on 16 December 1998, the Ikhwan were quick to suspect the Ba'athist regime of having slain him and relations between the two parties deteriorated again.[43]

Upon Hafiz al-Assad's death in June 2000, brief hope was raised again that a leadership change at the top of the Syrian state apparatus would bring about a policy shift with regard to the fate of exiled Muslim

Brotherhood members. From London, the leader of the organization, Ali Sadreddine al-Bayanouni, suggested that Bashar al-Assad's coming to power could mean that the time had come for the Islamic movement to finally settle accounts with the Ba'athist regime. "Bashar has come into the weighty inheritance of decades of totalitarian rule; he does not bear responsibility for what happened in the past at Hama and in other places but only for what happens after he is sworn in [to office],"[44] he then declared. Early signs seemed to indicate a certain willingness on the part of the regime to write a new chapter in its relations with the Islamic organization. According to Eyal Zisser, when in April 2001 the young President promulgated a decree ordering the issuing of one-year passports destined to encourage Syrian citizens abroad to return home to settle their affairs with the authorities, many interpreted this as a gesture indicating to Muslim Brotherhood members that they would be allowed to return to Syria as individuals. If a few of them did so, most of them nonetheless refrained from believing in the regime's promises. They had heard stories of a handful of Muslim Brothers returning home only to be interrogated, harassed, tortured and, in certain cases, killed by the security services which asked them to fully confess to participation in the bloody events of the early 1980s. When, after a brief period of liberalization known as the "Damascus Spring", it became clear that Bashar al-Assad had no serious intention of reforming the political system he inherited from his father, the Ikhwan started to call again for an overthrow of the Ba'athist regime. Having rejected violence, they started to form coalitions in exile with political forces distinct from theirs as a means to increase pressure on the Syrian Ba'ath from abroad, in line with the moderate spirit of their 2004 political project.

Such willingness to engage in a political dialogue with other Syrian opposition forces, even forces ideologically antagonistic to them, was not new to the Ikhwan. A few months after the Hama massacre, in March 1982, Muslim Brotherhood leaders had joined Amin al-Hafiz's dissident Ba'athist faction as well as the Arab Socialist troops of Akram al-Hawrani in forming the National Alliance for the Liberation of Syria (NALS). The effort was short-lived, however, as the Iraqi location of the Alliance's headquarters and the bitter infighting resulting in Akram al-Hawrani's departure from it a few years later raised doubts over its sustainability as a credible opposition in exile. In the early 2000s, the Ikhwan expressed a renewed eagerness to join the dialogue carried out in the framework of the "Damascus Spring" by other Syrian opposition forces, including various prominent secular left-wing figures such as the Christian Michel Kilo and the Communist Riad al-Turk. Negotiations over a common opposition platform most notably culminated in October 2005 with the signing of the "Damascus Declaration", in which the Muslim Brotherhood became a key participant. The declaration emphasized a set of democratic principles which dozens of exiled parties and independent personalities from all political, religious and ethnic backgrounds had agreed on. This marked a breakthrough in Syria's political life, regardless of the foreign location of many of the signatories. According to Joshua Landis, "for the first time in decades, it seemed that Syria's bickering political parties, outspoken intellectuals and civil society groupings were finding common ground." "Kurdish, Arab and Assyrian nationalists put aside their ethnic squabbling" and "socialists, communists, liberals and Islamists were willing to unite over a single platform of democratic change and respect for one another," wrote Landis. The pact between opposition groups represented in particular a tremendous boost for the Syrian Ikhwan. "The coalition set off alarm bells for a regime that had struggled for decades to deny the Muslim Brotherhood a foothold in Syrian society."[45]

The regime was even more unsettled when one of its most prominent members, Abdel Halim Khaddam, defected from Damascus and left for Paris in December 2005, shortly before announcing an alliance with the Muslim Brotherhood in exile. While a long-time member of the Syrian Ba'ath, a regime in which he assumed the positions of Foreign Minister and then Vice President, Khaddam had opposed Bashar's inheritance of power from his father upon the latter's death in June 2000. According to a prominent opposition activist in Damascus, Khaddam's defection represented a "thorn in the side of the Bashar al-Assad regime, especially because he has the ability to speak knowledgeably about inner circle corruption and to appeal to some Sunnis."[46] These were indeed the primary reasons behind the Muslim Brotherhood's willingness to team up with Khaddam. According to the former Vice President, it was the Brotherhood that initiated the dialogue after Ali Sadreddine al-Bayanouni and Abdel Halim Khaddam had both taken part in a show broadcast on Al-Jazeera in January 2006.[47] The two parties agreed to form a joint opposition platform which culminated with the creation of the National Salvation Front (NSF) at a meeting in Brussels in March 2006.

For the Brotherhood, the alliance with the former Ba'athist Vice President represented a golden opportunity to regain a measure of relevance in the landscape of Syrian politics. According to Obeida Nahas, who was Bayanouni's political adviser, "this was a serious enterprise as we thought our partnership with a former prominent Ba'athist would attract more defections on the part of regime officials".[48] At the time, the belief that the NSF was gaining momentum was also shared by many inside the Ba'athist regime who expressed "fear"[49] at the emergence of such an alliance precisely when Bashar al-Assad's grip on power was being greatly weakened by the forced Syrian withdrawal from Lebanon and the threats of external intervention coming from Washington. For a time, it seemed as if the unlikely alliance was gathering momentum. Even though the "Damascus Declaration" group did not join the new coalition, the NSF managed to gather several independent personalities, small political parties and a sizeable proportion of Kurds who were won over through the NSF's commitment to end discrimination against them—though one of the community's representatives pointed out that they did not end up having a "great impact"[50] on the opposition platform. For the Muslim Brotherhood, the stakes were high. According to Joshua Landis, "by linking up with the secular Khaddam, the Muslim Brotherhood showcased an eagerness to prioritize political pragmatism over narrow ideology" and "it may have alleviated the anxieties of Alawis and military leaders who believed that the Muslim Brothers' first move in power would be to purge regime loyalists."[51]

As Ikhwani hopes for "regime change" in Damascus gradually died down, however, it became "embarrassing"[52] for the Brotherhood to remain associated with a former prominent Ba'athist figure who had participated in the massacre of its own members. A cable from the US Embassy dated from April 2006—only a few months after the opposition coalition was set up—read that since "the Syrian Muslim Brotherhood has more support in Syria than Khaddam, so it had more to lose from risking an alliance with him [...] Many accused Bayanouni and the Muslim Brotherhood of unprincipled opportunism for their willingness to ally themselves with a pillar of the Hafiz al-Assad regime that was responsible for the violent suppression of their movement in the early 1980s."[53] In January 2009, Ikhwani leaders suspended their opposition activities, officially in order to show support for the Syrian regime's popular anti-Israel stance during the war in Gaza. "While we, the Muslim Brotherhood, sided with the people of Gaza who were defending themselves, Khaddam was blaming Hamas for the escalation of violence and refused to freeze his opposition to Assad for the duration of the war,"[54] Ali Sadreddine al-Bayanouni explained. This, however, was described as a "mere pretext"[55] by Abdel Halim Khaddam, who claims that the real reason behind the Brotherhood's withdrawal from the NSF was in fact Ikhwani willingness to negotiate their way back to Damascus with the Syrian regime. This is confirmed by Obeida Nahas, according to whom a "mediation" between the Ikhwani leadership and the Ba'athist rulers took place some time between 2009 and 2010, although he insisted that "the talks never moved beyond the mediation phase."[56]

UPRISINGS IN SYRIA

REVENGE ON HISTORY

When the Arab Spring protests began to spread throughout the Middle East while focusing, at first, on Tunisia, Jordan and Egypt, Bashar al-Assad felt confident enough to declare his country immune from the uprisings and suggested that this was perhaps because his regime's "ideology, beliefs and causes" were in tune with the mood on Syria's streets. What the Syrian ruler failed to foresee, however, was that the historical narrative at play during the uprisings of the late 1970s would quickly resurface and that, when protests did erupt in March 2011, it would fuel them to the extent that they eventually exacted "revenge on history". "We will not let the massacres of 1982 be repeated!"[1] shouted protesters when the symbolic city of Hama was besieged by regime troops throughout June 2011. "Hafiz died and Hama didn't. Bashar will die and Hama won't,"[2] shouted a rebel to sum up the way in which awareness of past events fuelled what quickly became an unyielding determination to get rid of the Syrian Ba'ath once and for all.

But the historical continuity seemingly at play throughout the unfolding of the Syrian uprisings was not limited to the opposition. In a rhetorical twist echoing that of the late 1970s, early on the regime justified its crackdown on the protests by arguing that it had to uproot the "jihadist elements" and "gangs" supposed to be active in the demonstrations. Interestingly enough, Bashar al-Assad accused the Syrian Brotherhood by name of being behind the demonstrations—without evidence, it should be stressed, and despite the Ikhwan's long exile from Syria. "We've been fighting the Muslim Brotherhood since the 1950s and we are still fighting with them,"[3] he claimed in October 2011 to justify his crackdown on the protests. It seemed as if the regime's obsession with the Islamist group was once again coming to the surface. To back up their narrative, regime elements went as far as setting up a fake Syrian Muslim Brotherhood website account which would later claim responsibility for the terrorist attacks that ravaged Damascus in December 2011—a responsibility immediately rejected by the Ikhwan on their real website.[4]

The irony is that, while at that point in time the Syrian Brotherhood's role in the unfolding of the protests was actually marginal, its profile was to rise spectacularly shortly thereafter. The regime's simultaneous attempt at radicalizing the role played by Islam in the protests, so as to pose as the ultimate guarantor of the country's "stability" and "moderation", would indeed fuel a wave of radical Islam leaving the centre ground open to the Brotherhood's message. In parallel, the political and socioeconomic chaos emerging out of the increasingly violent confrontation between the regime and the opposition in early 2012 would provide the long sought-after opportunity for the Ikhwan to make a historical comeback at the forefront of the anti-regime struggle. But will its rising profile and the heavy price it paid for its unyielding opposition to the Ba'ath automatically pave the way for electoral success?

Fostering Islamic radicalization

When they started in March 2011, the Syrian uprisings were not bound to become markedly religious in tone and nature. At first, even though the country's numerous mosques and prayer leaders played a key role in mobilizing parts of the population, the significance Islam would subsequently take on was not immediately obvious. In Dar'a, a relatively small tribal city on the border next to Jordan where popular anti-regime rallies first started before quickly spreading to the rest of Syria, the start of the protests was linked to local issues and demands voiced by local inhabitants. One of the city's most influential clerics, Moti' al-Batin, explained the way in which the uprisings there evolved into becoming noticeably religious in nature. "It all started when a group of twenty children painted the slogan 'we want freedom' on the wall of a street before they were caught by police officers who sent them directly to jail where they received bad treatment," he recounted. "There had for long been dissatisfaction with the corrupt regional and local government led by the head of the local security services, Atif Najib, also the son of Bashar's aunt, but this was too much […] The children's parents were not allowed to get their kids back and, when fathers took matters into their hands and went to Atif Najib asking him to order their release, he literally told them: 'Forget about your children, make others and, if you're not able to do that, bring me your wives!'"[5]

The inhabitants of Dar'a soon poured into the streets in an effort to support the parents' call for justice and dignity. As mosques were the only places where public gatherings were allowed, they quickly became the focal point for protesters who marched throughout the city's streets immediately after Friday prayers. For this reason, however, mosques themselves quickly became the targets of the regime. "Soldiers came into each and every of the city's three mosques while randomly shooting at people and shouting 'Allah is bad',"[6] explained Moti' al-Batin, himself the imam of a local mosque before he was shot in the back by an army sniper and managed to flee to Jordan and then Turkey. Ever since, displaying their religious devotion has become a way for Syrian protesters to express their strong opposition to a regime often seen as too secular, if not downright atheist and impious. Signs of the growing importance Islam was to play in the unfolding of anti-regime protests then multiplied. In many of the country's cities, the title of the weekly protests held after Friday prayers changed from "We won't kneel" into "We won't kneel except before God." In addition, the men of religion, while leading the prayers, were often forced into taking a stand: either supporting the regime—in which they might have a vested interest—or using their sermons to incite the faithful to defy regime snipers and tanks. "Sheikhs have a role," confirmed a cleric active in the Syrian opposition in Hama. "In an area where people are scared, a sheikh in his sermon can encourage them to go out."[7]

As protests multiplied across Syria, and in the enthusiastic aftermath of the toppling of dictators in Tunisia, Egypt and Libya, many analysts started to predict the quick demise of Bashar al-Assad's regime. What they had not foreseen, however, was the regime's unique capacity to look into its own past in order to find the resources needed to tame the rebellion. Today, more than ever before, the Syrian regime, composed of a number of officers and politicians who have themselves, or through the experiences of their relatives, lived through the internal crisis of the late 1970s and early 1980s, is looking at the current uprisings through the lens of its own history. At that earlier time, the deadly cycle of sectarian retribution opposing radical Sunni militants to those seen as supporting the regime, namely the Christian and Alawi minorities, had paradoxically reinforced Hafiz al-Assad's grip on power. The country's minority communities, as well as those Sunnis who feared the inroads made by an increasingly radical Islamic opposition, had indeed rallied solidly behind the "lesser evil" represented by the Syrian President—whatever their distaste for his brutal methods and authoritarian tendencies. Ever since uprisings began to shake Syria again, Bashar al-Assad has been keen to use the lessons learned by his late father. In regime circles, it is now believed that, by deliberately sowing the poisonous seeds of sectarian resentment and Islamic extremism in today's Syria, the President will ultimately be able to pose as the authoritative guarantor of the country's unity and stability. It is, however, a highly toxic and risky gamble for a country sitting on a sectarian powder keg.

Homs, a city of 650,000 people strategically standing between Damascus and Hama, has over the past year and a half emerged as the regime's main laboratory for its dangerous sectarian experiments. There, the cycle of mutual retribution pitting the city's various religious communities against one another (the Sunni majority versus the Christian and Alawi minorities) offers a gloomy prospect of what the future of Syria could look like. Throughout early 2012, the army's shelling of the Baba Amr quarter, a stronghold of the primarily Sunni opposition, coupled with the cruelties carried out by pro-regime militias against its inhabitants, have ignited a dangerous dynamic doomed to transform the country's peaceful protests into a distinctively sectarian and violent struggle. Already, there are reports suggesting that over 10,000 local Christians—or 90 per cent of the city's Christian community—have fled Homs for fear that the predominantly Sunni rebels might take revenge for their tacit support of the regime. The city's Alawis, needless to say, have lived in daily fear of being killed at rebel checkpoints. A rebel in Homs who admitted having carried out several executions of local Alawis belonging to the security forces explained: "I have been arrested twice, I was tortured for 72 hours, they hung me by the hands until the joints in my shoulders cracked. They burnt me with hot irons. Of course, I want revenge!"[8]

Over the past year, the *shabiha* (or "ghosts") unleashed by the regime have emerged as its most efficient way of sowing sectarian resentment in Homs and other cities. These pro-regime thugs, overwhelmingly Alawi in their composition, are ready to do whatever it will take to uphold Bashar al-Assad's grip on power. "They behave in a very sectarian way," explained Walid Safour, a London-based human rights activist originally from the city of Homs. "They want to dominate Syria and to show the extent to which they and Bashar al-Assad are the only rulers of this country: when they catch a Sunni rebel, they often beat him up in the street, humiliating him and insulting his religion." Walid Safour, who was himself the victim of the *shabiha* when, in October 1980, his belongings were stolen and he was beaten up by such a group of thugs, gave details of the prominent role pro-regime militias have taken since the 2011 uprisings started: "In the past, the shabiha numbered 40,000, today they are soon likely to reach a quarter of a million as the Assad regime has asked every Alawi family to send at least one of their sons to these groups."[9] The link between these pro-regime militias and the Assad family ruling over the country is clear. For long tasked with carrying out the criminal activities of the Assad clan—from robbery and blackmail to assassinations and organized crime—the actions of the *shabiha* have lately become distinctively sectarian in nature. The provocations of these pro-regime Alawi militias, until recently led by Fawaz al-Assad, Bashar's own cousin, have fuelled such sectarian resentment that they have also radicalized the role played by Islam in the unfolding of protest.

The regime's multiple provocations have indeed unleashed a wave of radical Islam which, by its very nature, potentially threatens the Syrian revolution's initially inclusive and democratic message—thus also playing into the rulers' hands. A small but rapidly growing number of radicalized protesters have started to shout slogans calling for revenge against the country's minority communities, hailing the legacy of the controversial Ibn Taymiyya, most famously known for his rulings condoning the killing of the "infidel" Alawis. International media covering the Syrian conflict have reported the shouting of catch-phrases such as: "Christians to Beirut, Alawis to coffins."[10] More recent protests held throughout the country have also seen the advent of Adnan al-Aroor as an increasingly popular figure among some members of the opposition. A 73-year-old religious scholar based in Saudi Arabia whose sermons are watched by many Sunni Syrians on a TV channel, he famously warned in July 2011 those Alawis who participate in repression that they would be "minced in meat grinders" and their flesh would be "fed to the dogs".[11] Whatever the efforts made by opposition leaders of all hues to avoid derailing the course of the Syrian uprisings, the anti-regime protests, at first representing a social movement not putting forward any particular religious demands, are on the verge of turning into a distinctively Sunni "awakening".

This dynamic, in turn, combined with the increasing militarization of the Syrian opposition in the aftermath of the regime's brutal crackdown against Homs and others cities from early 2012 onwards, contributed to fuelling an anti-regime religious rhetoric increasingly associated with the use of force. Calling for jihad against the Ba'ath has, for instance, become a main rallying cry for the opposition inside Syria. "Those whose intentions are not for God, they had better stay home whereas if your intention is for God, then you go for jihad and you gain an afterlife and heaven,"[12] a rebel leader shouted in Aleppo in July 2012 when exhorting his followers to fight back against the occupation of the city by government troops. Many of the rebel fighting units which have sprung up throughout the country under the shadowy umbrella of the Free Syrian Army (FSA) are now of an Islamist bent. These include groups relying on a relatively moderate Islamist ideology, such as the Farouk Battalion in Homs and the Tawheed Brigades in Aleppo. But organizations with a more conservative, sometimes Salafist-jihadist agenda are growing in Syria as there is no end in sight to the stalemate between mainstream rebel groups and regime forces. The north-western and overwhelmingly Sunni region of Jebel al-Zawiyah, surrounding Idlib, has in particular witnessed the rapid expansion of such groups. Some, such as Suqour al-Sham, do not seem to have a sectarian agenda in mind yet.[13] But others, such as Ahrar al-Sham, have been criticized for targeting specifically Alawis and Christians.[14] "The more time the revolution extends, the stronger the salafists will be," argued one activist who went on to explain that "each month that goes by, the movement turns more Islamic and more radical."[15]

Of these radical groups, it is the al-Qaeda affiliated Jabhat al-Nusrah that caught the attention of most Western media.[16] Its creation, announced in January 2012, was followed by a wave of suicide bombings claimed by the organization, which struck at the heart of Aleppo and Damascus. Shortly thereafter, a statement from Ayman al-Zawahiri, Usama Bin Laden's successor to the helm of al-Qaeda, appealed to Muslims across the region and particularly in Syria to raise the banner of holy war against the Syrian Ba'ath.[17] The Jabhat al-Nusrah quickly became highly effective in its violent and sometimes spectacular campaign against the regime. A study of its reach and capabilities showed that the organization increased the pace of its activities from seven attacks in March 2012 to sixty-six in June of the same year while concentrating the bulk of its efforts on Aleppo and Damascus.[18] The Jabhat al-Nusrah also came to embody the merger of the trends analysed in Chapter 7: not only is it successful in recruiting the skilled jihadists who, after 2003, made their way through Damascus to fight the American occupiers of Iraq with the blessing of the Syrian security services, but it also seems increasingly likely to attract the former Syrian members of the Fighting Vanguard who later joined the global jihad in the 1980s and patiently waited for the right time to return home to settle scores with the Ba'ath regime.

Significantly enough, this trend embodies precisely what the regime had been looking for to crush the wider protest movement while blaming its brutal repression on the existence of terrorist networks in Syria. This was made clear when, in February 2012, and as the government forces' siege of Homs was intensifying, the Syrian security forces deliberately released Abu Mus'ab al-Suri, a former jihadist of the Fighting Vanguard turned al-Qaeda ideologue, who had been in prison in Damascus since 2005.[19] The release of a figure whose custody for seven years in a Syrian prison probably did little to moderate his radicalism would, in due course, play into the regime's long-time argument that the rebellion is led by "Islamic terrorists" and "affiliates of al-Qaeda".

The Brotherhood's rebirth from ashes

While the painful stalemate between rebel groups of all hues and the Syrian regime lingered, the increasing political void left by the chaos came to represent, for the Muslim Brotherhood, a golden opportunity to make a historical comeback at the forefront of Syrian politics and society. But this was not a self-evident development, given the Ikhwan's long struggle for relevance from exile and the harsh repression of their social base at home. Law No. 49, punishing by death any known members of the Muslim Brotherhood, effectively prevented the organization from participating in the unfolding of the protests when they erupted in March 2011. In fact, its influence on the ground was at first considered so irrelevant that, when groups started to organize meetings in Doha in early September 2011 to negotiate the creation of a unified opposition umbrella, the Muslim Brotherhood was excluded from the talks.

However, the organization's leader, Muhammed Riyadh al-Shuqfah, had warned, "In the outside, nothing can happen without the Muslim Brotherhood."[20] Quickly, most opposition leaders came to the realization that, if the Ikhwan's presence inside Syria was indeed limited, their ideological influence, history of unyielding opposition to the Ba'ath, significant financial resources and organizational capacities would nonetheless make them an essential future component of any post-Assad settlement. Eventually, the Syrian Brotherhood was therefore invited to participate at a meeting held in Istanbul in early October 2011, which set up the Syrian National Council (SNC)—a body also comprising groups such as the secular Damascus Declaration, the mildly Islamist National Bloc, some Kurdish factions, a myriad of independent figures and representatives of the Christian and Alawi communities.

For the Ikhwan, much was at stake. From the outset, the Brotherhood had been targeted by the regime's rhetoric, according to which it was behind the instigation of the protests and the use of violence—despite its repeated denials and assertions that "no one owns the Syrian uprisings".[21] Remembering the harsh consequences they had suffered in the past from their lonely struggle against the regime, the Ikhwan saw it as more fit to act and speak within the framework of a broad-ranging opposition umbrella than as a single group. "Whatever we do and say in public," interviewed Syrian Brothers like to stress, "it is on behalf of the SNC."[22] The SNC, despite internal divisions between its secular and Islamist components and ideological squabbling over issues such as Kurdish autonomy and international intervention, rapidly gained support as the most comprehensive Syrian opposition platform. In April 2012, the Friends of Syria group comprising nations hostile to the Assad regime recognized the body as a legitimate representative of the Syrian people. With time, however, the SNC became the target of left-wing militants who accused it of being a mere "liberal front for the Muslim Brotherhood."[23] "The Brotherhood took the whole council!"[24] complained a small group of influential opposition figures when they broke away from the SNC.

A close look at the Ikhwan's role within the opposition, however, suggests that, if they wield great influence, it is nonetheless misleading to imply that they unilaterally took control. Indeed, Ikhwani representation inside the SNC's decision-making bodies does not, as such, exceed that of any other political blocs. As of September 2012, of the 310 members of the council, only twenty are Muslim Brothers and, if they are also represented by Farouk Tayfour as deputy head and member of the Executive Committee, they are only three out of thirty-three on the General Secretariat. The council's leader, at the time of writing Abdul Baseet Sieda, is not a Muslim Brother; nor was his predecessor, the secular Burhan Ghalioun. Why, then, are the Ikhwan often perceived by outsiders as the power behind the throne?

The answer lies partly in the confusion some observers make when analysing exiled Islamic political groups. As will be shown later, the landscape of political Islam has become highly heterogeneous and complex since the Brotherhood was forced out of Syria in the early 1980s. Many opposition figures classified as "Islamists", such as Imad Eddine al-Rashid or Haitham al-Maleh, actually do not belong to the Ikhwan and are even personally and politically hostile to them, if not ideologically so. In addition, the SNC also includes a group of former members of the Muslim Brotherhood who distanced themselves from the organization—out of ideological divergence and of lack of proper political opportunities—and have regrouped into a National Action Group for Syria often confused with the Ikhwan in media coverage. All in all, it can be estimated that the influence of Islamists of all hues over the SNC comprises 35 per cent of the council's membership and that the Brotherhood accounts for less than half of this proportion.

That said, it is fair to argue that the Ikhwan is the opposition's most powerful component. This is mainly because, whatever its history of internal divisions, the group has remained united in the uprisings—not a small achievement given the permanent shifts in loyalty seemingly gripping Syrian politics to this day. Such unity has, in turn, allowed the Ikhwan to act as a coherent, disciplined and organized unit within the SNC and, therefore, to wield great influence over its policies and decisions. "We bicker while the Brotherhood works,"[25] a liberal member of the council summed it up with frustration. While on the one hand the

Ikhwan deliberately did not put up a candidate for the chair of the SNC so as to not play into the regime's argument that the opposition is dominated by Islamists, they have, on the other, been keen to increase their representation within two of the council's most significant offices: military affairs and development aid. In turn, Brotherhood control over these two divisions—funded on a weekly basis through a purported $1 million regularly transferred to SNC bank accounts by outside donors[26]—meant that the Ikhwan was able to slowly start rebuilding its social base in Syria.

The Islamist organization helped funding, setting up and running camps for Syrian refugees fleeing the bloodshed to Turkey, Lebanon, and Jordan—where the group also counts on logistical and financial support from the local branches of the Muslim Brotherhood. The chaos in Syria also enabled the Ikhwan to reactivate their long-dormant networks throughout the country in order to give much needed medical assistance, food and money to the inhabitants of the besieged cities of Homs, Aleppo and Hama. Even activists long suspicious of the Syrian Brotherhood's intentions have started to accept the financial help offered to them by members of the Islamist organization. "I approached them and they instantly gave me 2,000 euros when I asked for help [...] and I am not even Ikhwan,"[27] recounted an activist in the region of Idlib. There are, of course, also many non-Brotherhood groups and individuals providing relief and assistance to Syrian activists, often benefiting from the donations of wealthy Syrian expatriates, Western organizations and countries such as Saudi Arabia and Qatar. But most are situated locally, limited to one domain, and very few have the national reach and organizational capacities of the Syrian Ikhwan. "There is effectively no Law No. 49 any more," said Obeida Nahas, an active opposition figure long close to the Brotherhood's leadership. "Over the past few months, the Brothers have been very active in recovering their civilian base: the revolution enabled them to reconnect with Syrian society."[28]

But keeping in touch with the Syrian street also meant that the Brotherhood had to adapt its approach and thinking as events unfolded on the ground. When, in early 2012, the regime shifted its response to the uprisings from a security to a military option, many militants inside Syria started to organize self-defence brigades—most of which regrouped under the banner of the Free Syrian Army (FSA). The militarization of the Syrian revolt could well have caught the Muslim Brotherhood off guard and reopened the old wounds of internal divisions. After all, the debate over armed struggle had split the Ikhwan throughout the 1980s and had been painfully closed with the reintegration of the "Hama clan" into the organization in the early 1990s and the signing of two documents in the 2000s stating the group's renunciation of violence to overthrow the Syrian Ba'ath. But, instead of proving a contentious topic, the Brotherhood's active support for the FSA and the fighters on the ground actually came smoothly, if not rather belatedly, at a meeting of the organization in late March 2012. The uprisings, against all odds, seem to have strengthened the Ikhwan's internal cohesion and discipline rather than fostering new divisions. This was certainly not a development expected by most outside observers given the tensions that rose as a result of an internal party election in July 2010, witnessing the advent of a leadership dominated by the "Hama clan".

Then, in the pre-Arab Spring mindset of the time, the election of the Hamawite Muhammed Riyadh al-Suqfah prompted fears that the return of the Hamawites to leadership would signal an ideological shift questioning Bayanouni's "moderate" legacy and would therefore prove to be a "setback" for the organization. Since then, of course, the meaning assumed by a word such as "moderation" has profoundly changed: would it be "moderate", today, to call for negotiations with a regime killing its own people, or "hard-line" to refuse all dialogue with a state trying to divide the opposition and rule? In the early context of the Syrian uprisings, few would now agree with that. Shuqfah's election, therefore, was perhaps the Brotherhood's single luckiest event in decades: when the time came for Syrians to rise as one man against the Ba'ath, the Islamist organization was not to be caught negotiating with the regime. At the time, however, the return of the "Hama clan" to leadership sent an uncompromising message to Damascus not shared by everyone in the organization: the time for mediation was over and the Brotherhood would resume its unyielding opposition to the Ba'ath—the truce with the regime having, for Shuqfah, ended the day the Israeli war on Gaza did. The ideological squabbling that then began between the Brotherhood's most uncompromising members and those more prone to dialogue with the regime quickly took the form of resurgent regional, clan and personal divisions between the "Hama clan" now in charge and the "Aleppo faction" it decided to sideline. Prominent Aleppine figures such as Ali Sadreddine al-Bayanouni and Zouheir Salem were marginalized from a leadership controlled by Muhammed Riyadh al-Shuqfah, who would count on the support of the powerful Farouk Tayfour as deputy leader, Muhammed Hatem al-Tabshi as head of the Shura Council and Moulhem al-Droubi as spokesman—all important figures close to the "Hama clan".

But, if it was fortunate for the Ikhwan to have been led by uncompromising figures precisely when the powerful wave of the Arab Spring reached Syrian shores, it also meant that, at the very beginning at least, the Brotherhood faced this historical event disunited and disorganized. Quickly, however, the Hamawite leadership realized the unprecedented importance of the uprisings in Syria: this was something long awaited by all its members and the divisions had been due more to the regime's divide and rule policy than to a real divergence on topics of state and society. To face a regime fighting for survival, the Syrian Brotherhood would, this time, need to be strongly united and disciplined. In a gesture of appeasement towards the "Aleppo faction", Muhammed Riyadh al-Shuqfah restructured the Ikhwani leadership in late March 2011. Ali Sadreddine al-Bayanouni was made the organization's first deputy—thereby formally exercising more authority than Farouk Tayfour, its second deputy—and Zouheir Salem became the organization's spokesman. Working for unity within Muslim Brotherhood ranks also embodied a shared sense among all members that the uprisings finally represented the historic event they had so long waited for: Syrians were finally taking revenge for the brutal crushing of the Islamist uprisings in the 1980s and the time would soon come for the Ikhwan to make their formal comeback at the forefront of Syrian politics and society—not only in Hama or Aleppo but also in the rest of the country.

The events on the ground prompted all members of the organization to rethink their approach to the regime in a fairly homogeneous way. On the one hand, the Ikhwan agreed they would not negotiate with the Ba'ath regime as long as repression continued and Bashar al-Assad remained in power. When, in late October 2011, the Brotherhood's leadership was made an offer by Iranian businessmen close to the regime in Tehran to form and lead a transitional government in Syria but with Assad remaining as President, the idea was outright rejected by the organization. On the other hand, it was decided that the Ikhwan would only endorse armed struggle when it became an absolute necessity and then only through a careful framework, so as not to repeat past mistakes.

This meant that, for quite some time, the Brotherhood's leadership insisted on the need for the Syrian revolution to remain peaceful and rejected growing calls to act violently against the regime—something the organization's most uncompromising figures also stressed.[29] Such caution, however, was not necessarily appreciated by those outside the group. A left-wing activist encountered in February 2012 put it this way: "We are liberals but we are more hard-line than the Ikhwan, it's crazy!"[30] Another opposition figure explained: "The Muslim Brotherhood is still busy trying to clean up its name, it has a major complex with violence."[31] When, in late March 2012, the Brotherhood finally endorsed the idea of supporting the FSA and providing weapons and funds to Syrian rebels on the ground, it did so under the collective framework of the SNC and stressed its commitment to a "democratic Syria" respecting the "rights of all ethnic and religious communities" in a published document—which, in a bid to stress the Ikhwan's inclusive message, did not include a single reference to Islam.[32]

Rhetorically, Brotherhood leaders stressed the coherence of their support for the FSA by insisting that "the right of self-defence does not contravene with the principle of the peacefulness of the revolution."[33] On the ground, however, some observers started to draw parallels with the situation prevailing in the early 1980s when fighting units affiliated with the Ikhwan's "military branch" flourished throughout the country. Figures suggest that, at the time of writing, the Muslim Brotherhood already supported close to 20 per cent of the fighting units throughout the country and up to 60–65 per cent of those located in the region of Homs—leading to accusations that the organization was now "administering the revolution".[34] It is also undeniable that the Ikhwan gave the bulk of their logistical and financial support to Islamist fighters. Syrian Brothers explain this by insisting that they prefer to provide help to their relatives and trusted contacts, who often happen to be fellow Islamists, rather than to unknown militants who could either be extremists or mobsters. "We have on the ground our networks," confirmed a prominent member of the Ikhwan, "and we make sure they don't distribute arms to those who are not within the streamline of the revolution."[35] A commander of the FSA summed it up this way: "al-Qaeda finances the jihadists, the Muslim Brotherhood funds the moderates."[36] In turn, the seeming caution of the Syrian Brotherhood when it comes to arming rebels and its attempts to strike a middle ground between secular groups and radical jihadists underline the extent to which its comeback as a social and political actor is felt not only in exiled SNC meetings but also at home.

Back to Syria: opportunities and challenges

In a reflection of its growing profile, the Syrian Brotherhood announced, at a four-day internal conference held in mid-July 2012 that it would create a political party to run for elections once Bashar al-Assad is gone. "We are ready for the post-Assad era," announced a prominent member of the Ikhwan, "we have plans for the economy, the courts, politics".[37] Critics of the organization have long pointed to its relatively modest electoral showings in the 1950s and early 1960s to suggest that it would score if allowed to compete in free and fair elections.[38] But recent Ikhwani estimates suggest that the Brotherhood's political platform could well gather as much as 25 to 30 per cent of the votes—hence giving the Islamist group enough seats, in a parliamentary system, to form and lead a coalition government.[39] And, in fact, there is evidence that, if the Ikhwan were allowed to return to Syria, they would certainly score many more votes than they did in the past.

Those analysts who forecast such a trend often point to the "Islamist Spring" which followed the toppling of secular autocrats in Egypt and Tunisia as an explanatory factor, suggesting the same would certainly happen with Syria. The seeds of the Islamist victories in these countries are indeed present, at least to a certain extent, in Damascus: the long history of Islamist opposition to autocratic secular rule, the seeming failure of leftist parties to address the concerns of the religious corners of society, or, again, the exponential growth of "poverty belts" around urban areas traditionally prone to vote for conservative parties. But there are other factors, all specific to Syria, which suggest that the Ikhwan would improve their electoral performance by comparison with their past experience—at least in the medium and long term.

One factor is that the Brotherhood would probably fare much better in Syria's countryside nowadays than it did in the past. In the 1950s and early 1960s, the organization's electoral reach was limited to the "big cities", essentially Aleppo, Damascus, Hama and Homs. During the uprisings it led in the late 1970s, the Muslim Brotherhood found its social base, once again, in the urban centres of Syria (see Chapter 3).

With time, however, the regime's pro-rural economic programme—which had helped Hafiz al-Assad gain the support of the countryside in the early 1980s—turned into mildly liberalized policies. In addition, throughout the 1990s and 2000s, the Ba'athist state seemed increasingly unable to cope with the harsh weather and the difficult socioeconomic conditions encountered in the countryside Growing rural dissatisfaction with the regime meant that, when the uprisings began to erupt in Syria in the framework of the Arab Spring, they were first and foremost located in the countryside before spreading to the cities. Rejecting the Ba'ath Party could therefore mean, for the inhabitants of rural Syria, embracing its historical rival: the Syrian Brotherhood. Such a trend would only be reinforced by the organization's recent inroads in the countryside. Sources within the Brotherhood indeed indicate that the Ikhwan had been trying to gather support for their cause in the countryside even before the current uprisings erupted. This is partially because the regime's security scrutiny was always less intense in rural areas, which made them more suited to underground activity. But, perhaps most importantly, this is also a by-product of the Islamist struggle of the early 1980s, when many members of the Brotherhood fled harsh repression in Hama and Aleppo to the rural periphery of these cities.

Critics of the Ikhwan who downplay the chances of Brotherhood success in a post-Assad election also suggest that the country's business community would be "more likely to ally itself with non-Islamist groups"[40] than with the Ikhwan. But, in fact, significant parts of the business class were already supportive of the Brotherhood throughout the 1950s and 1960s—despite the populist tone of the Ikhwan's "Islamic socialism"—and some businessmen even came to finance Islamist networks in the late 1970s (see Chapter 3). In a post-Assad Syria, that trend would only be likely to intensify as many exiled members of the Syrian Brotherhood have been active, over the past thirty years, in setting up business networks throughout the region. The challenge, here, will be to conquer the heart of the Damascene business class which has been co-opted by the regime for the past thirty years and which has been out of the Brotherhood's reach since the split of its "Damascus wing" in the late 1960s. There are indications, however, that the Ikhwan—and in particular the organization's youth—might be increasingly successful at making inroads within the Damascus merchant class, in particular the part affiliated with the religious Zayd movement active in the capital.

The Islamist organization is also well equipped to deal with regional divides typical of Syrian politics. In the past, the Ikhwan teamed up with the People's Party, an Aleppo-based pro-business platform, and this allowed the Islamist organization to increase its popularity in the northern metropolis and to double its participation in government, where it was represented by a Muslim Brother and by a sympathizer of the Ikhwan who was also a member of the People's Party (see Chapter 2).

But, perhaps most significantly, what could put the Syrian Brotherhood back under the electoral spotlight is its unique organizational capacity to run a coherent and nationwide campaign without shifts in loyalty of the sort to be expected in recently formed political groups. Some have, of course, predicted, on a regular basis, the breakup of the Ikhwan into two distinct movements. While there is indeed a history of divisions within the organization—and in particular, between the "Aleppo faction" and the "Hama clan" until recently—they were more the product of ideological and then clan quarrels resulting from the Ba'ath regime's repression than of diverging visions of the state, society, the economy or politics in general. Nothing, therefore, indicates that these two groups would split if the Brotherhood was allowed to go back to Syria and run for elections; nor would it be in their collective interest. There is, in addition, an element often overlooked in analyses of Muslim Brotherhood movements throughout the Middle East: the Ikhwan's political education teaches their members to be, first and foremost, loyal to the *tanzim* (the organization). Institutional belonging is therefore a key component of Ikhwani culture—especially in Syria where all members, whatever their ideological and regional inclination, are bound by the tears and blood of the Ba'athist repression. "It's normal that people sometimes get a little bit emotional or have personal feelings about things," explained a prominent Syrian Brother, "but, overall, respect dominates".[41] Of course, there is a price to pay for Ikhwani unity. When, as sometimes happens, some internal reforms or policy proposals put forward by the leadership alienate one or the other group—for ideological or clan-based reasons—they have to be put aside for the sake of unity.

At the same time, however, it is precisely this loyalty to the *tanzim* and, as a consequence, the Syrian Brotherhood's inherent difficulty in reinventing and reforming itself that increasingly seems to frustrate its younger members. Indeed, what observers who analyse the Syrian Ikhwan through the lens of the traditional division between the "Hama clan" and the "Aleppo faction" tend to overlook is the growing generation gap between leaders who were already in charge in the late 1970s but still run the organization and the group's ambitious youth. This reflects two of the Syrian Brotherhood's most pressing challenges. On the one hand, the youth's frustration underlines the extent to which a generational handover is, in the short term, vitally needed if the Ikhwan are to survive. With only 20 per cent of Brotherhood members under the age of forty-five, according to internal estimates, a challenge for the organization will be to ensure its generational renewal—something which will only be effective if young and talented conservative politicians also feel represented at the leadership level.

On the other hand, the wide age gap between the organization's leaders and its youngest members has also made the old-fashioned nature of the Brotherhood more obvious to some. Elderly leaders with a troubled past, clan divisions and a sometimes rigid ideology, played a role in fostering discontent in certain corners of the Ikwhani youth. "The Brotherhood's autocratic, tribal structure has become antiquated and ineffective," explained a Syrian Brother in his mid-forties, who fled Syria for Turkey thirty years ago. "The old generation is focused on leadership, we're focused on solutions,"[42] he stressed. Two broad trends emerged out of the Ikhwani youth as a result of its frustration. One wing is determined to remain within the Brotherhood's fold but wishes, in exchange for its loyalty, that the current leadership engages in serious reforms and promotes capable young members to leadership positions. The other wing seems, for its part, to have already lost patience—to the extent that some of its members might soon split from the Ikhwan and act, in due course, as the organization's most serious competitors.

Some even suggest that such a split has in fact already occurred when Ahmed Ramadan, an active opposition leader originally from Aleppo and now based in Bahrain, formed the National Action Group for Syria in February 2011, an important sub-group within the Syrian National Council (SNC) gathering young Syrian Brothers and other conservative activists. "Yes, there is a generational break within the Ikhwan," recognized the young, media-savvy Syrian Brother Obeida Nahas, who is also the director of the Levant Institute, a think tank in London, and a prominent member of Ahmad Ramadan's sub-group. "The National Action Group represents a new generation of conservative technocrats working on national projects for the future of Syria." He also insisted that "the ideological component [in the new generation] is almost non-existent."[43] Another young Syrian Brother, Hassan al-Hachimi, confirmed that the group came out of the frustration felt by the Ikhwan's "second generation" at the traditional way in which the "old leadership" had handled the organization since the Syrian uprisings. "It's not a split yet from the Muslim Brotherhood as some of our members are still part of the organization," he insisted, adding that "it is also not taking place within the Ikhwani framework [...] It's about doing something different [...] Our ambition is to be more political and less ideological than the Muslim Brotherhood but also more inclusive and democratic."[44] With a conservative, nationalist and pro-business rhetoric, allied with a social base expected to be strong in Aleppo where most of its activists originally come from, the National Action Group seems to want to replicate the successful pattern followed by the People's Party in the past.

In addition to possible splits within their ranks along generational lines, the Syrian Ikhwan are also faced with a fierce political and ideological competition from other Islamist actors who, as well as seeking to occupy the middle ground claimed by the Brotherhood, are also deeply hostile towards the organization. Some argue that, inside the country, the *ulama* are best positioned to increase their political influence in a post-Assad Syria. However, the men of religion are divided between those who have been co-opted by a Ba'ath regime in which they have a vested interest and those who have lent their support to the Syrian protesters.[45] Others argue that, outside Syria, the London-based Movement for Justice and Development (MJD) is increasingly acting as an efficient challenger to the Muslim Brotherhood's hegemony over the opposition in exile.

Formed in late 2005, the MJD was considered as early as 2009 as "small but politically connected and increasingly active"[46] in a cable from the American Embassy in Damascus. Led by Anas and Malik al-Abdeh, the sons of Muhammed al-Abdeh, a former prominent member of the Syrian Ikhwan's "Damascus wing", the MJD could at first glance be mistaken for representing the "second generation" of Issam al-Attar's disciples. This, however, is denied both by the MJD leaders and by al-Attar's closest associate, Muhammed Hawari, who insists that "even though we share common roots the fruits are different."[47] The founders of the MJD, for their part, are keen to emphasize that the creation of their group represents a triple break from the Muslim Brotherhood:

generational, ideological and organizational. "The Syrian Ikhwan has a fundamentally undemocratic way of operating," explained Malik al-Abdeh. "The same leaders have been in charge for decades: some of them even have a history of violence and are responsible for the exile of thousands of people in the early 1980s." The co-founder of the MJD even went further: "on the top of that, the Muslim Brotherhood is a very rigid and hierarchical organization operating in secrecy as freemasons with an interdiction to formulate criticism of the leadership."[48]

It is against this backdrop that the MJD insists it is more of a "network" than a "political party" strictly speaking: its founders are committed to quietly and progressively convincing Syrian elites of the MJD's pragmatic agenda. Ideologically, the organization sees itself in line with the Islamo-conservative Turkish AKP Party. "Our ambition is to emulate the success of the AKP in Turkey," Malik al-Abdeh explained. "Our members may be religiously devout or hold conservative views with regards to the role of religion, society and state but they want to be successful in politics without having to hold the narrow-religious view of Muslim Brotherhood members."[49] Despite its small size and the relatively young age of its members, the MJD has been increasingly successful at penetrating the core of exiled Syrian politics. When the Damascus Declaration group was formed in October 2005, Anas al-Abdeh was nominated as its chief coordinator. Very soon, however, the competition between the Ikhwan and the MJD was felt on both sides. "The Muslim Brotherhood adopted a very hostile attitude towards us right from the beginning," claimed Malik al-Abdeh.

But the reverse also seems to have been true. When, in late 2005, the Syrian Ikhwan expressed willingness for closer cooperation with the Damascus Declaration umbrella, they were faced with difficulties as the leader of the MJD, Anas al-Abdeh, then also the coordinator of opposition activities, seemed quite reluctant. According to a cable from the US Embassy in Damascus in November 2009, "the MJD does not enjoy a cooperative relationship with the Muslim Brotherhood." "As the Damascus Declaration has grown abroad, the MJD has tried to take an increasingly active role and endeavoured to prevent Muslim Brotherhood members from being elected to any Damascus Declaration committees," the dispatch read. "With the Damascus Declaration's increased exposure internationally, competition for influence is fuelling conflict between the two groups."[50] For a time, the Syrian Brotherhood must have felt

relieved as the MJD came under fire for having accepted "US government money," according to an article published by the *Washington Post*
in April 2011. "The whole story blew out of proportion," remembered
Malik al-Abdeh, who went on to explain that "we never hid the fact that
the Democracy Council had been financing the MJD-linked Barada
TV." According to him, the episode is now behind the MJD and one
could even argue that it might have, in fact, helped publicize its activities. "In the end, it worked to our advantage," argued Malik al-Abdeh.
"We became known and more Syrians became interested by our TV
programmes—some of which are now very popular since the advent of
the Syrian revolution."[51]

The MJD, in addition, recovered some of its political strength over
the past few months by capitalizing on the networks it has for long been
seeking to establish with mildly Islamist and conservative personalities
also opposed to the Brotherhood's perceived hegemony over the opposition. From Radwan Ziadeh to Imad al-Din al-Rachid and others, they
are part of the new generation of activists who left Syria only recently
and consider Islam as a cultural framework within which to define the
future Syrian state. While they put forward Islamic and democratic
values, they clearly refuse to be associated with the Muslim Brotherhood.[52] This, in turn, could reflect one other significant hurdle for the
Ikhwan: bridging the gap of mistrust with a Syrian elite long accus-
tomed to the regime's rhetoric depicting the organization as inherently
violent and radical. To counter this claim, the Brotherhood will have to
ensure a transition as smooth as possible from being an underground
political and social actor, with all its culture of secrecy, to being a visible
group whose leadership and membership are open to all Syrians. Eventually, this could even attract the multiple political and social actors
currently emerging in rebel-held enclaves of Syria and starting to run
these areas independently, away from the regime's scrutiny.

EPILOGUE

In recent decades, the "Muslim Brotherhood" has been widely perceived as a homogeneous movement putting forward a rigid ideology irrespective of the Middle Eastern country in which it operates. But a closer look at the Syrian Brotherhood's history and social base suggests that, for all the apparent similarities among the Ikhwan's various branches, there are also significant differences, for each is shaped by a different sociopolitical context and national culture. In the case of Syria's Muslim Brotherhood, it could even be argued that the organization was always more a Syrian party than simply an offshoot in Damascus of the wider Ikhwani movement. Indeed, it seems as if its political history, social composition and ideology have been more informed by the evolution of the country's peculiar sociopolitical and geographical landscape than by the rigid doctrine inherited from Hassan al-Banna more than eighty years ago.

The story of the Syrian Brotherhood's emergence is quite telling of the organization's fundamentally local origins. While its organizational structure was set up on the model of the Egyptian Ikhwan in the wake of Syria's independence from France, and personal and ideological ties also linked the two movements, the actual social and intellectual roots of the Syrian Brotherhood are found in much earlier times. The organization's original leaders were deeply inspired, both in their political practice and in their ideological leaning, by the "Salafiyya" trend in Damascus—a nineteenth-century reformist movement whose call for the adaptation of Islamic thought and practices to the evolving circumstances of the modern world led its supporters to embrace constitution-

201

alism and political liberalism. But this did not mean that the Syrian Brotherhood was going to put forward a progressive doctrine, for its social base was in the conservative constituencies of the Islamic clubs and societies which had flourished during the inter-war period. French control of education and the introduction of secular reforms did little to appease a populist tone eventually echoed by the Syrian Brotherhood's rhetoric upon its foundation. The peculiar intellectual and political background against which the Syrian organization was created ultimately meant that, in contrast to its Egyptian sister, the local Brotherhood would embrace early on the game of politics in its contemporary sense—abiding by the rules of parliamentary democracy, forming political parties and engaging in compromises.

The Syrian Brotherhood's local roots, however, meant that it also drew on more radical strands of Syrian Islamic thought. Damascus had been home to Ibn Taymiyya, a religious scholar influential in thirteenth- and fourteenth-century Syria who is often, though not uniquely, remembered for his literalist interpretation of the Qur'an and for his *fatwa* condoning the killing of the "infidel" Alawis. The memory of his teachings was revived by the 1963 takeover of the political system by the Ba'ath Party, a secular political platform which the Alawis rapidly came to dominate. These aspects, combined with the growing frustration felt by the Sunni urban middle class at the new regime's pro-rural bias, socialist programme, replacement of elites and ideological failure, all contributed to fuelling a wave of support for the Islamic opposition. The Syrian Brotherhood rapidly gained support as the opposition's most comprehensive and powerful component. Yet, despite the inclusive legacy of the organization's early participation in politics, the protest movement led by the Ikhwan in the 1970s was not immune from a rampant sectarian undertone aimed at the rulers' minority background.

There was something profoundly "Syrian" about the Brotherhood's radicalization. Such a process indeed resulted, at least partially, from a leadership crisis which, in the late 1960s, had pushed its "Damascus wing", the most moderate, to split from the rest of the organization— thereby stressing the extent to which the regional factor, always key in Syrian politics, was also part of the Syrian Brotherhood's development. The roots of the crisis were manifold and ideology, as such, was not a significant factor. But the result nonetheless had profound consequences for the organization: when the opportunity for a confrontation with the

Ba'ath arose in the late 1970s, its most moderate members would not be there to influence the group's choices. The increasingly radical bent assumed by the Brotherhood was also the product of a more regional phenomenon which had its roots in Sayyid Qutb's thought and found its first concrete application in Syria through the deeds of Marwan Hadid. Even though he was originally a Syrian Brother, the jihadist ambitions Hadid had charted for the Brotherhood were, at the time, not shared by the group's leadership, who quickly decided to sideline him. When he was murdered by regime forces in 1976, however, he became a martyr and his views spread more widely through local Islamic circles—to the extent that some vowed to take revenge for his death.

Small but violent cells affiliated with "Marwan Hadid's group", which would later become al-Tali'a al-Muqatila or the "Fighting Vanguard", spread throughout the country with the aim of pushing the whole Islamic movement into armed confrontation with a Ba'ath regime deemed to be infidel. At first, the jihadist platform acted independently from the Brotherhood's leadership and without its consent. But the rapidly growing popularity of some of its charismatic leaders, such as Adnan Uqlah, ultimately meant that members of the Ikhwan also started to join the jihadist group and thereby pushed the two organizations closer together. For the Brotherhood's leadership, the rapprochement with al-Tali'a was also inspired by a dose of political opportunism as, in the late 1970s and early 1980s, the struggle against the Ba'ath had reached its apex and the regime seemed about to implode. Of course some, within the Brotherhood's "Hama clan" in particular, may have sympathized with the kind of ideology put forward by al-Tali'a at that time, but they were first and foremost national politicians, not holy warriors or jihadist ideologues.

This distinction, in turn, was definitely made clear by the episode of the failed "*nafeer*". Shortly after the Hama massacre, Brotherhood leaders called the few thousand remaining Syrian Islamist fighters to gather in military camps based in Iraq and to prepare for a last-ditch battle with the regime so as to take revenge for the mass killings. The Ikhwani leadership, however, quickly realized the human and political cost such an operation would entail and decided to call the movement to a halt. The primarily political and pragmatic nature assumed by the organization's leadership, in turn, alienated the most radical corners of Islamist constituency who stopped sympathizing with the Brotherhood. They went on, instead, to join the global Islamic struggle taking place in Afghanistan while waiting for the right time to return to Syria to settle scores, once and for all, with the Ba'ath. The growing strength of this Syrian jihadist trend was reinforced by the regime's multiple attempts, after 2003, at pushing its home-grown Islamic radicals out of the country to fight the American occupiers in Iraq instead.

There, and before in Afghanistan, the Syrian jihadists acquired the additional military and ideological skills which would enable them to return home stronger than ever and well prepared to fight the Ba'ath. It is the merger of these trends that explains the prominence gained by jihadist groups in the framework of the Syrian uprisings. Not only is the sectarian aspect of their struggle evident and longstanding, it is also fuelled by a narrative of revenge for the past and by a rhetoric calling for the advent of an Islamic Caliphate over Syria. The regime's willingness to foster the radicalization of the Islamic movement, for domestic reasons in the late 1970s and for external reasons in the early 2000s, was bound to eventually backfire.

But the spectacular re-emergence of Syria's radical Islamic trend at the forefront of the uprisings is also the result of another long-standing dynamic: the fragmentation of the country's moderate Islamic landscape. Ever since the Brotherhood's exile and its long struggle for relevance, the country has been deprived of moderate voices on the Islamist front. There were, of course, religious scholars who always advocated the co-existence of religions and the peaceful proselytizing of society through social and cultural work, but most never engaged in politics. Some individuals of a moderate Islamist bent could also have acted as a point of reference for many young Syrians in search of identity, but they had neither a nationwide organization to carry their vision nor a social base to tap into for political mobilization. Such a state of paralysis, in turn, created a political and ideological void which the Syrian Brotherhood was quick to fill when the opportunity arose after the Arab uprisings erupted in Syria.

The Ikhwan's rebirth from the ashes can, of course, also be explained in reference to the memory of the struggle it led against the regime, to its historical legitimacy, or to its strong social base in cities such as Aleppo, Homs and Hama, which all act as major epicentres of the current uprisings. But perhaps the best explanation for the Brotherhood's historical comeback at the forefront of Syrian politics and society lies in

EPILOGUE

the group's unique organizational capabilities. Its potential to mobilize networks and resources in a coherent and disciplined way across the country is unparalleled. This does not mean, however, that the Ikhwan should expect Syrians to welcome them back cheerfully, should the organization ever be allowed to return home. The organization will have to overcome the mistrust of Syrian society in order to rebuild a social base. While such suspicion is partly the product of decades of regime propaganda aimed at tainting the group's image in markedly negative ways, it is also, and perhaps most crucially, the result of the organization's thirty-year reluctance to look in a critical way at its own history.

"The Syrian Brotherhood has changed,"[1] a leading opposition figure in exile, of Christian background, asserted confidently when asked whether he feared a takeover of Syria by the Muslim Brothers. But what exactly has changed? And changed from what? If the answer to that question is perhaps obvious to an exiled opposition figure who has held discussions on a regular basis with Syrian Brothers for the past thirty years in London, Istanbul and Paris, it might not be so evident to those corners of society long used to the Brotherhood's absence and to the regime's rhetoric. While this book has attempted to bring specific answers to these questions, and, as a result, raises new questions associated with them, the key challenge facing the Syrian Muslim Brotherhood will be their ability to address the remaining issues in a more open and public way in the years to come.

APPENDICES

APPENDIX 1

LIST OF THE SUCCESSIVE LEADERS OF SYRIA'S MUSLIM BROTHERHOOD

1945–1957: Mustapha al Sibai
1957–1969: Issam al-Attar
1972–1975: Abdel Fatah Abu Ghuddah
1975–1980: Adnan Saadeddine
1980–1985: Hassan Houeidi
1985–1986: Adeeb Jajeh (6 months)
1986:   Munir Ghadhban (6 months)
1986–1991: Abdel Fatah Abu Ghuddah
1990–1996: Hassan Houeidi
1996–2010: Ali Sadreddine al-Bayanouni
2010–Present: Riad al-Shuqfah

Source: Interview with Zouheir Salem, London, 28 July 2011.

APPENDIX 2

ABDULLAH AZZAM ON THE ROLE OF MARWAN HADID DURING THE 1964 HAMA RIOTS

Marwan [Hadid] went and gathered the youth who were around him. There was a mosque right at the foot of his apartment building where the youth would usually sleep, as he would bring them up and teach them there. He went to the Sultan [Mosque] and gathered them, each one of them carrying a grenade and a gun. Some of the youth were still in high school! They began saying Allahu Akbar! and announcing their fight against the state. So, the tanks came to Masjid as-Sultan and fired on it, with the youth standing on the minaret. The minaret fell with the youth in it, and the mosque was demolished with them inside.

By Allah, some of the trustworthy residents of Hamah narrated to me—and Allah Knows best—that, after a few days, when they were removing the rubble from on top of these youth who had been killed, they could hear tasbih and takbir from underneath the rubble.

Anyway, it was Written for Shaykh Marwan that he remains alive, so, they took him to court. This was done in the open, so that the Ba'thists could claim that they implement justice. They allowed some foreign journalists to attend the hearing. The judges in this case were Mustafa Tallas [Tlas] and Salah Jadid. Mustafa Tallas was the defence minister in Syria, and Salah Jadid was the most powerful Nusayri to have any position in the country.

They said to him: "Why did you carry weapons and go against the state?"

Shaykh Marwan answered: "Because there is a Nusayri dog named Salah Jadid—he is saying this to Salah Jadid!—and there is a dog who ascribes himself to *Ahl as-Sunnah* named Mustafa Tallas, and they desire to kill off Islam in this land, and we reject and will fight against Islam being wiped out in this land as long as we're alive".

He then dared the Revolutionary Guards to kill him inside the court-house, but the police guarded Shaykh Marwan in front of the foreign journalists, so that it would not be said to the world that he was killed in the courthouse.

They said to him: "You are working for someone else". He replied: "I am working for Allah, the Mighty and Exalted. As for the one who is serving others, then he is the leader of your party". They said: "You say that Muhammad al-Hamid is with you, but he hates you". Marwan replied: "{But if they turn away, then say: 'Allah is sufficient for me. There is none worthy of worship except He. Upon Him I depend, and He is the Lord of the mighty Throne.'"} [at-Tawbah; 129]"

It was a powerful court case. He was sentenced to death along with a group of the youth. Some of the youth were acquitted, however. Those who were acquitted began to weep, and those who were sentenced to death began to smile. The foreign journalists were in a state of shock: those who are acquitted are weeping, and those who are sentenced to death are smiling? So, the youth sentenced to death said to them: "We are being granted Paradise, and they are being prevented from Paradise", and they were taken to prison to await their executions.

Shaykh Marwan later said to me: "I never lived a time in my life that was sweeter to my heart and soul than those days in which the youth and I were awaiting our executions". And it might have been during those days that Shaykh Marwan wrote:

The soul shall rise tomorrow * And it shall meet Allah at its appointed time.

These are the words of Marwan Hadid. Anyway, one of the scholars of Hamah, Shaykh Muhammad al-Hamid, went to Amin al-Hafiz—who was the Syrian president at the time, from Hamah, as well—and said to him: "What do you want to do with Marwan Hadid?" He replied: "We sentenced him to death". Muhammad al-Hamid said: "Are you saying this with a sane mind? Do you think that Hamah will remain silent against you if you execute Marwan Hadid? You will face unending problems!" Amin replied: "What do you think, Shaykh?" He said: "I think you should release him and acquit him". Amin said: "Go and release him yourself". Saykh Marwan Hadid later said to me: "So, Shaykh Muhammad al-Hamid came and said: "My children—and he was their teacher, whom they all loved—come!" They said: "To where?" He said: "The state has acquitted you". So, we said to him: "May Allah Forgive you, as you have prevented us from Paradise".

Shaykh Marwan returned, and he knew no rest. He was basically a bomb about to explode.

Source: Abdullah Azzam, *Fi Dhilal Surat at-Tawbah*, pp. 21–25, available online at: http://forums.islamicawakening.com/f18/abdullah-azzam-on-marwan-hadeed-2222/ (Wording and style retained as in source).

APPENDIX 3

ABDULLAH AZZAM ON MARWAN HADID'S DEATH

The people of Hamah are just like the Afghans. They are bedouins who do not play around, just like the Afghans.

Anyway, after a while, [Marwan Hadid] disappeared, only to reappear in Damascus. He lived in an apartment, and began to gather and collect weapons. *Allahu Akbar*—he did not know of something called free time or boredom, and he did not know of fear. He gathered machineguns and grenades. Whenever he would hear of a place in Damascus where there was a grenade available, he would send one of the youth to go purchase it.

At this time, the intelligence was searching for him—*ya Salam!*—and at this time, I was at the University of Damascus. I was seeking to complete my degree at the university; I got my Bachelor's in Shari'ah from Damascus, and my Master's and Doctorate from al-Azhar. While I was standing in the university, a youth—one of Shaykh Marwan's students—came up to me and said: "Do you wish to see Shaykh Marwan?" I said: "What? Right away!" So, I went to him and entered his residence, and I looked at a face that did not belong to the people of this *dunya*. It was so pure and strange; the light emanating from his face. The first words he said to me—and he knew me from our days in Palestine—were: "O Abu Muhammad! Do you not long for Paradise?" And this was the last time I ever saw him.

Anyway, the police were searching for him, and what was he doing? Gathering weapons. He was searching for weapons that he could use to

215

get rid of the Nusayris. One day, the intelligence discovered his apartment and surrounded it. Shaykh Marwan had two of his students with him, as well as his wife, with whom he had not yet consummated the marriage. He had said to her: "I do not wish to consummate with you, as I feel that this would prevent me from other things", so, he remained a virgin. Yes, he married, but did not consummate.

One of his students went down to buy some breakfast for them. He saw the cars waiting outside, so, he retreated. He saw six cars used by the intelligence, waiting. He tried to go back into the apartment building, but they caught him. This youth was carrying a pocketknife—the residents of Hamah usually carry knives in their back pockets—and the car was filled with six intelligence officers. So, his youth stood next to them, pulled out his knife, slaughtered each one of them, then he escaped. The sirens then began going off all over Damascus. The police began chasing him until they finally caught up with him in a building, where he jumped from the third or fourth floor to escape. He managed to get away from them, finally making it to Jordan.

Back to Shaykh Marwan: the police cars began surrounding his apartment building after the Fajr, and they began calling out through the microphone: "O residents of this building! Get out, as there is an Iraqi spy who we wish to arrest!"—at this time, there were disputes between Syria and Iraq. So, Shaykh Marwan grabbed his own microphone (he had his own microphone that he would use to call to prayer), saying: "O intelligence officers! O police! O you who are surrounding the building! We will give you fifteen minutes, and you must leave within these fifteen minutes. After this, we will begin fighting you if you do not leave". And he actually waited fifteen minutes, and after fifteen minutes, he began with the grenades and machinegun fire. Calls were being made to local police stations, and, eventually, over 1,000 police and intelligence officers were surrounding the house, against Marwan and one other brother with him, along with his wife. They tried entering the building, so, the other brother went down and met them at the entrance with some TNT. They then tried entering from above, landing on the building's roof with a helicopter—but who would be the brave one to enter first? One thousand against two.

By the time it was afternoon, they were still unable to enter the apartment building. They would fire from below, and he would fire back from above. After the afternoon, they finally entered the apartment. This was the excuse of Shaykh Marwan: he became injured in his hand, rendering it useless. He came out with his head up high. They took along with them his wife, who he had not consummated his marriage with.

The news was relayed to Hafiz al-Asad, who went crazy, as many officers were killed in the process. Hafiz al-Asad said: "I wish to solve this with him personally". So, he went to him personally, saying to him: "O Marwan! Let us open a new page with each other! Let Allah Forgive what has happened, and we will not take you to account for anything you did, with one condition: that you abandon your weapons". Marwan replied: "I agree, with one condition: that you assist me in establishing an Islamic state in Syria". Hafiz al-Asad gathered himself and left the room.

The Military Council gathered, including Naji Jamil—the commander of the Air Force—and Mustafa Tallas [Tlas] was also present, as well as a large group of the Nusayri officers and generals. They came to Shaykh Marwan. He sat down, looked to Naji Jamil and Mustafa Tallas, and said: "Woe to you, you dog, Naji Jamil! Do you think that we will let you live? I made the youth promise that they would start with you, you and Mustafa Tallas. Because of you, you dogs, we have been humiliated by these Nusayris; they violated our honor. As for you, you Nusayri generals, I made the youth promise that they would kill at least 5,000 of you". Naji Jamil said: "Take this insane man; take him away from me".

Afterwards, they would bring his wife into the cell next to him, trying to violate her while he was in captivity, and his soul began to tighten. Someone like this, with a free and honorable soul, sees her honor being violated, and he can do nothing about it. He is in captivity.

Hc lost so much weight that he reached 45 kg (99 lbs), and his weight used to be around 100 kg (around 220 lbs).

He finally died in prison, without anyone knowing whether he was killed or had died a natural death. Towards the end, his veins would not even accept glucose. When he died, they sent to his father to take his body. He asked them: "Did you kill him?" They replied: "No", and they buried his body in a graveyard in Damascus, with a hundred soldiers guarding his funeral, out of fear that the youth would take his body and demonstrate in Damascus".

Source: Abdullah Azzam, *Fi Dhilal Surat at-Tawbah*, pp. 21–5, available online at: http://forums.islamicawakening.com/f18/abdullah-azzam-on-marwan-hadeed-2222/ (Wording and style retained as in source).

APPENDIX 4

ABU MUS'AB AL-SURI ON THE TRAINING TACTIC OF AL-TALIA AL-MUQATILA

Al-Talia created its own system for training; the physical fitness part of training was encouraged by the leadership but depended largely on the individuals' effort. The members were trained to disassemble then reassemble weapons in safe houses, then they would be taken along on a military operation (e.g. assassination attempt) as an observer, this breaks the psychological barrier. The second time, the trainee will be armed but this time he has a mission: to protect those people carrying out the military operation, then he will be asked by the seniors of his group to carry out the assassination himself. Many times, the first shots fired by the mujhaideen hit the heads of the infidels, very quickly trainees will learn. Many military operations were carried out using trainees, the most successful were lead by the martyr captain Ibrahim Youssef (May Allah have mercy on his soul), he was able to establish and supervise a limited organized training program in the small mountains near Aleppo. Unfortunately the lack of forests and mountains prevented al-Talia from establishing its own camps on the inside. Later, al-Talia members were sent to Iraq for professional military training, they trained on different types of weapons especially the effective use of rocket propelled grenades (R.P.G.), they attended military lectures on the tactics of war, some of them got trained on tank warfare, some returned and participated in the fight, others stayed abroad, settled down and went about their daily lives and thus lost all they have learned.

Source: Abu Mus'ab al-Suri, "Lessons learned from the Jihad ordeal in Syria" (Document captured by US troops in Afghanistan in 2002, referenced as AFGP-2002–600080, full translation), p. 33, available at: http://www.ctc.usma.edu/posts/lessons-learned-from-the-jihad-ordeal-in-syria-english-translation (Wording and style retained as in source).

APPENDIX 5

ABU MUS'AB AL-SURI ON THE BATTLE OF HAMA
IN FEBRUARY 1982

The battle of Hama proved, beyond a shadow of doubt, the conventional wisdom that any revolution that goes into an open all out confrontation in a defined geographical location that needs to be defended, without any intervention by outside forces to aid it, and without starting marginal confrontations in other areas to force the army to relocate some of its forces, and on timing not its own, is doomed to utter failure and destruction. Even though the mujahideen were forced into the battle through a well-orchestrated plan by the regime, this does not change the fact that it lead to total failure. A lesson we should take to heart. The leader of the mujahideen in Hama, Abu Bakr Umar Jawad (May Allah have mercy on his soul) distributed eight thousand Russian machine guns the morning of the day the battle broke out, there were one thousand mujahideen and many thousands of armed civilians trying to defend the city, there was plenty of arms and munitions, they had medium duty weapons like R.P.G.s and heavy machine guns, but the city could not withstand the onslaught, they had no supply or reinforcement routs, they ran out of anti armor weapons after four days only. The organization that lead the fight was a strong one with ten years of experience, they had spent three years preparing for the battle, they could not hold out, the city was sacked, most of the mujahideen got martyred, many civilians threw down their arms and surrendered, half the city was totally destroyed, and it was a real disaster. And even

221

though the enemy suffered heavy losses there is no comparison between their losses and ours.

Source: Abu Mus'ab al-Suri, "Lessons learned from the Jihad ordeal in Syria" (Document captured by US troops in Afghanistan in 2002, referenced as AFGP-2002–600080, full translation), p. 33, available at: http://www.ctc.usma.edu/posts/lessons-learned-from-the-jihad-ordeal-in-syria-english-translation (Wording and style retained as in source).

APPENDIX 6

THE SYRIAN MUSLIM BROTHERHOOD'S MOST IMPORTANT STATEMENT REGARDING THEIR EVOLUTION AND THEIR VISION OF SYRIA'S FUTURE

The Political Perspective for Syria

The Muslim Brotherhood's Vision of the Future

Preamble

In obedience to God's instructions: "Call people to the path of your Lord with wisdom and goodly exhortation, and argue with them in the most kindly manner". (Q. 16: 125);

In line with our comprehensive and self-renewing understanding of Islam, its noble faith and values, as well as its legal code based on justice, kindness and compassion;

Recognizing that Islam enshrines the basic concept of faith that 'God is the Lord of all the worlds', that Muhammad, God's final Messenger who preached the pure divine faith, was sent to all mankind as manifestation of God's grace, and that 'all creatures are God's dependents. Among them, the ones God loves most are those who bring the most benefit to His dependents';

In fulfilment of the goals of Islamic law, which aims to remove stress and hardship from people's lives;

And continuing our long march that adopts a positive, centralist and open approach that is free of rigidity and extremism;

We, the Muslim Brotherhood in Syria, present our political programme. It reflects our clear and enlightened vision, commitment to the truth and to our principles and a positive response to the changing needs of our society. It represents a step towards the rebuilding of our country at all three levels: the individual, the social and the state. It is indeed a contribution to the work aiming to lay the foundation of a solid national structure that is based on participation by all in making the future better and happier. We thus stretch our hand offering what is good and aiming for what is good. We strongly adhere to our identity, proud of belonging to our nation, stressing both its Islamic and Arab dimensions that characterise its civilisation and role. We pledge to make Syria the home of all Syrians, while stressing our right to function as a national group committed to dialogue, recognizing the unity of our nation and rejecting all forms of unilateralism, oppression and dictatorship that have long plagued our country.

Ever since its inception in 1945, the Muslim Brotherhood in Syria stood out as a nationalist group ready to defend our nation and representing a broad popular trend opposed to imperialism and all its schemes and designs, as also to tyranny and dictatorship. It has positively interacted with all political, social and cultural groups. It has demonstrated its commitment to keep Syrian society free of religious and sectarian fanaticism, open to all.

Mustafa al-Sibaie, Muhammad al-Mubarak, Issam al-Attar, Abd al-Fattah Abu Ghuddah, Muhammad al-Hamid and many other leading Islamic figures were fully engaged in the national and political debate. They presented their views in reply to other views, but when they were met with harm and oppression they reacted with patience and forbearance, committing themselves always to remain within the law and advocating free and fair elections.

Despite the negative aspects of the Patriotic era, it witnessed the action of the Muslim Brotherhood in Syria and its advocacy of intellectual enlightenment to counter both narrow rigidity on the one hand and immorality on the other. In so doing, it demonstrated its commitment to the reformist approach based on an enlightened understanding of Islam. At the same time, it worked hard for the eradication of superstitions and practices that were given a religious guise despite being alien to Islam. It worked for the eradication of ignorance, the spread of knowledge and education, the alleviation of poverty, the elimination of unemployment and the combating of other social ills, including complacency and weakness. It attended to the needs of Muslim women, supporting their emancipation, and rights of education, employment and full participation in public life. It sought to give women their proper position realising that the general concept of women's role in society represented a confused mess of traditional practices that have no Islamic basis. Despite being forced into the underground, the Muslim Brotherhood remained committed to a moderate policy and strategy based on dialogue, guided by the Qur'anic instruction: "Call people to the path of your Lord with wisdom and goodly exhortation…" (Q. 16: 125).

However, since the military coup of 8 March 1963, a policy of tyrannical rule that allowed no opposition was imposed on Syria. People have endured much injustice and hardship, compounded by multi-faceted corruption that placed human, social and political relations on the wrong basis. No room was allowed for expression or change. Prisons were filled with people for no reason other than holding a different point of view. They were also subjected to all forms of torture. The advocates of Islamic revival were the main sufferers of all these practices, long before any act of violence.

Uncompromising tyrannical policies that sought to suppress religion and silence its advocates led to a state of social and political intolerance leading in turn to acts of violence committed by certain individuals who did not belong to our group. Such violence culminated in June 1979 into the massacre of students at the Artillery Academy, but the government used this event as a pretext to impose an extermination policy in our country that has continued ever since.

Although the Muslim Brotherhood was quick to denounce the massacre, issuing a formal statement dissociating itself of any such acts, and despite the fact that we never resorted to violent action nor advocated any policies of violence, the regime insisted on holding us responsible for it, as well as the violent actions that preceded it. The Minister of Interior at the time issued a statement to this effect, threatening the total extermination of the Muslim Brotherhood, chasing its members in the country and outside it. Tens of thousands of innocent citizens were rounded up to join the large numbers of Syrians who were already in prison. Many prominent figures were assassinated in Syria and elsewhere. This policy culminated in issuing Decree 49 of 1980 which imposes the capital punishment for nothing more than the membership of the Muslim Brotherhood. This decree was intended to provide a legal cover for the numerous massacres carried out in the streets and prisons in many villages, towns and cities in Syria, the worst of which was that committed in Hama in February 1982.

The security authorities have ever since followed a policy of no compromise that included the majority of Syrians. Although we continued to adhere to our peaceful policy, without ever entertaining any thought of resorting to military confrontation with the regime, we, together with large numbers of Syrian citizens, found ourselves forced to resort to self defence in a situation of spiralling violence that was certainly not of our making. It was indeed the policy followed by the government that led to such violence that culminated in a popular uprising that enjoyed broad support that included trade unions and other social groups which had always opposed the despotic policies of the regimes. On the other side, there was an extremist trend in government advocating a policy of extermination against us. Such people pursued policies that ensured the continuation of despotic policies that undermined all efforts that aimed to stop the spiral of violence and to bring about direct negotiations between us and the government. They also worked hard to undermine initiatives made by different figures aiming to achieve reconciliation. We, on our part, always responded positively to such efforts.

The Syrian authorities should have dealt with the early cases of violence as would suit individual and limited cases, looking at their causes and adopting remedies to ensure that they would not spread. Instead, elements intoxicated by power resorted to carry out a pre-planned policy that ensured the spread of violence and confrontation.

As we place such information before the world, we express our continued grief at the fact that tens of thousands of Syrians have been wrongfully imprisoned, forced to leave the country, killed or were lost without trace as a result of this confrontation in which they had no role. We certainly sympathise with all innocent victims of this confrontation. We also call for the formation of a national, independent, legal inquiry into these events, with access to all relevant information in order to put the facts of those bloody events before our people. This is the only way to ensure that each party is made to bear the moral, political and legal responsibility for its own actions and their results.

Today, a quarter of a century after those tragic events, our nation is facing serious threats and challenges which require a full review of policies and attitudes by all parties so as to be able to shoulder our historic responsibilities. This is the only way that will help the wounds suffered by our nation to heal. The Muslim Brotherhood in Syria have already carried out a thorough review of its policies, and outlined a set of principles the details of which are outlined in the National Charter of Honour. Today, we are presenting this political project that explains our vision for the future. All this is made as a contribution to a wider effort to re-establish a solid national foundation for our country. It is undertaken in implementation of our principles and fulfilment of our aims, hoping for a better future for Syria.

Our political project emphasises the need to build a modern state in which we see a clear reflection of an Islamic state that is fundamentally different from the theocracies of the middle ages. The modern state we seek considers citizenship as the basis of justice and equality, ensures separation between the different authorities, and implements a national pluralistic contract that allows peaceful change of government. In our view, the most important challenge faced by Arab countries generally, and Syria in particular, is to put in place a sound mechanism to allow such peaceful change of government, ensuring a two-way democratic system that cannot be suspended or bypassed by any group or person.

In our project, it is society that provides the solid foundation of the state. Hence, we have a clear vision of an integrated network of social relations based on partnership, justice and equality. In such a society, women enjoy equal status with men and have equal rights and full participation in public life at the social, economic and political levels. However, appropriate values must be put in place to ensure that man and woman continue to fulfil the mutually complementary roles God has assigned to them.

In our project, all individuals enjoy their positions of honour. We emphasise the freedom of belief dimension as well as our cultural identity and affiliation, advocating the need for better information, clearer awareness, mutual tolerance, common achievement and strengthening social values.

We look at government, its apparatus and institutions, and how to reform it, as well as the policies that we consider to be the best to bring about an end to the prevailing state of tension in our country.

Corruption, which has taken different shapes and forms, has landed our country in a deplorable state of affairs. No national initiative to eradicate corruption will succeed unless it is carried out by strong and sincere people who are able to undertake reforms and carry them through. The vicious circle of corruption can only be broken by sincere people who are committed to serve the interests of their nation.

It is our belief that re-building our country and society on a proper moral and constitutional basis, ensuring the eradication of policies of complacency and corrupt practices, is the only practical way to give back to the citizens of Syria their freedom and to liberate the occupied territories of our homeland.

On 3 May 2001, the Muslim Brotherhood in Syria issued its National Charter of Honour outlining a set of rules and measures of control for political action, which were presented for discussion. Similarly, our political project, which is issued today, is a human effort based on our Islamic viewpoint. It aims for positive and constructive change, and it is certainly open for discussion and revision.

London
4 Dhul-Qaadah 1425 H.
16 December 2004.

Source: "The political perspective for Syria: the Muslim Brotherhood's vision of the future" (London, 16 December 2004, copy given to author) (Wording and style retained as in source).

In the name of God the Merciful

Covenant and charter

For a free country, free life for every citizen. In this crucial stage of the history of Syria, where the dawn is born from the womb of suffering and pain, on the hands of the Syrian heros, men and women, children, youth and old men, in a national overwhelming revolution, with the participation of all components of the Syrian people, for all the Syrians. We "the muslim brotherhood in Syria", from Islam religion true principles, based on freedom, justice, tolerance and openness. We present this covenant and charter, to all of our people, committed to it in the letter and sprit, a covenant which safeguards the rights, and a charter which dispels fears as a source of reassurance and satisfaction.

This covenant and charter represents a national vision, common denominators, adopted by "the Muslim Brotherhood in Syria", and introduced as a new social contract, establishing a modern and safe national relationship, among the Syrian society components, with its all religious and ethnic factions, and all current intellectual and political currents.

"The Muslim Brotherhood in Syria" are committed to Syria in the future to be:

1. A civil modern state with a civil constitution, coming from the will of the Syrian people, based on national harmony, written by a freely and impartially elected constituent assembly, protecting the fundamental rights of individuals and groups of any abuse or override, ensuring an equitable representation to all components of society.

2. A democratic pluralistic deliberative country, according to the finest modern thoughts of human, a representative republic, in which people choose those who govern and represent through the ballot box, in an impartial free transparent election.

3. A state of citizenship and equality, in which all people are equal, regardless of their ethnicity, religion, ideology or orientation, going by citizenship principles which are the basis of rights and duties, in which all citizens are allowed to reach the highest positions, based on the rule of elections and efficiency.

4. A country that respects human rights—as approved by God laws and international charters—of dignity and equality, freedom of thought and expression, of belief and worship, of media, political participation, equality of opportunities, social justice and providing the basis needed for a decent living. In which no citizen is oppressed in his belief nor worship, or restricted in a private or general matter. A country that refuses discrimination, prevents torture and criminalizes it.

5. A country based of dialogue and participation, not on exclusivity, exclusion or transcendence, all its people participate equally, in building and protecting it, enjoying its wealth and goods, committing to respecting all its ethnic, religious and sectarian component, and the privacy of those components, with all their civilizational, cultural and social dimensions, and the expression of these components. Considering this diversity an enriching factor, an extension to a long history of co-existence, in a generous frame of human tolerance.

6. A state in which people govern themselves, choose their way, determine their future, with no guardianship of any autocratic ruler or one party system, and be their own decision-makers.

7. A country with respect to institutions, based of the separation of the executive, legislative and judicial powers, where the officials are in the service of people, and their permissions and following mechanisms are specified in the constitution, and the military and security departments responsibility is protecting homeland and people not protecting authority and regime, and do not interfere in the political competition between parties and national groups.

8. A country that renounces terrorism and fights it, and respects international covenants, charters, treaties and conventions. As factor of security and stability in its regional and international perimeter. Establishes the best equal relations with its friends, in the forefront the neighbour Lebanon, for its people suffered—as the Syrian people—from the scourge of the system of corruption and tyranny, and works on achieving its people's strategic interest and restoring its occupied land in all legal means, and supporting the legal demands of the Palestinian brotherly people.

9. A state of justice and law, where there is no room for hatred, revenge and retaliation. Even those whose hands are contaminated with people's blood, of any part, it is their right to have a fair trial, before an impartial and independent tribunal.

10. A country of intimacy and love, between the sons of the big Syrian family, in the light of a massive reconciliation. Where all false pretexts adopted by the system of corruption and tyranny, to intimidate the citizens of one nation of each, to prolong his rule and to sustain its control on everyone.

This is our vision and aspiration to our desired future, and this is our covenant in front of God, and our people, and in front of all people. A vision that we assure today, after a history full of national working for decades, since the founding of the brotherhood, by the hands of Dr. Mustafa Assiba'ey God's mercy be upon him in 1945. We presented its features clearly and ambiguously, in the "national honor charter 2001", and in our political project in 2004, and in the official papers approved by the brotherhood, on various social and national issues.

And these are our hearts opened, our hands outstretched to all our brothers and partners in our beloved homeland, for it to take its decent position between the civilized human societies.

APPENDIX 6

"Help your one another in virtue, righteousness and piety* and do not in sin and aggression."

25 March 2012

Source: Covenant and charter of the Muslim Brotherhood Movement in Syria, copy given to the author, 25 March 2012 (Wording and style retained as in source).

NOTES

PROLOGUE

1. "Syria: Why is there no Egypt-style Revolution?", *BBC News*, 4 March 2011.
2. Thomas Friedman, *From Beirut to Jerusalem* (New York: Anchor, 1990), p. 76.
3. I will use throughout the book the term Islamist to describe those who engage in political activism as articulated through an Islamic frame of reference and discourse. The term does not necessarily refer to those who wish to put forward such vision through political violence.
4. "American Ambassador to Syria visits focal point in uprising", *New York Times*, 7 July 2011.
5. "Kidnapping, spats on docket of Syria rebel boss", *Wall Street Journal*, 17 Aug. 2012.
6. "No one likes violence…but people know there is no going back", *The Independent*, 10 Sept. 2012.
7. "Assad: Challenge Syria at your peril", *Daily Telegraph*, 29 Oct. 2011.
8. Ibid.
9. "Syria's Muslim Brotherhood accuses regime of seeking to implicate it in bombings", *Nahar*, 24 Dec. 2011.
10. See, among others, "Syria's Muslim Brotherhood claims responsibility for deadly blasts", *Herald Sun*, 25 Dec. 2011.
11. "Concerns about Al-Qaeda in Syria underscore questions about rebels", *New York Times*, 21 Aug. 2012.
12. Itamar Rabinovich, *Syria under the Ba'th, 1963–66: The Army-Party Symbiosis* (Jerusalem: Israel Universities Press and New Brunswick: Transaction Books, 1972) and Raymond Hinnebusch, *Authoritarian Power and State Formation in Ba'thist Syria: Army, Party and Peasants* (San Francisco: Westview Press, 1990).

13. Hanna Batatu, *Syria's Peasantry, the Descendants of its Lesser Rural Notables, and their Politics* (Princeton: Princeton University Press, 1999) and Michael Van Dusen, "Syria: Downfall of a Traditional Elite" in Frank Tachau (ed.), *Political Elites and Political Development in the Middle East* (New York: Shenkman Publishing Company Inc., 1975).

14. Patrick Seale, *Asad of Syria: The Struggle for the Middle East* (I.B. Tauris, London, 1988) and Eberhard Kienle, *Baath vs. Baath* (I.B. Tauris, London, 1991).

15. Michel Seurat, *L'Etat de barbarie* (Paris: Seuil, 1989) and Martin Kramer, "Syria's Alawis and Shi'ism" in Martin Kramer (ed.), *Shi'ism, Resistance and Revolution* (Boulder: Westview Press, 1987).

16. Umar Faruk Abd-Allah, *The Islamic Struggle in Syria* (Berkeley: Mizan Press, 1983); Raymond Hinnebusch, "The Islamic Movement in Syria: Sectarian Conflict and Urban Rebellion in an Authoritarian-Populist Regime", in Ali Dessouki (ed.), *Islamic Resurgence in the Arab World* (Princeton: CIS, 1982); Hana Batatu, "Syria's Muslim Brethren", MERIP Reports (No. 110, Nov.–Dec. 1982) and Johannes Reissner, *Ideologie und Politik der Muslimbrüder Syriens* (Freiburg: Klaus Schwarz, 1980).

17. Eyal Zisser, "Syria, the Baath Regime and the Islamic Movement: Stepping on a New Path?", *The Muslim World* (Vol. 95, No. 1, 2005) and Robert G. Rabil, "The Syrian Muslim Brotherhood" in Barry Rubin (ed.), *The Muslim Brotherhood: The Organization and Policies of a Global Movement* (New York: Palgrave Macmillan, 2010). It should be noted, however, that Alison Pargeter's chapter on the Syrian Brotherhood in her book provides an excellent overview of the organization's evolution throughout history. See Alison Pargeter, *The Muslim Brotherhood: The Burden of Tradition* (London: Saqi Books, 2010).

18. There are many works of excellent quality on the Egyptian Brotherhood but three useful references are Richard Mitchell, *The Society of the Muslim Brothers* (New York: Oxford University Press, 1993); Gilles Kepel, *Muslim Extremism in Egypt: The Prophet and the Pharaoh* (Los Angeles: University of California Press, 1993); and Brynjar Lia, *The Society of the Muslim Brothers in Egypt: The Rise of an Islamic Mass Movement* (London: Ithaca, 2006).

1. THE EMERGENCE OF A POLITICIZED ISLAM IN SYRIA (1860–1944)

1. For a full account of the life and thought of Jamal al-Din al-Afghani, see Nikki R. Keddie, *An Islamic Response to Imperialism: Political and Religious Writings of Sayyid Jamail al-Din "al-Afghani"* (Berkeley: University of California Press, 1983).

2. Paul Salem, *Bitter Legacy: Ideology and Politics in the Arab World* (Syracuse: Syracuse University Press, 1994), pp. 91–4.
3. Ahmed al-Rahim, "Islam and Liberty", *Journal of Democracy* (Vol. 17, No. 1, 2006), p. 166.
4. Paul Salem, *op. cit.*, pp. 94–5.
5. David D. Commins, *Islamic Reform: Politics and Social Change in late Ottoman Syria* (New York: Oxford University Press, 1990), p. 25.
6. David D. Commins, *The Wahhabi Mission and Saudi Arabia* (London: I.B. Tauris, 2006), pp. 132–3.
7. Ibid., p. 29.
8. Nazih Ayubi, *Political Islam: Religion and Politics* (New York: Routledge 1991), pp. 125–6.
9. For a detailed discussion on Damascene Salafists' views on Sufism, see David D. Commins (1990), *op. cit.*, pp. 80–81. For the minority view held by al-Zahrawi, see David D. Commins (1990), *op. cit.*, pp. 57–9.
10. For an example representative of the Damascene Salafists' early rebuttal of the practice of *takfir*, see Jamal al-Din al-Qasimi quoted in Itzchak Weissmann, *Taste of Modernity: Sufism, Salafiyya and Arabism in Late Ottoman Damascus* (Leiden: Brill, 2011), pp. 292–4.
11. David D. Commins (1990), *op. cit.*, p. 144.
12. Ibid., pp. 126–7.
13. Itzchak Weissmann goes even further by arguing that the "Salafi trend of Damascus constituted a religious response to the political alliance forged between the Ottoman State under the modernizing autocracy of Sultan Abdullhamid II and orthodox sufi sheikhs and ulama who were willing to mobilize the masses in his support." See Itzchak Weissmann (2011), *op. cit.*, p. 273.
14. David D. Commins (1990), *op. cit.*, p. 141.
15. Itzchak Weissmann, *Taste of Modernity: Sufism, Salafiyya and Arabism in Late Ottoman Damascus* (Leiden: Brill, 2011), pp. 285–6.
16. Elizabeth F. Thompson, *Colonial Citizens: Republican Rights, Paternal Privilege and Gender in French Syria and Lebanon* (New York: Columbia University Press, 2000), p. 103.
17. Interview with Ali Sadreddine al-Bayanouni, London, 30 Nov. 2011.
18. UK mission to Syria cable to Foreign Office, "Weekly Political Summary", No. 15, E1369/207/89, 26 Feb. 1942.
19. Elizabeth F. Thompson, *op. cit.*, p. 105.
20. Ibid., p. 153.
21. Ibid., p. 152.
22. Philip S. Khoury, *Syria and the French Mandate: The Politics of Arab Nationalism, 1920–1945* (London: I.B. Tauris, 1987), p. 609.

23. All of the quotes in this paragraph are drawn from the report of a political officer at the British mission in Damascus who reported on the events of the week. See UK mission to Syria cable to Foreign Office, "Weekly political summary No. 7: Syria and the Lebanon", E 3231/207/89, 21 May 1942.
24. UK mission to Syria cable to Foreign Office, "Weekly political summary No. 7: Syria and the Lebanon", E 3231/207/89, 21 May 1942.
25. Philip S. Khoury, *op. cit.*, p. 611.
26. Elizabeth F. Thompson, *op. cit.*, p. 262.
27. UK mission in Damascus cable to Foreign Office, "Weekly political summary No. 3", E3208/23/89, 26 May 1944.

2. ISLAM AND DEMOCRACY: THE MUSLIM BROTHERHOOD IN POST-INDEPENDENCE SYRIA (1946–1963)

1. Richard P. Mitchell, *The Society of the Muslim Brothers in Egypt* (London: Oxford University Press, 1969), p. 325.
2. Paul Salem, *Bitter Legacy: Ideology and Politics in the Arab World* (Syracuse: Syracuse University Press, 1994), p. 119.
3. Interview with Kamal al-Helbawy, London, 2 Sept. 2011.
4. Richard P. Mitchell, *op. cit.*, p. 326.
5. Hassan al-Banna quoted in Brynjar Lia, *The Society of the Muslim Brothers in Egypt: The Rise of an Islamic Mass Movement, 1928–1942* (Reading: Ithaca Press, 1998), p. 202.
6. Paul Salem, *op. cit.*, p. 99.
7. Richard P. Mitchell, *op. cit.*, p. 13.
8. Brynjar Lia, *op. cit.*, p. 215.
9. Although Mohammed al-Hamid played an active part in setting up the Syrian branch of the Muslim Brotherhood through publicizing its activities in his home town of Hama and helping to recruit members for the group, he never joined the organization as a full-blown member, as he instead preferred to devote his time to religious teaching at the Hama Sultan mosque. "He was not a member of the Muslim Brotherhood but he was very much loved and admired by all the Syrian Brothers," said Issam al-Attar, the former leader of the Brotherhood. Interview with Issam al-Attar, Aachen, 19 Dec. 2011.
10. Umar F. Abd-Allah, *The Islamic Struggle in Syria* (Berkeley: Mizan Press, 1983), pp. 97–8.
11. UK Embassy cable to Foreign Office, "Briefing on the Ikhwan al-Muslimin, dispatch No. 123", E 9414/1211/89, 23 September 1946.
12. Interview with Ali Sadreddine al-Bayanouni, London, 30 Nov. 2011. Dar

al-Arqam was founded by two local Islamic thinkers, Omar Bhaa Alidine al-Amari and Abd Qadar Asabsabi, who, in the early 1930s, strove to increase the social base for political Islam in their home town of Aleppo by doing more than just preaching or political activism. It was reported, for instance, that they set up night schools to teach Arabic to workers so as to decrease the levels of illiteracy in the northern metropolis—for both men and women. Interview with Zouheir Salem, London, 3 Oct. 2011.

13. UK Embassy cable to Foreign Office, "Briefing on the Ikhwan al-Muslimin, dispatch No. 123", E 9414/1211/89, 23 Sept. 1946.

14. Mustapha al-Sibai quoted in "Muslim Brothers faithful to chief: an interview with Mustapha al-Sibai", *New York Times*, 27 Feb. 1955.

15. Mustapha al-Sibai quoted in UK Embassy cable to Foreign Office, "Briefing on the Ikhwan al-Muslimin, dispatch No. 123", E 9414/1211/89, 23 Sept. 1946.

16. Mustapha al-Sibai quoted in UK Embassy cable to Foreign Office, "Briefing on the Ikhwan al-Muslimin, dispatch No. 123", E 9414/1211/89, 23 Sept. 1946.

17. Ibid.

18. Joshua Teitelbaum, "The Muslim Brotherhood in Syria, 1945–1958: Founding, Social Origins, Ideology", *Middle East Journal* (Vol. 65, No. 2, 2011), p. 222.

19. Arnaud Lenfant, "L'évolution du salafisme dans la Syrie contemporaine", in Bernard Rougier (ed.), *Qu'est ce que le salafisme?* (Paris: Presses Universitaires de France, 2008), p. 166.

20. Mustapha al-Sibai quoted in Umar F. Abd-Allah, *op. cit.*, p. 95.

21. Said Hawwa quoted in Itzchak Weismann, "The Politics of Popular Religion: Sufis, Salafis and Muslim Brothers in 20th Century Hamah", *International Journal of Middle Eastern Studies* (Vol. 37, 2005), p. 52.

22. Ibid.

23. For more on Abdel Qadir al-Jazairi's plea for good Christian-Muslim relations, see David D. Commins, *op. cit.*, p. 27.

24. See Brynjar Lia on the refusal to form a political party. For the Egyptian Ikhwan's vision of democracy, see Richard P. Mitchell, *op. cit.*, pp. 246–8.

25. Itzchak Weissmann, "Democratic Fundamentalism? The Practice and Discourse of the Muslim Brothers Movement in Syria", *The Muslim World* (Vol. 100, No. 1, 2010), p. 8.

26. Umar F. Abd-Allah, *op. cit.*, p. 95.

27. Stephen Humphreys, "Islam and Political Values in Saudi Arabia, Egypt and Syria", *Middle East Journal* (Vol. 33, No. 1, 1979), p. 6.

28. Philip S. Khoury, *op. cit.*, p. 604.

29. UK Embassy cable to Foreign Office, "Mr. Weld-Foster to Mr. Eyres (enclosure in No. 38)", E 111 31 Feb. 89; 25 Oct. 1946.

30. For more on the "Union of Ulama", see Thomas Pierret, *Baas et Islam en Syrie: la dynastie Assad face aux oulémas* (Paris: Presses Universitaires de France/Collection Proche Orient, 2011), pp. 225–36.
31. UK Embassy cable to Foreign Office, "Syria: weekly political summary", No. 5, E7787/171/89; 25 Aug. 1947.
32. UK Embassy cable to Foreign Office, "Briefing on the Ikhwan al-Muslimin, dispatch No. 123", E 9414/1211/89, 23 Sept. 1946.
33. Mustapha al-Sibai quoted in Joshua Teitelbaum, "The Muslim Brotherhood and the 'Struggle for Syria', 1947–1958: Between Accommodation and Ideology", *Middle Eastern Studies* (Vol. 40, No. 3, 2004), pp. 137–8.
34. UK Embassy cable to Foreign Office, "Events leading to the formation of the Khalid al-Azm Cabinet", No. 158, EY 1015/4; 7 Jan. 1950.
35. See, for example, the description in a cable from the British Embassy in Damascus of the Brotherhood's programme in August 1947 as "highly reactionary". UK Embassy cable to Foreign Office, "Weekly political summary/secret", E7787/171/89, 25 Aug. 1947.
36. Mustapha al-Sibai quoted in Joshua Teitelbaum (2004), *op. cit.*, p. 143.
37. UK Embassy cable to Foreign Office, "Events leading up to the formation of Khalid al-Azm's Cabinet"; EY 1015/4, No. 158, 7 Jan. 1950.
38. Joshua Teitelbaum (2004), *op. cit.*, p. 144.
39. Mustapha al-Sibai quoted in Radwan Ziadeh, *Power and Policy in Syria: the Intelligence Services, Foreign Relations and Democracy in the Modern Middle East* (New York: I.B. Tauris, 2011), p. 136.
40. Thomas Pierret (2011), *op. cit.*, pp. 232–3.
41. "Sheikh Mustafa Sibai" in UK Embassy cable to Foreign Office, "Leading personalities in Syria", No. 132 Confidential, UY1012/1, 24 Aug. 1956.
42. Interview with Nawal al-Sibai, email correspondence, 12 Dec. 2011.
43. UK Embassy cable to Foreign Office, "Weekly political summary (secret)", No. 234, E 10682/213/89, 30 Oct. 1946.
44. UK Embassy cable to Foreign Office, "Weekly political summary", No. 7, E 2101/171/89, 11 Feb. 1947.
45. UK Embassy cable to Foreign Office, "Weekly political summary (secret)", No. 225, E8688/213/89, 6 Aug. 1946.
46. UK Embassy cable to Foreign Office, "Weekly political summary", No. 7, E 10404/171/89, 7 Nov. 1947. See also UK Embassy cable to Foreign Office, "Weekly political summary (secret)", No. 225, E 8688/213/89, 6 Aug. 1946 and UK Embassy cable to Foreign Office, "Syria and the Palestine Question", No. 143, E 11851/11283/89, 15 Dec. 1947.
47. For more on the pro-Palestinian activism of the Ba'ath Party in the late 1940s see UK Embassy cable to Foreign Office, "Disturbances in Syria", No. 136, E 15809/2603/89, 13 Dec. 1947.

48. Interview with Zouheir Salem, London, 3 Oct. 2011.
49. Mustapha al-Sibai, "Islamic Socialism", in Kemal H. Karpat (ed.), *Political and Social Thought in the Contemporary Middle East* (London: Pall Mall, 1968), p. 124.
50. Mustapha al-Sibai quoted in Joshua Teitelbaum (2011), *op. cit.*, p. 224.
51. This led, among other things, to mass demonstrations by the Ikhwan in front of the Communist Party headquarters in Damascus and the Friends of Soviet Russia building. See "Syria and the Palestine Question", No. 143, E 11851/11283/89, 15 Dec. 1947.
52. UK cable to Foreign Office, "Observations on Communism in Syria (secret)", No. 75, PR 57/17/6, 6 May 1952.
53. "Ma'ruf Dawalibi" in UK Embassy cable to Foreign Office, "Leading personalities in Syria (secret)", No. 103, EY 1012/1, 9 July 1951.
54. "Muhammed Mubarak", in UK Embassy cable to Foreign Office, "Leading personalities in Syria", No. 132 Confidential, UY1012/1, 24 Aug. 1956.
55. UK Embassy cable to Foreign Office, "Weekly political summary", No. 3, E 3208/23/89, 26 May 1944.
56. UK Embassy cable to Foreign Office, "Briefing on the Ikhwan al-Muslimin, dispatch No. 123", E 9414/1211/89, 23 Sept. 1946.
57. Mustapha al-Sibai, "Islamic Socialism", Chapter 19 in Kemal H. Karpat (ed.), *Political and Social Thought in the Contemporary Middle East* (London: Pall Mall, 1968), p. 126.
58. UK Embassy cable to Foreign Office, "Weekly political summary", No. 241, E12267/213/89, 3 Dec. 1946.
59. UK Embassy cable to Foreign Office, "Trade union activities in Syria", No. 20, E 1349/1349/89, 13 Feb. 1947.
60. UK Embassy cable to Foreign Office, "Weekly political summary (secret)", No. 234, E 10682/213/89, 30 Oct. 1946.
61. Umar F. Abd Allah, *op. cit.*, p. 94.
62. Ibid., p. 93.
63. Mustapha al-Sibai, "Islamic Socialism", in Kemal H. Karpat (1968) Ibid., p. 126.
64. Muhammed al-Mubarak quoted in Joshua Teitelbaum (2011), *op. cit.*, p. 223. It should be noted that Muhammed al-Mubarak joined the People's Party in 1951 even though he remained close to the Ikhwan. See "Muhammed Mubarak", UK Embassy cable to Foreign Office, "Leading personalities in Syria", No. 132 Confidential, UY1012/1, 24 Aug. 1956.
65. "Muhammed Mubarak", UK Embassy cable to Foreign Office, "Leading personalities in Syria", No. 132 Confidential, UY1012/1, 24 Aug. 1956.
66. "Sheikh Mustafa al-Sibai", UK Embassy cable to Foreign Office, "Ledaing personalities in Syria", No. 132 Confidential, UY 1012/1, 24 Aug. 1956.

67. Besides being a prominent sympathizer of the Muslim Brotherhood, Ma'aruf al-Dawalibi was also a member of the People's Party in which he wielded great influence—most notably thanks to his good relations with Rushdi Kekbis who became the party's leader in August 1948. See "Ma'ruf Dawalibi", UK Embassy cable to Foreign Office, "Leading personalities in Syria (secret)", No. 103, EY 1012/1, 9 July 1951. Muhamad al-Mubarak, another prominent member of the Ikhwan, joined the People's Party in 1951 and contributed to reinforcing the links between the two platforms. See "Muhammed Mubarak", UK Embassy cable to Foreign Office, "Leading personalities in Syria", No. 132 Confidential, UY1012/1, 24 Aug. 1956.

68. Interview with Obeida Nahas, London, 30 June 2011.

69. UK Embassy cable to Foreign Office, "Political situation in Syria", Confidential No. 4, EY 1016/1, 10 January 1952.

70. UK Embassy cable to Foreign Office, "Syria: annual review for 1953", Confidential No. 31, VY 1011/1, 22 Feb. 1954.

71. Joshua Teitelbaum (2004), *op. cit.*, p. 151.

72. UK Embassy cable to Foreign Office, "Her Majesty's Ambassador's analysis of the events in Syria which brought about the resignation of President Shishakli and his suggestions as to what the character of the new regime may prove to be", Confidential No. 46, UY1016/85, 13 March 1954.

73. Joshua Teitelbaum (2004), *op. cit.*, p. 139.

74. UK Embassy cable to Foreign Office, "Work of the new government", No. 11, EY 1015/9, 16 July 1952.

75. UK Embassy cable to Foreign Office, "Legislative decree issued by the new Syrian government", Confidential No. 47, EY 1017/1, 29 March 1952.

76. "Muslim Brothers Faithful to Chief: An Interview with Mustapha al-Sibai", *New York Times*, 27 Feb. 1955.

77. In 1955, the assassination of the Ba'athist-affiliated Colonel Malki by Colonel Ghassan al-Jadid, himself affiliated with the Parti Populaire Syrien, had enabled Ba'athist commanders to carry out a first purge inside the Syrian armed forces. See UK Embassy cable to Foreign Office, "The assassination of Colonel Malki", Confidential No. 61, VY 1015/3, 2 May 1955. For more on the "small but powerful group of Syrian officers who supports the Ba'ath Socialist Party", see UK Embassy cable to Foreign Office, "Syria, annual review for 1954", Confidential No. 19, VY 1011/1, 14 Feb. 1955.

78. UK Embassy cable to Foreign Office, "Political situation", Confidential No. 135, V1054/4, 9 March 1954.

3. THE ISLAMIC REACTION TO THE BA'ATHIST REVOLUTION

1. Muhammad al-Mubarak quoted in Nazih Ayoubi, *Political Islam: Religion and Politics in the Arab World* (New York: Routledge, 1991), p. 89.

2. Olivier Carré and Gérard Michaud, *Les Frères Musulmans (1928–1982)* (Paris: Gallimard, 1983), p. 134.

3. Michel Aflaq quoted in Philip S. Khoury, *op. cit.*, pp. 605–6.

4. Michel Aflaq, "The Socialist Ideology of the Ba'th", in Kemal H. Karpat (ed.), *Political and Social Thought in the Contemporary Middle East* (London: Pall Mall, 1968), p. 193.

5. Stephen Humphreys, "Islam and Political Values in Saudi Arabia, Egypt and Syria", *Middle East Journal* (Vol. 33, No. 1, 1979), p. 13.

6. Interview with Abdel Halim Khaddam, Paris, 23 June 2011.

7. Patrick Seale, *Asad of Syria: The struggle for the Middle East* (London: I.B. Tauris, 1988), pp. 92–4.

8. Interview with Muhammed Riyad al-Shuqfeh, Istanbul, 9 Sept. 2011.

9. Interview with Abdel Halim Khaddam, Paris, 23 June 2011.

10. Thomas Pierret, *Baas et Islam en Syrie: la dynastie Assad face aux oulémas* (Paris: Presses Universitaires de France/Collection Proche Orient, 2011), pp. 237–9.

11. For more on the advent of the "neo-Ba'ath" and its policies, see Gordon Torrey, "The Neo-Ba'ath—ideology and practice", *Middle East Journal* (Vol. 23, No. 4, 1969), pp. 445–4.

12. Eyal Zisser, "Syria, the Ba'th Regime and the Islamic Movement: Stepping on a New Path?", *The Muslim World* (Vol. 85, No. 1, 2005), p. 45.

13. Ibrahim Khlass, "The path towards the creation of our new Arab man", *Jaysh al-Sha'b* (Apr. 1967), quoted in Olivier Carré and Gérard Michaud, *op. cit.*, pp. 132–3.

14. Ibrahim Khlass, "The path towards the creation of our new Arab man", *Jaysh al-Sha'b* (Apr. 1967), quoted in Mordechai Kedar, "In Search of Legitimacy: Asad's Islamic Image in the Syrian Official Press", in Moshe Ma'oz, Joseph Ginat and Onn Winckler (eds), *Modern Syria: From Ottoman Rule to Pivotal Role in the Middle East* (Brighton: Sussex Academic Press, 1999), p. 19.

15. Thomas Pierret, op. cit., p. 241.

16. Eyal Zisser, *op. cit.*, p. 44.

17. Moshe Ma'oz, *Asad: The Sphinx of Damascus* (London: Weidenfeld and Nicolson, 1988), pp. 150–51.

18. Mordechai Kedar, *op. cit.*, p. 23.

19. Thomas Pierret, "Sunni Clergy Politics in the Cities of Ba'thi Syria", in Fred H. Lawson (ed.), *Demystifying Syria* (London: Saqi Books and the Middle East Institute at SOAS, 2009), pp. 70–83.

20. Hafiz al-Assad quoted in Thomas Pierret (2011), *op. cit.*, p. 242.

21. John Donohue, "The new Syrian Constitution and the religious opposition", *CEMAM Reports* (No. 1, 1972), pp. 81–3.

22. Itzchak Weismann, "Sa'id Hawwa: the Making of a Radical Muslim Thinker in Modern Syria", *Middle Eastern Studies* (Vol. 29, No. 4, 1993), p. 618.

23. Thomas Pierret (2011), *op. cit.*, pp. 241–6.

24. Hafiz al-Assad quoted in Radwan Ziadeh, *op. cit.*, p. 140.

25. Interview with a former senior Syrian diplomat, London, 14 June 2011.

26. Philip S. Khoury, *op. cit.*, p. 50.

27. Michael Van Dusen, "Syria: Downfall of a Traditional Elite" in Frank Tachau (ed.), *Political Elites and Political Development in the Middle East* (New York: Shenkman Publishing Company Inc, 1975), p. 159.

28. Michael Van Dusen, *op. cit.*, p. 153.

29. Alasdair Drysdale, "The Asad Regime and its Troubles", *MERIP Reports* (No. 110, Nov.-Dec. 1982), pp. 5–25.

30. Raymond Hinnebusch, "Rural Politics in Ba'thist Syria: a Case Study in the Role of the Countryside in the Political Development of Arab Societies", *The Review of Politics* (Vol. 44, No. 1, 1982), p. 117.

31. Ziad Keilany, "Land Reform in Syria", *Middle Eastern Studies* (Vol. 16, No. 3, 1980), p. 210.

32. Raymond Hinnebusch (1982), *op. cit.*, p. 117.

33. Syed Aziz al Ahsan, "Economic Policy and Class Structure in Syria: 1958–1980", *International Journal of Middle East Studies* (Vol. 16, No. 3, 1984), p. 307.

34. Robert Springborg, "Baathism in Practice: Agriculture, Politics and Political Culture in Syria and Iraq", *Middle Eastern Studies* (Vol. 17, No. 2, 1981), p. 197.

35. Elizabeth Longuenesse, "The Class Nature of the State in Syria", *MERIP Reports* (May 1979), p. 4.

36. Fred H. Lawson, "The Social Basis for the Hamah Revolt", *MERIP Reports* (No. 110, Dec. 1982), p. 24.

37. Hanna Batatu, "Syria's Muslim Brethren", *MERIP Reports* (No. 110, Nov.-Dec. 1982), p. 15.

38. Michel Aflaq (1968), *op. cit.*, p. 195.

39. Raymond Hinnebusch, *Authoritarian Power and State Formation in Ba'thist Syria: Army, Party and Peasants* (San Francisco: Westview Press, 1990), p. 291.

40. Hanna Batatu (1982), *op. cit.*, p. 16.

41. Ibid., p. 19.

42. Umar F. Abd-Allah, *op. cit.*, p. 162.

43. Ibid., p. 162.

44. Raymond Hinnebusch (1990), *op. cit.*, p. 284.

45. UK Embassy cable to Foreign Office, "Political Situation—confidential", EY 1015/32, No. 232, 1950.

46. Interview with Obeida Nahas, London, 30 June 2011.
47. Fred H. Lawson (1984), *op. cit.*, pp. 465–7.
48. Ibid., *op. cit.*, p. 469.
49. Patrick Seale, *op. cit.*, p. 320.
50. Michael Van Dusen, *op. cit.*, p. 144.
51. Patrick Seale, *op. cit.*, p. 321.
52. George Joffé, "Arab Nationalism and Palestine", *Journal of Peace Research* (Vol. 20, No. 2, 1983), pp. 164–7.
53. Daniel Pipes, *Greater Syria: The History of an Ambition* (Oxford University Press, 1990), p. 151.
54. Patrick Seale, *op. cit.*, p. 282.
55. Alasdair Drysdale, "The Asad regime and its troubles", *MERIP Reports* (No. 110, Nov.-Dec. 1982), p. 4.
56. Patrick Seale, *op. cit.*, p. 285.
57. Salah Eddine al-Bitar, *Le Monde*, 21 Sept. 1976 quoted in Patrick Seale, *op. cit.*, pp. 286–7.
58. Hanna Batatu, *Syria's Peasantry, the Descendants of its Lesser Rural Notables and their Politics* (Princeton: Princeton University Press, 1999), p. 259.
59. Interview with Abdel Halim Khaddam, Paris, 23 June 2011.
60. Ibid.
61. Ibid.
62. Patrick Seale, *op. cit.*, p. 319.
63. See Table 2 and 3 in Nikolaos Van Dam, "Sectarian and Regional Factionalism in the Syrian Political Elite", *Middle East Journal* (Vol. 32, No. 2, 1978), pp. 204–6.
64. Raymond Hinnebusch, "State and Islamism in Syria", in Abdul Salam Sidahmed and Anoushiravan Ehteshami (eds), *Islamic Fundamentalism* (Boulder: Westview Press, 1996), p. 205.
65. Fred H. Lawson (1984), *op. cit.*, p. 466.
66. Ibid., p. 24
67. Itzchak Weismann, "The Politics of Popular Religion: Sufis, Salafis and Muslim Brothers in 20th Century Hamah", *International Journal of Middle Eastern Studies* (Vol. 37, No. 1, 2005), p. 52.
68. Michel Seurat, *L'Etat de barbarie* (Paris: Seuil, 1989), p. 73.
69. Olivier Carré and Gérard Michaud (1982), *op. cit.*, p. 31.
70. Interview with Abdel Halim Khaddam, Paris, 23 June 2011.
71. Interview with Ahmed al-Uthman, Paris, 2 June 2011.
72. Interview with Abdel Halim Khaddam, Paris, 23 June 2011.
73. Fred H. Lawson (1982), *op. cit.*, p. 27.
74. Philippe Droz-Vincent, *Pouvoirs autoritaires, sociétés bloquées* (Paris: PUF, 2004), p. 266.

75. Interview with Abdel Halim Khaddam, Paris, 23 June 2011.

76. See Table 3 in Nikolaos Van Dam (1978), *op. cit.*, p. 206.

77. Michel Seurat (1989), *op. cit.*, p. 73.

4. "A MINORITY CANNOT FOREVER RULE A MAJORITY"

1. Michel Seurat, "Vague d'agitation confessionnelle en Syrie", *Le Monde Diplomatique*, Oct. 1979.

2. Hanna Batatu, "Some Observations on the Social Roots of Syria's Ruling Military Group and the Causes for its Dominance", *Middle East Journal* (Vol. 35, No. 3, 1981), p. 334.

3. Yaron Friedman, *The Nusayri-Alawi: An Introduction to the Religion, History and Identity of the Leading Minority in Syria* (Leiden: Koninklijke Brill NV, 2010), pp. 223–35.

4. Mahmud Faksh, "The Alawi Community in Syria: A New Dominant Political Force", *Middle Eastern Studies* (Vol. 20, No. 2, 1984), p. 135.

5. See, for instance, Pierre May, *L'Alaouite: ses croyances, ses mœurs, les cheikhs, les lois de la tribu et les chefs* (Beirut: Imprimerie Catholique, 1931), pp. 42–3 as well as Jehan Cendrieux, *Al Ghadir ou le sexe-Dieu* (Paris: Bibliothèque Charpentier, 1926), p. 11.

6. For a complete English translation of Ibn Taymiyya's *fatwa*, see Yaron Friedman, *op. cit.*, pp. 303–9. For a politico-theological analysis of the *fatwa*, see Yaron Friedman, "Ibn Taymiyya's Fatwa against the Nusayri-Alawi Sect", *Der Islam* (Vol. 82, No. 2, 2005), pp. 349–63.

7. Although the "State of the Alawis" was formally reintegrated into Syria in 1936, it continued to enjoy a particular dose of autonomy from Damascus until 1946. In 1939 and 1942, laws were enacted to grant the Alawi territory and the Jebel Druze administrative and financial autonomy. Upon Syria's independence from France, one of the first acts of the newly elected Chamber of Deputies was to revoke such laws and fully reintegrate these two territories into the Syrian state.

8. UK Embassy cable to Foreign Office, "Capture and trial of Suleiman Murshid", No. 26, E12530/0204/80, 19 Dec. 1946.

9. UK Embassy cable to Foreign Office, "Weekly political summary (secret), No. 218, E6193/213/89, 11 June 1946.

10. UK Embassy cable to Foreign Office, "Weekly political summary (secret)", No. 99, E1487/23/89, 7 March 1944.

11. Michael Van Dusen, *op. cit.*, p. 128.

12. UK Embassy cable to Foreign Office, "Weekly political summary (secret)", No. 99, E 1487/23/89, 7 March 1944.

13. UK Embassy cable to Foreign Office, "Mr. Shone to Mr. Bevin", No. 18, E1872 Feb. 89, 1 March 1946.

14. UK Embassy cable to Foreign Office, "Syria: weekly political summary", No. 5, E 1511/171/89, 19 Feb. 1947.
15. UK Embassy cable to Foreign Office, "Weekly political summary (secret)", No. 218, 11 June 1946.
16. UK Embassy cable to Foreign Office, "Weekly political summary (secret)", No. 212, E4471/213/89, 30 Apr. 1946.
17. UK Embassy cable to Foreign Office, "Capture and trial of Suleiman Murshid", No. 26, E12530/0204/80, 19 Dec. 1946.
18. Martin Kramer, "Syria's Alawis and Shi'ism" in Martin Kramer (ed.), *Shi'ism, Resistance and Revolution* (Boulder: Westview Press, 1987), p. 245.
19. See Matti Moosa, *Extremist Shiites: The Ghulat Sects* (Syracuse: Syracuse University Press, 1988), p. 297.
20. See Annie Laurent, "Syrie-Liban: les faux-frères jumeaux", *Politique Etrangère* (Vol. 48, No. 3, 1983), pp. 597–8.
21. See Daniel Pipes, *Greater Syria, the History of an Ambition* (New York: Oxford University Press, 1990), pp. 166–80.
22. UK Embassy cable to Foreign Office, "Syria: weekly summary", E 7787/171/89, No. 33, 25 Aug. 1947.
23. Hanna Batatu (1999), *op. cit.*, p. 142.
24. UK Embassy cable to Foreign Office, "Capture and trial of Suleiman Murshid", No. 26, E12530/0204/80, 19 Dec. 1946.
25. See Michael Van Dusen, "Syria: Downfall of a Traditional Elite" in Frank Tachau (ed.), *Political Elites and Political Development in the Middle East* (New York: Shenkman Publishing Company Inc, 1975), p. 136 and also Hanna Batatu (1999), *op. cit.*, pp. 157–60.
26. Hanna Batatu (1999), *op. cit.*, pp. 144–61.
27. See Table 5 and 6 in Nikolaos Van Dam (1978), *op. cit.*, pp. 208–210.
28. Fabrice Balanche, *La région alaouite et le pouvoir syrien* (Paris: Editions Karthala, 2006), pp. 52–64.
29. Michel Seurat (1989), *op. cit.*, p. 67.
30. Michel Seurat, "Vague d'agitation confessionnelle en Syrie", *Le Monde Diplomatique* (Oct. 1979).
31. Interview with Ahmed al-Uthman, Paris, 2 June 2011.
32. Jacques Weulersse, *Le pays des Alaouites* (Damascus: Institut Français de Damas, 1940), p. 77.
33. These figures are drawn from an analysis of Tables 3, 4, 5, 6 and 7 in Nikolaos Van Dam, *The Struggle for Power in Syria: Politics and Society under Asad and the Ba'th Party* (London: I.B. Tauris, 1996), pp. 82–6.
34. Interview with a former senior Syrian diplomat, London, 14 June 2011.
35. Martin Kramer, *op. cit.*, pp. 246–9.
36. Thomas Pierret, "Sunni Clergy Politics in the Cities of Ba'thi Syria", in Fred

H. Lawson (ed.), *Demystifying Syria* (London: Saqi Books and the Middle East Institute at SOAS, 2009), pp. 70–83.

37. *Al-Nadhir*, No. 1, 6 Sept. 1979 and No. 6, 8 Nov. 1979, quoted in Nikolaos Van Dam (2011, 4ᵗʰ Edition of 1996), p. 90.
38. "The Manifesto of the Islamic Revolution in Syria" quoted in Umar F. Abd-Allah, *op. cit.*, p. 211.
39. Interview with a former senior Syrian diplomat, London, 14 June 2011.
40. Patrick Seale, *op. cit., pp. 316–17.*
41. Gérard Michaud and Jim Paul, "The Importance of Bodyguards", *MERIP Reports* (No. 110, Nov.-Dec. 1982), p. 30.
42. Hanna Batatu (1982), *op. cit.*, p. 336.
43. Interview with Abdel Halim Khaddam, Paris, 23 June 2011.
44. Interview with a deputy-leader of the "Muslim Brotherhood", *Radio Damascus*, 7 Sept. 1979, quoted in Nikolaos Van Dam (2011), *op. cit.*, p. 91.
45. James A. Paul, *Syria Unmasked: The Suppression of Human Rights by the Assad Regime* (New Haven: Yale University Press, 1991), p. 10.
46. Michel Seurat (1989), *op. cit.*, p. 73.
47. Michel Seurat, "Vague d'agitation confessionnelle en Syrie", *Le Monde Diplomatique*, Oct. 1979.
48. Interview with Walid Safour, London, 22 Sept. 2011.
49. Patrick Seale, *op. cit.*, p. 327.
50. *Tishrin*, 9 March 1980 quoted in James A. Paul, *op. cit.*, p. 12.
51. James A. Paul, *op. cit.*, p. 13.
52. General Shafiq Fayadh quoted in Patrick Seale, *op. cit.*, p. 328.
53. James A. Paul, *op. cit.*, p. 15.
54. Ibid., p. 20.
55. Syrian Human Rights Committee, "The Massacre of Hama (1982): Law Application Requires Accountability", (London, 1999). The report is available online at: http://www.shrc.org/data/aspx/d1/1121.aspx
56. Interview with Abdel Halim Khaddam, Paris, 23 June 2011.

5. THE RADICALIZATION OF THE ISLAMIC MOVEMENT (1963–1980)

1. Interview with Mohammed Hawari, Aachen, 19 Dec. 2011.
2. Itzchak Weismann, *Taste of Modernity: Sufism, Salafiyya and Arabism in Late Ottoman Damascus* (Leiden: Brill, 2001), p. 223.
3. For more on the Damascene Salafis' early advocacy of ideas stemming from political liberalism, see David D. Commins, *op. cit.*, pp. 124–31.
4. For more on the thought of al-Tamaddun al-Islami, see Ahmad Mouaz al-Khatib (translation by Thomas Pierret), "Al-Tamaddun al-Islami: passé et

présent d'une association réformiste damascène", *Maghreb-Machrek* (No. 198, Winter 2008–2009), pp. 2–5.

5. Itzchak Weismann, "Democratic Fundamentalism? The Practice and Discourse of the Muslim Brothers movement in Syria", *The Muslim World* (Vol. 100, No. 1, 2010), p. 8.

6. Nazih Ayoubi, *Political Islam: Religion and Politics in the Arab World* (New York: Routledge, 1991), p. 89.

7. Ahmad Mouaz al-Khatib, *op. cit.*, p. 8.

8. Interview with Mohammed Hawari, Aachen, 19 Dec. 2011.

9. From an expression coined by Henri Laoust and quoted in Stéphane Lacroix, "L'apport de Muhammed Nasir al-Din al-Albani au salafisme contemporain", in Bernard Rougier (ed.), *Qu'est ce que le salafisme?* (Paris: PUF, 2008), p. 49.

10. Interview with Issam al-Attar, Aachen, 19 Dec. 2011.

11. Ibid.

12. Ibid.

13. Umar F. Abd Allah, *op. cit.*, pp. 102–3.

14. Interview with Ali Sadreddine al-Bayanouni, London, 30 Nov. 2011 and interview with Zouheir Salem, London, 3 Oct. 2011.

15. Interview with Muhammed Hawari, Aachen, 19 Nov. 2011.

16. Interview with Issam al-Attar, Aachen, 19 Dec. 2011.

17. Interview with Muhammed Riyad al-Shuqfah, Istanbul, 9 Sept. 2011.

18. Interview with Muhammed Hawari, Aachen, 19 Nov. 2011.

19. Umar F. Abd Allah, *op. cit.*, p. 102.

20. Interview with Issam al-Attar, Aachen, 19 Dec. 2011.

21. Interview with Ali Sadreddine al-Bayanouni, London, 30 Nov. 2011.

22. Interview with Issam al-Attar, Aachen, 19 Dec. 2011.

23. Interview with Muhammed Hawari, Aachen, 19 Nov. 2011.

24. Interview with Issam al-Attar, Aachen, 19 Dec. 2011.

25. Ibid.

26. Interview with Muhammed Riyad al-Shuqfah, Istanbul, 9 Sept. 2011.

27. Umar F. Abd Allah, *op. cit.*, pp. 107–8.

28. Interview with Muhammed Hawari, Aachen, 19 Nov. 2011.

29. Ibid.

30. Hassan al-Houeidi was one of the rare Damascene Brothers who was formally reintegrated into the Syrian Muslim Brotherhood after the split of the early 1970s. He was to leave Issam al-Attar for good in 1981 after the "Damascus wing" split from a short-lived union between Ikhwani and jihadist forces. Houeidi remained an important voice in the Syrian Muslim Brotherhood, becoming one of the organization's leaders in the early 1990s.

31. Although Muhammed Surur Zein al-Abideen belonged to the "Damascus wing", he was originally from Dar'a.

32. Interview with Malik al-Abdeh, London, 6 Dec. 2011.
33. Interview with Muhammed Hawari, Aachen, 19 Nov. 2011.
34. Thomas Pierret, *Baas et Islam en Syrie: la dynastie Assad face aux oulémas* (Paris: PUF, 2011), pp. 241–5.
35. Itzchak Weismann, "Sa'id Hawwa: The Making of a Radical Muslim Thinker in Modern Syria", *Middle Eastern Studies* (Vol. 29, No. 4, 1993), p. 618.
36. Itzchak Weismann, "Sa'id Hawwa and Islamic Revivalism in Ba'thist Syria", *Studia Islamica* (No. 85, 1997), p. 152.
37. Sayyid Qutb quoted in Gilles Kepel, *Muslim Extremism in Egypt: The Prophet and the Pharaoh* (Los Angeles: University of California Press, 1985), p. 53.
38. Sayyid Qutb in Nazih Ayubi, *Political Islam: Religion and Politics* (New York: Routledge, 1991), p. 140.
39. Sayyid Qutb quoted in Gilles Kepel, *op. cit.*, p. 54.
40. Gilles Kepel, *op. cit.*, p. 56.
41. Umar F. Abd Allah, *op. cit.*, pp. 104–5.
42. Ibid., p. 105.
43. While most Hamawite members of the Ikhwan assert, until today, that Marwan Hadid had been part of the organization throughout his life, other members, most often from Aleppo or Damascus, claim that his membership was revoked following the April 1964 uprising in Hama.
44. Unknown author, document found in Usama Bin Laden's home in Abbottabad, Pakistan, referenced by West Point's Center for Counter Terrorism as [SOCOM-2012–0000017], available online at: http://www.ctc.usma.edu/posts/letters-from-abbottabad-bin-ladin-sidelined
45. Ayman al-Shorbaji, *The diary of Ayman al-Shorbaji, the leader of the Muslim Brotherhood's Vanguard fighters in Damascus in the 1980s which formed the height of the conflict between the Vanguards and the Syrian regime* (Date and place of publication unknown, copy given to the author, translation by Emira Bahri).
46. Interview with Muhammed Riyad al-Shuqfah, Istanbul, 9 Sept. 2011.
47. Dr. Manna, "Histoire des Frères Musulmans en Syria", *Sou'al* (Vol. 5, 1985), p. 76.
48. Olivier Carré and Gérard Michaud, *op. cit.*, p. 152.
49. Interview with Ali Sadreddine al-Bayanouni, London, 21 July 2011.
50. Abu Mus'ab al-Suri, "Lessons learned from the armed Jihad ordeal in Syria" (Document captured by US troops in Afghanistan in 2002, referenced as AFGP-2002–600080, full translation), p. 29. The document was accessed on the US Department of Defence's Harmony Database website of the Combating Terrorism Center at West Point.
51. Ayman al-Shorbaji, *op. cit.*, p. 10.
52. Abu Mus'ab al-Suri, *op. cit.*, p. 18.

53. Ayman al-Shorbaji, *op. cit.*, pp. 27–9.

54. Interview, name withheld on request, Nov. 2011.

55. Even though, within al-Tali'a, power formally lay in the hands of Abd us-Sattar az-Za'im and, upon his death, of his successors Hisham Jumbaz, Tamim al-Shuqraqi and Umar Jawad, it is widely reported that it was Adnan Uqlah who in fact exercised the most influence and authority inside the jihadist organization from the late 1970s, to the extent that he is often referred to as the actual leader of al-Tali'a in media reports and intelligence dispatches. See, for instance, US Defense Intelligence Agency (DIA), "Syria: Muslim Brotherhood pressure intensifies" (Secret), DDB-2630–34-B2, 22 Apr. 1982.

56. Gérard Michaud, "The Importance of Bodyguards", *Merip Reports* (Dec. 1982), p. 29.

57. Abu Mus'ab al-Suri, *op. cit.*, p. 21.

58. Ibid., p. 45.

59. Interview with Obeida Nahas, London, 30 June 2011.

60. Hanna Batatu (1999), *op. cit.*, p. 270.

61. Interview with Muhammed Riyad al-Shuqfah, Istanbul, 9 Sept. 2011.

62. Abu Mus'ab al-Suri, *op. cit.*, p. 41.

63. Ibid., pp. 39–40.

64. Abu Mus'ab al-Suri, *op. cit.*, p. 13 and p. 40.

6. ENDORSING JIHAD AGAINST THE BA'ATH (1980–1982)

1. Interview with Muhammed Riyadh al-Shuqfah, Istanbul, 9 Sept. 2011.

2. See *The Political Perspective for Syria: The Muslim Brotherhood's Vision of the Future* (London, Dec. 2004, copy given to the author), pp. 3–4.

3. Umar F. Abd-Allah, *op. cit.*, p. 109.

4. Interview with Abdel Halim Khaddam, Paris, 23 June 2011.

5. Interview with Yahya Bedir, Istanbul, 9 Sept. 2011.

6. Unknown author, document found in Usama Bin Laden's home in Abbottabad, Pakistan, referenced by West Point's Center for Counter Terrorism as [SOCOM-2012–0000017], available online at: http://www.ctc.usma.edu/posts/letters-from-abbottabad-bin-ladin-sidelined

7. See, for instance, Barry Rubin, *The Truth About Syria* (New York: Palgrave MacMillan, 2007), p. 57 and Daniel Pipes, *Greater Syria: The History of an Ambition* (New York; Oxford University Press, 1992), p. 182. Other authors who studied the period in detail, such as Itzchak Weissmann, have also not questioned the Brotherhood's involvement in the massacre: see Itzchak Weissmann, "Sa'id Hawwa: The Making of a Radical Muslim Thinker in Modern Syria", *Middle Eastern Studies* (Vol. 29, No. 4, 1993), p. 618. Works pub-

lished in English disputing the regime's thesis in details are rare. See Hanna Batatu (1999), *op. cit.*, pp. 266–8 and Alison Pargeter, *The Muslim Brotherhood: The Burden of Tradition* (London: Saqi Books, 2010), pp. 78–9.

8. Interview with Zouheir Salem, London, 3 Oct. 2011.
9. James A. Paul, *op. cit.*, p. 10.
10. Interview with Walid Safour, London, 22 Sept. 2011.
11. James A. Paul, *op. cit.*, p. 55.
12. Interview with Walid Safour, London, 22 Sept. 2011.
13. James A. Paul, *op. cit.*, p. 56.
14. Ali Sadreddine al-Bayanouni quoted in Alan George, *Syria: Neither Bread nor Freedom* (London: Zed Books, 2003), p. 91.
15. Interview with Issam al-Attar, Aachen, 19 Nov. 2011.
16. For more information, see Syrian Human Rights Committee, "The Tadmur (Palmyra) prison massacre on its 27th anniversary", 26 June 2007, also available at: http://www.shrc.org/data/aspx/d3/3243.aspx
17. Quoted in Paul A. James, *op. cit.*, p. 16.
18. Rif'at al-Assad in an editorial in *Tishrin*, 1 July 1980 quoted in Paul A. James, *op. cit.*, p. 16.
19. Interview with Abdel Halim Khaddam, Paris, 23 June 2011.
20. Interview with Mohammed Aldik, Paris, 8 Feb. 2012.
21. Syrian Human Rights Committee, "Special Report: repressive laws in Syria", 19 Feb. 2001, also available at: http://www.shrc.org/data/aspx/d4/254.aspx#D2
22. Interview with Ahmed al-Uthman, Paris, 2 June 2011.
23. Interview with Ali Sadreddine al-Bayanouni, London, 30 Nov. 2011.
24. Ibid.
25. Interview with Muhammed Riyad al-Shuqfah, Istanbul, 9 Sept. 2011.
26. Abu Mus'ab al-Suri, *op. cit.*, pp. 13–14.
27. Ibid., p. 35
28. Unknown author, document found in Usama Bin Laden's home in Abbottabad, Pakistan, referenced by West Point's Center for Counter Terrorism as [SOCOM-2012–0000017], available online at: http://www.ctc.usma.edu/posts/letters-from-abbottabad-bin-ladin-sidelined
29. Abu Mus'ab al-Suri, *op. cit.*, p. 37.
30. Interview with Zouheir Salem, London, 3 Oct. 2011.
31. Interview with Muhammed Hawari, Aachen, 19 Nov. 2011.
32. Interview with Issam al-Attar, Aachen, 19 Dec. 2011.
33. Abu Mus'ab al-Suri, *op. cit.*, p. 41.
34. Michel Seurat (1989), *op. cit.*, p. 57.
35. US Defense Intelligence Agency (DIA), "Syria: Muslim Brotherhood pressure intensifies" (Secret), DDB-2630–34-B2, 22 Apr. 1982.

36. Interview with Obeida Nahas, London 23 June 2011.
37. Interview with Ahmed al-Uthman, Paris, 2 June 2011.
38. A deputy leader of al-Tali'a quoted in Chris Kutschera, "Les Frères Musulmans et l'alliance politique", *Le Monde Diplomatique*, March 1983.
39. Abu Mus'ab al-Suri, *op. cit.*, p. 16.
40. For the full text of the Islamic Front's Charter, see Umar F. Abd-Allah, *op. cit.*, pp. 148–90.
41. Interview with Muhammed Hawari, Aachen, 19 Dec. 2011.
42. Abu Mus'ab al-Suri, *op. cit.*, p. 40.
43. Interview, name withheld on request, Jan. 2012.
44. Abu Mus'ab al-Suri, *op. cit.*, p. 42.
45. Ibid., p. 40.
46. Ibid., p. 16.
47. Ibid., p. 15.
48. Ibid., p. 16.
49. Interview with Zouheir Salem, London, 3 Oct. 2011.
50. Interview with Muhammed Riyad al-Shuqfah, Istanbul, 9 Sept. 2011 and interview with Zouheir Salem, London, 20 July 2011. See also Alison Pargeter, *The Muslim Brotherhood: The Burden of Tradition* (London: Saqi Books, 2010), pp. 85–6.
51. Abu Mus'ab al-Suri, *op. cit.*, p. 41.
52. Interview with Zouheir Salem, London, 3 Oct. 2011.
53. Interview with Muhammed Riyad al-Shuqfah, Istanbul, 9 Sept. 2011.
54. Interview with Muhammed Riyad al-Shuqfah, Istanbul, 9 Sept. 2011 and interview with Zouheir Salem, London, 3 Oct. 2011.
55. Adnan Saadeddine for instance stated "[Marwan Hadid] stayed in the Ikhwan and he didn't leave it. We never kicked him out": Adnan Saadeddine quoted in Alison Pargeter, *op. cit.*, p. 77.
56. Interview with Muhammed Riyad al-Shuqfah, Istanbul, 9 Sept. 2011.
57. Interview with Ali Sadreddine al-Bayanouni, London, 30 Nov. 2011. Ali Sadreddine al-Bayanouni's suggestion that, in Hama, there was cooperation, if not fusion, between the local branches of al-Tali'a and the Syrian Brotherhood is partially confirmed by the release of an intelligence cable from the US Defense Intelligence Agency according to which Adnan Saadeddine "had acquired considerable experience with [al-Tali'a al-Muqatila]" and Said Hawwa, "his deputy", had even "served as an assistant to Sheikh Marwan Haddid" up to the latter's death. See US Defense Intelligence Agency (DIA), "Syria: Muslim Brotherhood pressure intensifies" (Secret), DDB-2630-34-B2, 22 Apr. 1982.
58. Interview with Muhammed Aldik, Paris, 8 Feb. 2012.
59. Interview with Ali Sadreddine al-Bayanouni, London, 30 Nov. 2011.

60. US Defense Intelligence Agency (DIA) cable, "Syria: Muslim Brotherhood pressure intensifies" (Secret), DDB-2630–34-B2, 22 Apr. 1982.
61. This account is based on extensive discussions with Obeida Nahas, Ali al-Bayanuni and Zouheir Salem. Interview with Zouheir Salem, London, 21 July 2011; interview with Ali al-Bayanuni, London, 21 July 2011 and interview with Obeida Nahas, London, 23 June 2011.
62. Interview with Muhammed Riyad al-Shuqfah, Istanbul, 9 Sept. 2011.
63. Interview with Zouheir Salem, London, 20 July 2011.
64. Interview with Ali Sadreddine al-Bayanouni, London, 30 Nov. 2011.
65. US Defense Intelligence Agency (DIA) cable, "Syria: Muslim Brotherhood pressure intensifies" (Secret), DDB-2630–34-B2, 22 Apr. 1982.
66. James A. Paul, *op. cit.*, p. 20.
67. Patrick Seale, *op. cit.*, p. 335.
68. Eberhard Kienle, *Ba'th v. Ba'th: The Conflict between Syria and Iraq, 1968–1989* (London: I.B. Tauris, 1990), p. 35.
69. Amazia Baram, "Ideology and Power Politics in Syrian-Iraqi Relations, 1968–1984" in Moshe Ma'oz and Avner Yaniv (eds), *Syria under Assad; Domestic Constraints and Regional Risks* (London: Palgrave Macmillan, 1986), p. 128.
70. Interview with Abdel Halim Khaddam, Paris, 23 June 2011.
71. Hanna Batatu (1999), *op. cit.*, p. 269.
72. Interview with Obeida Nahas, London 23 June 2011.
73. Interview with Muhammed Riyadh al-Shuqfah, Istanbul, 9 Sept. 2011.
74. Correspondence with Muhammed al-Jundi through an intermediary, Muhammed Aldik, 16 March 2012.
75. Hafiz al-Assad quoted in Raymond Hinnebusch (1990), *op. cit.*, p. 290.
76. Abu Mus'ab al-Suri quoted in Brynjar Lia, *Architect of Global Jihad: the Life of al-Qaeda Strategist Abu Mus'ab al-Suri* (London: Hurst & Co., 2008), p. 44.
77. President Sadat was eventually assassinated in October1981 by members of Islamic Jihad, a violent offshoot of Egypt's Muslim Brotherhood set up in 1980 by the jihadist ideologue Muhammad Abdel Salam Faraj.
78. Brynjar Lia (2008), *op. cit.*, p. 45.
79. Interview with Abdel Halim Khaddam, Paris, 23 June 2011.
80. Interview with Obeida Nahas, London, 23 June 2011.
81. Ibid.
82. Abu Mus'ab al-Suri, *op. cit., p. 9.*
83. Ibid., p. 10.
84. Ibid., p. 22.

7. MILITANT ISLAM AFTER HAMA

1. Thomas Friedman, *From Beirut to Jerusalem* (New York: Anchor, 1990), p. 76.
2. It has been reported that former members of al-Tali'a, who participated in the Syrian jihad of the early 1980s, have now made their way back to fight the Ba'ath regime. For instance, a group including former Syrian jihadist fighters is called the Harakat al-Mu'uminun Yusharikun (the "Believers Participate Movement") led by a former al-Tali'a member, Lu'ay al-Zu'bi. See Abdulrahman Alhaj, "Political Islam and the Syrian Revolution", *Al Jazeera Center for Studies*, 10 June 2012.
3. Interview with a former senior British Intelligence official, name withheld on request, Nov. 2011.
4. US Embassy cable to State Department, "The Syrian Muslim Brotherhood", DAMASCUS 575, 26 Feb. 1985.
5. Abu Mus'ab al-Suri, *op. cit.*, p. 13.
6. Ibid., p. 36.
7. US Defense Intelligence Agency (DIA), "Syria: Muslim Brotherhood pressure intensifies" (Secret), DDB-2630–34-B2, 22 Apr. 1982.
8. Interview with Ali Sadreddine al-Bayanouni, London, 4 Sept. 2012.
9. Interview, name withheld on request, Dec. 2011 and Feb. 2012.
10. Interview, name withheld on request, Feb. 2012.
11. Abu Mus'ab al-Suri, *op. cit.*, p. 13. A cable from the US Embassy in Damascus disputes Abu Mus'ab al-Suri's claim that only a "few members" of al-Tali'a returned to Syria after having negotiated with the Assad regime. It instead suggests the number of former jihadist fighters who gave up their fight against the Ba'ath was then much higher: "we even have a report that some 'few hundred' al-Tali'a members have returned to Syria from refuge in Saudi Arabia", the cable states. See US Embassy cable to State Department, "The Syrian Muslim Brotherhood", DAMASCUS 575, 26 Feb. 1985.
12. Abu Mus'ab al-Suri, *op. cit.*, p. 35.
13. Interview with Abdullah Anas, London, 2 Oct. 2011.
14. Ibid.
15. "Join the caravan" was the title of a book authored by Abdullah Azzam and also one of his catchphrases to implore Muslims across the world to rally around his call for jihad aimed at protecting Islamic lands from foreign domination. A copy of his volume translated into English is available at: http://www.hoor-al-ayn.com/Books/Join%20the%20Caravan.pdf
16. Interview with Abdullah Anas, London, 2 Oct. 2011.
17. Bernard Rougier, "Le jihad en Afghanistan et l'émergence du salafisme-jihadiste", in Bernard Rougier (ed.), *Qu'est ce que le salafisme?* (Paris: PUF, 2008), pp. 65–86.

18. Abdullah Azzam, "The solid base", *al-Jihad* (Apr. 1988, No. 41), quoted in Rofl Mowatt-Larssen, "Al-Qaeda's Religious Justification of Nuclear Terrorism", *Working Paper*, Belfer Center for Science and International Affairs, Harvard Kennedy School (12 Oct. 2010).

19. Bernard Rougier, "Le jihad en Afghanistan et l'émergence du salafisme-jihadisme" in Bernard Rougier (ed.) *Qu'est ce que le salafisme?* (Paris: PUF, 2008), p. 69.

20. Interview with Abdullah Anas, London, 2 Oct. 2011.

21. Brynjar Lia, *op. cit.*, p. 74.

22. Ibid., p. 73.

23. Abu Mus'ab al-Suri quoted in Brynjar Lia, *op. cit.*, pp. 74–5.

24. Brynjar Lia, *op. cit.*, p. 75.

25. Ibid., p. 104.

26. US Embassy (Madrid) cable to State Department, "Spain: an active front in the war on terror", Secret, 05 Madrid 3260, 15 Sept. 2005.

27. Ibid.

28. Brynjar Lia, *op. cit.*, pp. 132–3.

29. Abu Mus'ab al-Suri quoted in Nibras Kazimi, *Syria Through Jihadist Eyes: A Perfect Enemy* (Stanford: Hoover Institution Press, 2010), p. 35.

30. Abu Mus'ab al-Suri quoted in Nibras Kazimi, *op. cit.*, p. 33.

31. Abu Baseer al-Tartousi quoted in Nibras Kazimi, *op. cit.*, pp. 38–9.

32. Interview with a Salafist-jihadist, name withheld on request, Tunis, March 2012.

33. Abu Jandal quoted in Nibras Kazimi, *op. cit.*, pp. 40–41.

34. Murad Batal al-Shishani, "Abu Mus'ab al-Suri and the Third Generation of Salafi-jihadists", *Terrorism Monitor* (Vol. 3, No. 16, 2005).

35. For the full detailed figures see Brian Fishman (ed.), *Bombers, Bank Accounts and Bleedout: Al-Qaeda's Road in and out of Iraq* (West Point: Combating Terrorism Centre at West Point, July 2008), pp. 33–6, and US Embassy Cable to State Department, "Syria: 2008 country report on terrorism", 08STATE120019, 29 Dec. 2008.

36. Michael Rubin, "Syria's Path to Islamist Terror", *Middle East Quarterly* (Winter 2010), p. 30.

37. Interview with a former senior British Intelligence official, name withheld on request, Nov. 2011.

38. Ghaith Abdul-Ahad, "From here to eternity", *The Guardian*, 8 May 2005.

39. Matthew Levitt, "Syria's Financial Support for Jihad", *Middle East Quarterly* (Winter 2010), p. 41.

40. US Embassy cable to State Department, "Syria: 2008 country report on terrorism", 08STATE120019, 29 Dec. 2008.

41. The full translated transcript of Muayed al-Nasseri is available: "The 'Army

of Muhammed' confesses: we received aid in money and arms from Syria and Iran", *Memri TV*, 14 Jan. 2005.

42. US Embassy (Baghdad) cable to State Department, "The great game in Mesopotamia: Iraq and its neighbours, Part II", 09BAGHDAD2561, 24 Sept. 2009.

43. US Embassy (Damascus) cable to State Department, "Syria: 2008 country report on terrorism", 08STATE120019, 29 Dec. 2008.

44. Matthew Levitt, "Syria's Financial Support for Jihad", *Middle East Quarterly* (Winter 2010), p. 44.

45. US Embassy (Baghdad) cable to State Department, "The great game in Mesopotamia: Iraq and its neighbours, Part II", 09BAGHDAD2561, 24 Sept. 2009.

46. US Embassy (Damascus) cable to State Department, "Syrian intelligence chief attends Ct dialogue with S/Ct Benjamin", 10DAMASCUS159, 24 Feb. 2010.

47. Ghait Abdul-Ahad, "From here to eternity", *The Guardian*, 8 May 2005.

48. "In secular Syria, an Islamic revival", *Christian Science Monitor*, 3 Oct. 2003.

49. "The 'Army of Muhammed' confesses: we received aid in money and arms from Syria and Iran", *Memri TV*, 14 Jan. 2005.

50. Abu Ibrahim quoted in Ghait Abdul-Ahad, "From here to eternity", *The Guardian*, 8 May 2005.

51. Arnaud Lenfant, "L'évolution du salafisme en Syrie au XXème siècle", in Bernard Rougier (ed.) *Qu'est ce que le salafisme?* (Paris: PUF, 2008), p. 174.

52. Abu al-Qaqaa quoted in "In secular Syria, an Islamic revival", *Christian Science Monitor*, 3 Oct. 2003.

53. "Syria, long ruthlessly secular, sees fervent Islamic resurgence", *New York Times*, 24 Oct. 2003.

54. US Embassy cable to State Department, "Syrian roundup", 06DAMASCUS2858, 15 June 2006 and Sami Moubayed, "The Islamic Revival in Syria", *Middle East Monitor* (Vol. 1, No. 3, Sept. 2006).

55. Accounts diverge on the exact identity of Abu al-Qaqaa's assassin. See "Radical Syrian cleric shot dead", *BBC*, 29 Sept. 2007, and "The killing of Abu al-Qaqaa", *Asharq al-Awsat*, 3 Oct. 2007.

56. US Embassy cable to State Department, "Syria: 2008 country report on terrorism", 08STATE120019, 29 Dec. 2008.

57. All of the quotes from Ali Mamlouk are drawn from US Embassy cable to State Department, "Syrian intelligence chief attends Ct dialogue with S/Ct Benjamin", 10DAMASCUS159, 24 Feb. 2010.

58. US Embassy cable to State Department, "Syrian intelligence chief attends Ct dialogue with S/Ct Benjamin", 10DAMASCUS159, 24 Feb. 2010.

59. Ahmed Kuftaro quoted in Eyal Zisser, "Syria, the Ba'ath Regime and the

Islamic Movement: Stepping on a New Path?", *The Muslim World* (Vol. 95, No. 1, 2005), p. 51.

60. Ibid.

61. Sami Moubayed, "The Islamic Revival in Syria", *Middle East Monitor* (Vol. 1, No. 3, Sept. 2006).

62. Ahmad Hassoun quoted in Radwan Ziadeh, *Power and Policy in Syria: Intelligence Services, Foreign Relations and Democracy in the Modern Middle East* (New York: I.B. Tauris, 2011), p. 151.

63. Said Ramadan al-Buti quoted in Eyal Zisser, *op. cit.*, p. 50.

64. Salah Kuftaro quoted in "Syria, long ruthlessly secular, sees Islamic resurgence", *New York Times*, 24 Oct. 2003.

65. Thomas Pierret (2011), *op. cit.*, p. 110.

66. Eyal Zisser, *op. cit.*, p. 57.

67. Abdul Kader al-Kittani quoted in "Syria's ruling party solidifies its power", *New York Times*, 5Apr. 2006.

68. Radwan Ziadeh, *op. cit.*, p. 151.

69. Muhammad al-Habasch quoted in "Syria's ruling party solidifies its power", *New York Times*, 5 Apr. 2006.

70. "Closing Pandora's box?", *Al-Ahram*, 18 Aug. 2010.

71. "Islamic revival in Syria is led by women", *New York Times*, 29/08/2006.

72. Muhammad al-Habasch quoted in "The Qubaysi ladies take up Islamic preaching in Syria with government approval", *al-Hayat*, 3 May 2006.

73. Thomas Pierret, "Les mystérieuses Qoubeysiyyat divisées face à la révolution", 22 Dec. 2011. Article accessed on 14 March 2012 and available at http://blogs.mediapart.fr/blog/thomas-pierret/221211/les-mysterieuses-qoubeysiyyat-divisees-face-la-revolution.

74. Quoted in Eyal Zisser, *op. cit.*, p. 58.

8. STRUGGLING FOR RELEVANCE: THE MUSLIM BROTHERHOOD'S EXILE

1. Interview with Burhan Ghalioun, Paris, 2 June 2011.

2. Parts of this chapter are drawn from material I have published elsewhere previously. See Raphaël Lefèvre, "After Hama: regime—Muslim Brotherhood relations, 1982, 2012" in Line Khatib *et al.*, *State and Islam in Ba'athist Syria: Cooptation or Confrontation?* (Boulder: Lynne Rienner, 2012).

3. Adnan Saadeddine quoted in Alison Pargeter, *The Muslim Brotherhood: the Burden of Tradition* (London: Saqi Books, 2010) p. 85.

4. Adnan Saadeddine quoted in Hanna Batatu (1999), *op. cit.*, p. 269.

5. Interview with Muhammed Riyad al-Shuqfah, Istanbul, 9 Sept. 2011.

6. Ibid.

7. Adnan Saadeddine, *Mesirat jama'at al-ikhwan al-Muslimeen fi Suria* (Private publisher, July 1998). See Alison Pargeter, *op. cit.*, pp. 85–7.
8. Abu Mus'ab al-Suri, *op. cit.*, p. 13.
9. Interview with Muhammed Riyad al-Shuqfah, Istanbul, 9 Sept. 2011.
10. Interview with Walid Safour, London, 22 Sept. 2011.
11. Interview with Muhammed Riyad al-Shuqfah, Istanbul, 9 Sept. 2011.
12. Interview with Abdel Halim Khaddam, Paris, 23 June 2011.
13. Interview with a source close to the Syrian Brotherhood, name withheld on request, Nov. 2011.
14. Adnan Saadeddine quoted in Chris Kutchera, "Whither the Syrian Muslim Brothers", *Middle East Magazine* (Apr. 1988), available online at: http://www.chris-kutschera.com/A/syrian_brothers.htm
15. Interview with Muhammed Riyad al-Shuqfah, Istanbul, 9 Sept. 2011.
16. Interview with Zouheir Salem, London, 9 Sept. 2011.
17. Ali Duba quoted in Chris Kutschera, "Syrie: l'éclipse des Frères Musulmans", *Cahiers de l'Orient* (No. 7, Volume 3, 1987), also available online at: http://www.chris-kutschera.com/syrie_eclipse_fm.htm
18. Interview with Ali Sadreddine al-Bayanouni, London, 30 Nov. 2011.
19. Interview with Muhammed Riyad al-Shuqfah, Istanbul, 9 Sept. 2011.
20. Adnan Saadeddine, *Al-Ikhwam al-Muslimoon Fi Souriya: Muthakerat wa Thekrayat* ("The Muslim Brotherhood in Syria: Memoirs and Reminiscences") (Amman: Dar Ammar, 2010), pp. 95–6.
21. Chris Kutschera, "Syrie: l'éclipse des Frères Musulmans", *Cahiers de l'Orient* (No. 7, Volume 3, 1987), also available online at: http://www.chris-kutschera.com/syrie_eclipse_fm.htm
22. Interview with Zouheir Salem, London, 2 Oct. 2011.
23. Interview, name withheld on request, Aug. 2012.
24. *The National Charter of Syria* (London, Aug. 2002, copy given to the author), p. 2. For a detailed analysis of the National Honour Charter's programme and ideology, see Thomas Pierret, "Le 'projet politique pour la Syrie de l'avenir' des Frères Musulmans", in Baudouin Dupret *et al* (eds), *La Syrie au présent* (Paris: Sinbad Actes Sud, 2007), pp. 729–38.
25. See *The Political Perspective for Syria: the Muslim Brotherhood's Vision of the Future* (London, Dec. 2004, copy given to the author), pp. 3–4 and *The National Charter of Syria* (London, Aug. 2002, copy given to the author), p. 6.
26. Interview with Zouheir Salem, London, 20 July 2011.
27. *The Political Perspective for Syria: the Muslim Brotherhood's Vision of the Future* (London, Dec. 2004, copy given to the author), p. 2.
28. For more information on this period, see the excellent work of Teitelbaum: Joshua Teitelbaum, "The Muslim Brotherhood and the 'Struggle for Syria',

1947–1958: between Accommodation and Ideology", *Middle Eastern Studies* (Vol. 40, No. 3, 2004).

29. Ali Sadreddine al-Bayanouni is quoted from an interview he gave to *Le Monde*, 13 May 1981, quoted by Rateb Boustani, "L'opposition islamique et l'alliance politique", Chapter VII in Baudouin Dupret *et al.* (eds), *La Syrie au présent* (Paris: Sinbad Actes Sud, 2007), p. 747. Said Hawwa is quoted in Hans Günter Lobmeyer, "*Al-dimuqratiyya hiyya al-hall?* The Syrian Opposition at the End of the Asad Era", in Eberhard Kienle (ed.), *Contemporary Syria: Liberalization between Cold War and Cold Peace* (London: British Academic Press, 1993), p. 90.

30. Hans Gunter Lobmeyer, "*Al-dimuqratiyya hiyya al-hall?* The Syrian Opposition at the End of the Asad Era", in Eberhard Kienle (ed.), *Contemporary Syria: Liberalization between Cold War and Cold Peace* (London: British Academic Press, 1993), p. 90.

31. Interview with Zouheir Salem, London, 20 July 2011.

32. *The National Charter of Syria* (London, Aug. 2002, copy given to the author), p. 1.

33. Ibid., pp. 2–3.

34. Ibid., p. 5.

35. Ali Sadreddine al-Bayanouni quoted in Itzchak Weismann (2010), *op. cit.*, p. 8.

36. Interview with Zouheir Salem, London, 20 July 2011.

37. Ali Sadreddine al-Bayanouni quoted in Piotr Zalewski, "Islamic Evolution", *Foreign Policy*, 13/2011.

38. *The Political Perspective for Syria: The Muslim Brotherhood's Vision of the Future* (London, Dec. 2004, copy given to the author), p. 5.

39. Interview with Zouheir Salem, London, 20 July 2011.

40. US Embassy cable to State Department, "The Syrian Muslim Brotherhood", DAMASCUS 575, 26 Feb. 1985.

41. The estimate of 10,000 prisoners suspected of belonging to the Muslim Brotherhood comes from a spokesman for the Fighting Vanguard, quoted in US Embassy cable to State Department, "The Syrian Muslim Brotherhood", DAMASCUS 575, 26 Feb. 1985. For the figures related to Hafiz al-Assad's release of political prisoners, see: Eyal Zisser, "Syria, the Baath Regime and the Islamic Movement: Stepping on a New Path?", *The Muslim World* (Vol. 95, No. 1, 2005), p. 49.

42. Eyal Zisser, *op. cit.*, p. 52.

43. Interview with Muhammed Riyad al-Shuqfah, Istanbul, 9 Sept. 2011.

44. Eyal Zisser, *op. cit.*, p. 55.

45. Joshua Landis, "The Syrian Opposition: The Struggle for Unity and Relevance, 2003–2008" in Fred H. Lawson (ed.), *Demistifying Syria* (London: Saqi Books, 2009), pp. 130–31.

46. Riyad Seif quoted in US Embassy cable to State Department, "SARG is feeling confident is the message to Staffdel Talwar", 06DAMASCUS5349, 3 Dec. 2006.

47. Interview with Abdel Halim Khaddam, Paris, 23 June 2011.

48. Interview with Obeida Nahas, London 23 June 2011.

49. US Embassy cable to State Department, "Khaddam's and Bayanouni's Faustian pact", C-NE6–00262, 18 Apr. 2006.

50. Interview with Abdul Baasit Sieda, Tunis, 24 Feb. 2012.

51. Joshua Landis, "The Syrian Opposition: the Struggle for Unity and Relevance, 2003–2008" in Fred H. Lawson (2009), *op. cit.*, p. 134.

52. Interview with Obeida Nahas, London, 23 June 2011.

53. US Embassy cable to State Department, "Khaddam's and Bayanouni's Faustian pact", C-NE6–00262, 18 Apr. 2006.

54. Interviews with Ali Sadreddine al-Bayanouni, London, 30 Nov. 2011.

55. Interview with Abdel Halim Khaddam, Paris, 23 June 2011.

56. Interview with Obeida Nahas, London, 23 June 2011.

9. UPRISINGS IN SYRIA: A REVENGE ON HISTORY

1. "American Ambassador to Syria visits focal point in uprising", *New York Times*, 7 July 2011.

2. "1982 Hama massacre looms over Syria revolt", *The Guardian*, 2 Feb. 2012.

3. "Assad: Challenge Syria at your peril", *Daily Telegraph*, 29 Oct. 2011.

4. The 23 December 2011 terrorist attacks in Damascus, which killed forty-four people, was claimed by the "Syrian Muslim Brotherhood" on the website www.ikhwan-sy.com whereas the organization's actual website is www.ikhwansyria.com. It is reported that the fake Brotherhood website was set up by Emile Qass Nasrallah, a journalist who bought the website rights for a year only and was working for Dounia TV, a television channel owned by Sleiman Mahmoud Maarouf—a major financier of the pro-regime *shabihha* militias and a close relative of one of Bashar al-Assad's closest security advisers, General Mohammed Nasif Khayr Bek. For more on this story, see Ignace Leverrier, "Le terrorisme frappe à nouveau en Syrie. Mais lequel?", *Un Oeil sur la Syrie*, 8 Jan. 2012. Despite the Brotherhood's repeated assertions that it was not behind the December 2011 terrorist attacks, some media outlets nonetheless published the story as it was initially presented to them. See, for instance, "Syria's Muslim Brotherhood claims responsibility for deadly blasts", *Herald Sun*, 25 Dec. 2011. It was only a few days later that most media reported the mistake. See, for example: "Muslim Brotherhood denies Syria bombing claim", *Al-Watan Daily*, 25 Dec. 2011.

5. Interview with Moti' al-Batin, Istanbul, 9 Sept. 2011.

6. Ibid.
7. Nir Rosen, "Islamism and the Syrian Uprisings", *Foreign Policy*, 8 March 2012.
8. "The burial brigade of Homs: An executioner for Syria's rebels tells his story", *Spiegel Online*, 29 March 2012.
9. Interview with Walid Safour, London, 22 Sept. 2011.
10. "Promise of Arab Spring is threatened by divisions", *New York Times*, 21 May 2011.
11. "Syrian Sunni cleric threatens: 'we shall mince [the Alawis] in meat grinders", *MEMRI TV Videos*, 13 July 2011. The video is available online at: http://www.youtube.com/watch?v=Bwz8i3osHww
12. "As Syrian war drags on, jihadists take bigger role", *New York Times*, 29 July 2012.
13. Asher Berman, *Rebel Groups in Jebel al-Zawiyah* (Washington: Institute for the Study of War, 26 July 2012), p. 6.
14. "As Syrian war drags on, jihadists take bigger role", *New York Times*, 29 July 2012.
15. Nir Rosen, "Islamism and the Syrian Uprisings", *Foreign Policy*, 8 March 2012.
16. Even though the Jabhat al-Nusrah is often described in the media as an al-Qaeda's offshoot inside Syria, some analysts have cast doubts on the group's origins and, in some cases, have even suggested it might have been initially set up and encouraged by the Syrian regime. For instance, see "Are reports of al-Qaida in Syria exaggerated?" *Der Spiegel*, 15 Aug. 2012.
17. "Al-Nusrah Front claims suicide attack", *Long War Journal*, 26 Feb. 2012.
18. "Syria conflict: jihadists' role growing", *BBC*, 2 Aug. 2012.
19. "Abu Mus'ab al-Suri released from custody: report", *Long War Journal*, 6 Feb. 2012.
20. Interview with Muhammed Riyad al-Shuqfah, Istanbul, 9 Sept. 2011.
21. Ali al-Bayanouni, "No one owns the Syrian uprisings", *The Guardian*, 16 Apr. 2011.
22. Interview with Ahmed al-Uthman, Paris, 8 Sept. 2012.
23. Kamal Labwani quoted in "Islamists seek influence in Syria uprisings", *AP*, 23 March 2012.
24. Kamal Labwani quoted in "Syria opposition group is routed and divided", *New York Times*, 14 March 2012.
25. Fawaz al-Tello quoted in "Syria's Muslim Brotherhood rise from the ashes", *Reuters*, 6 May 2012.
26. "Ghalioun emails: Qatari money and lost democracy", *Al-Akhbar*, 19Apr. 2012.
27. Othman al-Bidewi quoted in "Syria's Muslim Brotherhood rise from the ashes", *Reuters*, 6 May 2012.

28. Interview with Obeida Nahas, London, 12 Sept. 2012.

29. Farouk Tayfour, for instance, explained his stance clearly in February 2012: "The Muslim Brotherhood's position hasn't changed since the 2001 document on renouncing the use of violence was signed. When the revolution started, we always insisted on its peacefulness and we still do. Violence on the opposition's side in Syria comes from individual acts and small groups who have no ties whatsoever to the Muslim Brotherhood". Interview with Farouk Tayfour, Tunis, 24 Feb. 2012.

30. Interview with Sayyed al-Sibai, Tunis, 24 Feb. 2012.

31. Interview with Ashraf Almoqdad, Tunis, 24 Feb. 2012.

32. "Covenant and Charter of the Muslim Brotherhood in Syria" (London, 25 March 2012, copy given to the author).

33. Interview with Ali Sadreddine al-Bayanouni, email exchange, 14 May 2012.

34. "Muslim Brotherhood seeks to fill post-Assad vacuum", *Daily Star*, 10 Aug. 2012.

35. Moulhem al-Droubi quoted in "Syria's Muslim Brotherhood is gaining influence over anti-Assad revolt", *Washington Post*, 13 May 2012.

36. Rebel commander Abu Mussab quoted in "Muslim Brotherhood undermining Syrian rebel unity", *Al-Akhbar*, 20 Aug. 2012.

37. Moulhem al-Droubi quoted in "Syrian Muslim Brotherhood to launch political party", *Ahram Online*, 20 July 2012.

38. See, for instance: Hassan Hassan, "Syrians are torn between a despotic regime and a stagnant opposition", *The Guardian*, 23 Aug. 2012.

39. Moulhem al-Droubi quoted in "Syrian Muslim Brotherhood to launch Islamist party", *Al-Akhbar*, 20 July 2012.

40. Hassan Hassan, "Syrians are torn between a despotic regime and a stagnant opposition", *The Guardian*, 23 Aug. 2012.

41. Interview with Farouk Tayfour, Tunis, 24 Feb. 2011.

42. Khaled Khoja quoted in Piotr Zalewski, "Islamic evolution", *Foreign Policy*, 11/08/2011.

43. Interview with Obeida Nahas, Tunis, 24 Feb. 2012.

44. Interview with Hassan al-Hachimi, Tunis, 24 Feb. 2012.

45. For an excellent analysis of the role played by Syrian *ulama* in the current protests, see Thomas Pierret, "Syrie: l'Islam dans la revolution", *Politique Etrangère* (Vol. 4, 2011), pp. 879–91.

46. US Embassy cable to State Department, "Murky alliances: Muslim Brotherhood, the Movement for Justice and Democracy and the Damascus Declaration", DE RUEHDN 000477, 8 July 2009.

47. Interview with Muhammed Hawari, Aachen, 19 Dec. 2011.

48. Interview with Malik al-Abdeh, London, 6 Dec. 2011.

49. Interview with Malik al-Abdeh, London, 6 Dec. 2011.

50. US Embassy cable to State Department, "Movement for Justice and Development seeking to expand role in Syria", DE RUEHDM 00185, 3 Nov. 2009.
51. Interview with Malik al-Abdeh, London, 6 Dec. 2011.
52. Thomas Pierret, "Syrie: l'Islam dans la revolution", *Politique Etrangère* (Vol. 4, 2011), pp. 879–891.

EPILOGUE

1. Interview, name withheld on request, Feb. 2012.

INDEX

personnel of, 146; resources provided to Jama'at e Jihad al-Suri, 146

al-Batin, Moti': 182–3; shooting of, 183

al-Bayanouni, Ali Sadreddine: 91, 113, 127, 132, 140, 168, 171–3, 176, 191; first deputy of Syrian Muslim Brotherhood, 192; leader of Syrian Muslim Brotherhood, 24, 92, 115, 170; signatory of Charter of Islamic Front, 120

al-Bayanuni, Muhammad Abu al-Nasr: supporters of, 58

Bedin, Yahya: 111

Belgium: Brussels, 93, 177

al-Bittar, Abd al-Razzq: 9, 84

al-Bittar, Bahjat: 84

al-Bittar, Salah Eddine: 129; co-founder of Ba'ath Party, 28, 37, 46, 55, 68

al-Bukhari, Salim: 9–10, 84

al-Bukhtiar, Hisham: 165

al-Buti, Said Ramadan: 48, 72, 157; background of, 155

Camp David Accords (1979): 130; signatories of, 131

Christianity: 14, 25, 30, 65, 173, 186, 205

Cold War: 34, 132

Correction Movement: launch of (1970), 47; members of, 47

Da'abul, Muwfaq: 91

Dahda, Abu: exile of, 146

Damascus Declaration: 178; formation of (2005), 177, 199; member of SNC, 188; personnel of, 199

Damascus Spring: 176–7

Dar al-Arqam: aims of, 24; founding of (1935), 13

Darwish, Sulayman Khalid: 151

al-Dawalibi, Ma'aruf: 34, 36–7; electoral performance of (1954), 39; Syrian Minister of National Economy, 30

al-Din, Nazira Zayn: 15–16

al-Droubi, Moulhem: 192

Druze: 68, 72; presence in Syrian governmental cabinets, 71; territory inhabited by, 25

Duba, Ali: head of Syrian Military Intelligence, 75, 141, 165; negotiations with Syrian Muslim Brotherhood, 165–6, 168

Egypt: 8, 20, 25, 54, 100; borders of, 142; Cairo, 22–3, 34, 69, 99, 131; Free Officers coup (1952), 38; Muslim population of, 23; Revolution (2011) xi, 181, 183, 194

Egypt-Israel Treaty (1979): 159

Enlightenment: 4, 7

Fadlallah, Mohammad Hussein: spiritual leader of Hizbullah, 159

Farouk Battalion: 186

Fatah: training camps of, 102

Fatah al-Islam: affiliates of, 153

Fayadh, General Shafiq: commander of Third Army Division, 76, 128

Federal Republic of Germany (West Germany): Bonn, 165

Fighting Vanguard: xvi, 58, 82, 88, 102, 106–7, 109, 111–12, 119, 125–6, 138–9, 163–5, 172, 187; connections with Muslim Brotherhood, 73; ideology of, 88; members of, 95, 103–5, 116–18, 120–2, 124, 126, 133, 138, 140, 143–4, 162, 187; origins of, 203

First World War (1914–18): 65

France: 5, 68; Paris, 14, 55, 158, 177, 205

Free Syrian Army (FSA): 186; formation of, 190; supporters of, 191, 193

Friends of Syria: 188

General Peasants Union: formation of, 51

INDEX

Germany: Aachen, 93, 95, 113, 165;
Berlin, 166; Frankfurt, 168
al-Ghadban, Munir: 165, 168
Ghadiyya, Abu: 151
Ghalayini, Mustafa: 15
Ghalioun, Burhan: leader of SNC, 189
Gharrah, Major Muhammad: assassination of (1976), 103
al-Gharra: 16, 24; aims of, 14; anti-French demonstrations organised by (1939), 14; founding of (1924), 14; members of, 16, 86; veil campaign of, 15
Groupe Islamique Armé (GIA): 145

Habannaka, Sheikh Hassan: 47
al-Habasch, Muhammad: 157–9
al-Hachimi, Hassan: 198
Hadid, Marwan: 99, 101–2, 123, 142; arrest of (1975), 102; death of (1976), 103, 203; influence of, 143; leader of Fighting Vanguard, 95, 102, 120; return to Syria (1963), 99–100; role in Hama riot (1964), 45, 72, 124; supporters of, 58; visit to Cairo, 99
al-Hafiz, General Amin: role in repression in Hama riots (1964), 46; Syrian Prime Minister, 45
Hama Massacre (1982): 43, 57, 73, 76–7, 122, 125, 137–8, 141, 161, 163–4, 176, 203; casualty figures of, 77, 128; events of, 127–8, 139; military units involved in, 128; political impact of, xvi, 59, 109–10, 166–7, 175
Hamas: 159; members of, 160; Syrian Ba'ath support for, 148
al-Hamid, Muhammad: 26, 171; ideology of, 36; supporters of, 58
Hariri, Rafiq: Lebanese Prime Minister, 157

Hassoun, Ahmad: 155
Hawari, Muhammed: 120
al-Hawrani, Akram: 33, 68; head of Arab Socialist Party, 28, 37, 138
Hawwa, Said: 73, 89, 94, 98, 101, 123, 125, 127, 139, 163, 172; background of, 97; *Jund Allah*, 98; resignation from Executive Committee of Syrian Muslim Brotherhood (1983), 127; signatory of Charter of Islamic Front, 120; supporters of, 58, 98
Haydar, Ali: leader of Syrian Special Forces, 75
Haydar, Muhammad: Syrian Deputy Prime Minister for Economic Affairs, 56
Hinnawi, Colonel Sami: 29
Hizbullah: 159; members of, 159; Syrian Ba'ath support for, 148
al-Houeidi, Hassan: 91, 122, 165, 169; head of Executive Committee of Syrian Muslim Brotherhood, 126; role in Joint Command of Syrian Muslim Brotherhood, 118
al-Hudaybi, Hassan: head of Muslim Brotherhood (Egyptian), 36, 39; *Preachers, not Judges*, 100
Hussein of Jordan, King: 132; death of, 132; destruction of *fedayeen* camps, 101
Hussein, Saddam: 129, 164–5; regime of, 150

ijtihad: 7–8, 27, 85; concept of, 84; support for, 10–11
imperialism: 9, 35, 37, 39; British, 5
India: British Raj, 5
Iran: Iraqi Invasion of (1980), 129; Islamic Revolution (1979), 130; Tehran, 129, 192
Iran-Iraq War (1980–8): 54, 169; Iraqi Invasion of Iran (1980), 129

266

INDEX

INDEX